African Tales

A Xhosa storyteller, October 28, 1975

African Tales

Compiled by Harold Scheub

THE UNIVERSITY OF WISCONSIN PRESS

The University of Wisconsin Press
1930 Monroe Street
Madison, Wisconsin 53711

www.wisc.edu/wisconsinpress/

3 Henrietta Street
London WC2E 8LU, England

5   4   3   2   1

Printed in the United States of America

Library of Congress Cataloging-in-Publication Data
African tales / compiled by Harold Scheub.
p. cm.
Includes bibliographical references.
ISBN 0-299-20940-7 (hardcover : alk. paper) — ISBN 0-299-20944-X
(pbk. : alk. paper)
1. Tales—Africa. I. Scheub, Harold.
GR350.A366   2005
398.2′096—dc22   2004025639

And Shahrazad saw the dawn of day and stopped her storytelling. Then Dunyazad said, "My sister, how pleasant your tale is, and how tasteful, how sweet, how generous!" Shahrazad replied, "And what is this compared to what I could tell you in the night to come, if I live and if the king spare me?" The king thought, "By Allah, I shall not kill her until I hear the rest of her tale, for it is truly wonderful." So they rested that night in mutual embrace until the dawn. After this, the king went to his court, and the minister and the troops came in and the court was crowded. The king gave orders and judged and appointed and deposed, bidding and forbidding during the rest of the day. Then the council broke up, and the king entered his palace. When it was the third night, and the king had had his will of Shahrazad, Dunyazad, her sister, said to her, "Finish for us that tale of yours," and Shahrazad continued her story. . . .[1]

Contents

Illustrations

Story and Storyteller

The Collection of Stories from the Oral Tradition

Collecting stories from the oral tradition is an arduous task when one considers the complexity of the storytelling performance. It is not simply the words of the storyteller that are the critical aspect of this artistic event: there is also the body of the performer to consider, the dancelike movements of the body, the use of the voice, the deeply emotional relationship between storyteller and audience. It is a performance that one seeks to capture in words, not simply the words. Too frequently, the stories that are taken from the oral tradition are scripts, rather than performances.

Those who have gathered African stories have been aware of these challenges. Melville J. Herskovits and Frances S. Herskovits wrote, "Our method of recording was to take the text directly on the typewriter as our interpreters translated the narrator's flow of the story."[2] In an earlier time, Henry Callaway collected Zulu stories in a similar way: "A native is requested to tell a tale; and to tell it exactly as he would tell it to a child or a friend; and what he says is faithfully written down."[3] But those who witnessed the storytelling performances realized that simply writing the words down was not sufficient, and the problem was intensified if the stories were not being told before audiences in a typical way. Still, even with such a crude means of collection, Callaway captured for all time the splendid stories of the Zulu performer Lydia umkaSethemba. Leo Frobenius, the German anthropologist, made twelve expeditions to Africa and was deeply aware of the dimensions of performance. His hope was that "every expedition will be equipped with a staff of artists who will transfer to paper and canvas that which cannot be recorded accurately with the camera."[4] Two other early collectors of African stories showed a similar awareness of the difficulty of capturing the total performance in words.

Edward Steere, who compiled an important collection of Swahili stories, wrote, "I have tried . . . to make the translation as literal as possible, and to reproduce in English something like the mixture of familiar phrases and unfamiliar ideas which make up the originals."[5] Edouard Jacottet worked among the Sotho people of southern Africa and edited an impressive gathering of stories. He wrote of "how the tales . . . have been collected. Nearly all of them have been written down at the dictation of competent natives either by me or by friends. . . . We have thus the *ipsissima verba* of the Natives themselves, the very Se-Suto as it is spoken in every day life, without any admixture of European ideas or speech."[6]

Through such methods of collection, much of what we know about African oral tradition has been preserved. By often coarse means, stories were collected, storytellers were immortalized, and the work of such splendid storytellers as Lydia umkaSethemba awkwardly preserved. One of the great early San storytellers was //kabbo, who, while imprisoned on Robben Island in South Africa for livestock theft, was visited by a German philologist, W. H. I. Bleek, who wrote down //kabbo's stories.[7]

I was very much aware of these difficulties when I set out to make a collection of stories from the oral traditions of the Xhosa, Zulu, Swati, and Ndebele peoples of southern Africa. I had better equipment than the earlier collectors—a tape recorder, a motion picture camera, and a still camera. But, even with such supplies, the accurate reproduction of oral performances remains thoroughly challenging. It is indeed possible to tape every word of the storyteller, possible to capture on film some of the gesture, the body movement. But of course the spontaneity of the performance is gone, as is the vibrant and critical relationship with the audience. I always sought to be invited to storytelling sessions that I myself had not initiated. And I attempted to remain very much in the background. It was the decision of storytellers and audiences that I should record the performances: often I did not. I walked throughout the rural reaches of southeastern Africa, fifteen hundred miles during each of four one-year trips, working with storytellers, historians, poets, philosophers in the oral tradition. The countless performances to which I was fortunately witness comprise some eight thousand stories, histories, biographies, poems, and memoirs. And I was able to record on film many parts of those performances.

But I was also aware that I was lifting the performances out of their social and historical contexts. When I expressed this concern to storytellers, a number of them firmly informed me that stories did not belong to one time or place, nor did they belong to one people or culture. Stories, they argued, are for all times and for all people, and they therefore have no one immovable context. And an earlier collector echoed these observations: "If carefully studied and compared with corresponding legends among other people," wrote Henry Callaway in 1868, "they will bring out unexpected relationships, which will more and more force upon us the great truth, that man has every where thought alike, because every where, in every country and clime, under every tint of skin, under every varying social and intellectual condition, he is still man,—one in all the essentials of man,—one in that which is a stronger proof of essential unity, than mere external differences of nature,—one in his mental qualities, tendencies, emotions, passions."[8] This is the message that was delivered to me by Xhosa and Zulu storytellers one hundred years later.

Translation of Stories from the Oral Tradition

The problems for the translator of oral performance into written form are enormous, some of them insurmountable except by extensive multimedia productions, and even then the impact of the original performance is diminished. The problems of developing literary correspondences for nonverbal artistic techniques in the oral tradition are staggering, for the translation of a single narrative performance involves profound transformations that seemingly defy equivalence. The major problem centers not so much on the translation of an African language into English but on the translation from the oral form to the written word.

The translation of a narrative performance freezes in the written word the creation of a tradition that is fluid and flexible, and suggests a permanence that is not characteristic of the oral system that produced it. The artist obviously has no script; his materials include ancient images, his body and voice, his imagination, and an audience. Within a broad thematic and artistic framework, he is free to deal with the images as he chooses, and he is praised by the audience for the originality with which he objectifies what is ancient and familiar. Little is memorized: the artist must depend on his memory and imagination and on the controlled cooperation of the members of the audience to develop the skeletal mythic image that he has drawn from a repertory of remembered images that he has inherited from a venerable artistic tradition. The plotting of images, while important, may not be the most compelling part of a performance. Performers are storytellers first of all, and they are also intellectuals and artists, roles that have been defined for them for generations. They are craftsmen who can use the narrative's surface as a tool, a language to be utilized and manipulated to reveal a theme, create an argument, elicit an emotional or intellectual response from the audience. The image that is being evoked has never before been produced in just that fashion and will never again be created that way. The surface of the story can be exploited by the artist and made to project a certain idea at one time, a unique emotion when it is produced the next time, a solution to a problem currently plaguing the society, the communication of the artist's own preoccupation, but seldom losing its universal appeal. The narrative cores are really the language of artists who communicate not by words but by images, which are evoked with the assistance of nonverbal as well as verbal techniques.

From the creation, combination, and maneuvering of images emerge ideas, values, arguments, affirmation of social institutions, and, most important, emotional relationships. These are stated and developed in a manner that is logical and rational within the context of the oral tradition. Remembered are images that contain implicitly the conflicts and resolutions that become evident only when the performer develops them in a performance, giving the ancient image renewed life with his body, with the rhythm of the language. As the artist plots the images in a linear development, underlying structures simultaneously guide the imaginations of the members of the audience in a rhythmical, circular fashion, so that the surface of the story becomes a means of metaphor. What is sometimes dismissed as a simple fascination with a world of fantasy is actually a metaphorical language, sophisticated, useful, transmitted through the ages.

As the performer projects the remembered image, he is constantly in need of the assistance of the audience, and if he is a talented, confident artist, he makes use of the many potentially disruptive tensions that exist between him and the members of the audience. That audience has the same repertory of mythic images as the artist, so that the response to the images is complex, at once familiar and novel.

The translator not only must be aware of the images and symbols developed on the surface of the story; he must also be sensitive to their poetic use, to the deeply metaphorical nature of these oral narratives. In addition, he must be sensitive to the aesthetic principles that guide the creation of the work, for what might appear on the written page as an awkwardly conceived or a fragmented story may not be so regarded by the audience in attendance at the original presentation. Problems of artistic proportion are indeed considerations by members of African oral societies, but these frequently go beyond the plotting of images; they become involved in the intricate logic and interworking of the imaged language itself. What initially appears a simple matter of verbal equivalence is actually a unique metaphorical language that the unwary translator may hopelessly bungle.

This relationship between artist and audience becomes further complicated for the translator when one considers its nonverbal quality. The performer expects that the members of an audience will physically, emotionally, sometimes vocally assist him in the development of images. It is necessary to the success of his production that he wholly involve the audience in the work of art. The artist exploits the rhythmic possibilities of the oral language so that it becomes a language of sounds that constantly threaten to dissolve into song. He moves his body, arms, face, shoulders rhythmically, at times a dancing-in-place, that rhythmic movement routinely threatening to dissolve into pure dance. Song and dance are significant artistic underpinnings of the oral story. These musical characteristics of the performance have their own beauty, but they are also used to bring the members of the audience into a fuller participation in the developing images. Those images are also enveloping: the members of the audience move their bodies in harmony with that of the performer. In various ways, they are in physical and emotional accord with the artist and his creation, their emotions a part of the images, those emotions thereby rendering the audience an integral part of the metaphorical transformation at the heart of the story. The audience knows the hackneyed plots, its members having witnessed their production countless times. But there is a freshness about the work that is perhaps not evident on the surface; moreover, the artistic delight in the performance goes deep, and the rhythms set in motion by the performer sustain images that are very complex.

How, then, does one effectively and authentically translate the verbal and nonverbal elements of such a tradition to the written word? Dynamic rather than formal equivalence is obviously a necessity, since formal correspondences would merely distort the receptor language and remain remote from the original production. It is impossible to consider the verbal aspects of the performance in isolation from the nonverbal. The superficial plotting of images seems the easiest of tasks for the translator, yet a dynamic translation might obscure the underlying structures that give logic and meaning to the work. Characterization may seem to the reader of African oral narratives to be flat, undeveloped. But this is a problem for the reader, not one for the member of the audience during the actual production. The performer is himself the characters in the story, giving them life and fullness, his body giving them dimension. And consider the movement of the artist, the nuance of the hand, a flitting motion that tells much about a character; consider the rhythm of the language, an oral language that emphasizes the ear rather than the eye: can this be caught in translation? The language is well adapted to oral performance, and once that performance is removed from a context of sound and rhythm, it is in danger of ceasing to have life, in danger of becoming something else. It might then wither on the page of a book, becoming a mere outline. The audience, so important in so many ways to the artist, is gone; the extemporaneous atmosphere of the oral production evaporates; and the dynamic suspense of an unfinished performance with the maze of tensions between artist and audience has largely been eliminated.

The unique tensions of the live, oral, public performance and the many nonverbal aspects of the work of art cannot be rendered in any precise way on paper. One must seek a solution by devising something of a hybrid form, neither the original narrative performance nor a literary story, yet borrowing from both. The translator must accept the fact that the oral nature of the narrative is gone the minute sound is gone, and the shift is from the ear to the eye. But there is an inner ear, and it is the challenge to the translator to work on that.

African Tales

A Xhosa storyteller, October 28, 1975

1

Kwaku Ananse and Aso[9]

Asante (Ghana)[10]

There once lived a certain man called Akwasi-the-jealous-one. His wife was Aso, and he did not want anyone to see Aso or anyone to talk to her. So he went and built a small settlement for Aso to live in. No one ever went into the village. Now Akwasi-the-jealous-one could not beget children. Because of that, if he and his wife lived in town, someone would take her away.

Sky-god told young men, "Akwasi-the-jealous-one has been married to Aso for a very, very long time. She has not conceived by him and borne a child. Therefore, he who is able, let him go and take Aso, and, should she conceive by him, let him take her as his wife."

All the young men tried their best to lay hands on her, but not one was able.

Now, Kwaku Ananse was there watching these events, and he said, "I can go to Akwasi-the-jealous-one's village."

Sky-god said, "Can you really do so?"

Ananse said, "If you will give me what I require."

Sky-god said, "What kind of thing?"

He said, "Medicine for gun and bullets."

And Sky-god gave it to him. Ananse took the powder and bullets to various small villages, saying, "Sky-god has told me to bring powder and bullets to you, and you are to go and kill meat. On the day that I return here, I shall take the meat and depart." He distributed the powder and the bullets among very many small villages, until all were finished. All the villagers got him some meat.

On a certain day, Ananse wove a palm-leaf basket. Its length was from here to over yonder. Ananse took it to the small villages where he had distributed the powder and bullets, to receive all the meat which they had killed. Father Ananse took the meat and palm-leaf basket and set it on his head, and set out on the path leading to Akwasi-the-jealous-one's

3

settlement. When he reached the stream from which Akwasi and his wife drank, he picked out some meat and put it in. Ananse strove hard and brought the palm-leaf basket full of meat and passed through the main entrance leading into Akwasi-the-jealous-one's compound.

And Aso saw him. She said, "Akwasi! Come and look at something that is coming to the house here. What can it be?"

Ananse said, "It is Sky-god who is sending me. I am weary and am coming to sleep here."

Akwasi-the-jealous-one said, "I have heard my lord's servant."

Aso said to Ananse, "Father man, some of your meat has fallen down at the main entrance to the compound."

The spider said, "Oh, if you happen to have a dog, let it go and take that meat and chew on it."

So Aso went and got it and gave it to her husband.

Then Ananse said, "Mother, set some food on the fire for me."

Aso put some on, and Ananse said, "Mother, is it *fufuo* that you are cooking, or *eto*?"

Aso replied, "*Fufuo.*"

Ananse said, "Then it is too little. Go and fetch a big pot."

Aso went and fetched a big one.

Ananse said, "Come and get meat." There were forty hindquarters of great beasts. He said, "Take these only and put them in, and if you had a pot big enough, I would give you enough meat to chew to make your teeth fall out."

Aso finished preparing the food, turned it out of the pot, and placed it on a table, splashed water, and put it beside the rest of the food. Then Aso took her portion and went and set it down near the fire. And the men went and sat down beside the table. They touched the backs of each other's hands.[11]

While they were eating, Kwaku Ananse said, "There is no salt in this *fufuo.*"

Akwasi said to Aso, "Bring some salt."

But Ananse said, "No, when the woman is eating, you should not tell her to get up to bring salt. You yourself should go and bring it."

Akwasi got up, and Ananse looked into his bag and took out a pinch of purgative medicine and put it in the *fufuo*.

Then he called Akwasi, saying, "Come, I had brought some salt with me."

When Akwasi came, Ananse said, "Oh, I shall eat no more. I am full."

Akwasi, who suspected nothing, continued eating.

When they finished eating, Akwasi said, "Friend, we and you are sitting here, and yet we do not know your name."

Ananse said, "I am called Rise-up-and-make-love-to-Aso."

Akwasi said, "I have heard, and you, Aso, have you heard this man's name?"

Aso replied, "Yes, I have heard."

Akwasi rose to go and prepare one of the spare bedrooms and to make all comfortable.

He said, "Rise-up-and-make-love-to-Aso, this is your room. Go and sleep there."

The spider said, "I am the Soul-washer to Sky-god, and I sleep in an open verandah room. Since mother bore me and father begat me, I have never slept in a closed bedroom."

Akwasi said, "Then where will you sleep?"

He replied, "Were I to sleep in this open verandah room here, that would make you equal to Sky-god, for it would mean that I was sleeping in Sky-god's open verandah room. Since I am never to sleep in any one's open room except that of Sky-god, I shall just lie down in front of this closed sleeping room where you repose."

The man took out a sleeping mat and laid it there for him.

Akwasi and his wife went to rest, and Ananse, too, lay down there. Ananse lay there, and he slipped in the cross-bar of the bedroom door. Then he lay there and took his musical bow and sang,

"Akuamoa Ananse, today we shall achieve something, today,
Ananse, the child of Nsia, the mother of Nyame, the sky-god,
Today we shall achieve something, today.
Ananse, the Soul-washer to Nyame, the sky-god,
Today I shall see something."

Now he stopped playing his musical instrument and laid it aside, and then he lay down. He slept for some time, when he heard Akwasi-the-jealous-one calling, "Father man."

Not a sound in reply except the chirping of the cicada, dinn!

"Father man."

Not a sound in reply except the chirping of the cicada, dinn!

Akwasi-the-jealous-one is dying; the medicine has taken effect on him, but he calls, "Father man."

Not a sound in reply except the chirping of the cicada, dinn!

At last he said, "Rise-up-and-make-love-to-Aso."

The spider said, "Mm! Mm! Mm!"

Akwasi said, "Open the door for me."

Ananse opened the door, and Akwasi went somewhere.

And the spider rose and went into the room there.

He said, "Aso, did you not hear what your husband said?"

She replied, "What did he say?"

Ananse replied, "He said I must rise up and make love to you."

Aso said, "You don't lie."

And he did it for her, and he went and lay down.

That night, Akwasi rose up nine times. The spider also went nine times to where Aso was.

When things became visible, next morning, Ananse set off.

It was about two moons later when Aso's belly became large.

Akwasi questioned her, saying, "Why has your belly got like this? Perhaps you are ill, for you know that I who live with you here am unable to beget children."

Aso replied, "You forget that man who came here and whom you told to rise up and make love to Aso. Well, he took me, and I have conceived by him."

Akwasi-the-jealous-one said, "Rise up and let me take you and give you to him."

They went to Sky-god's town. On the way, Aso gave birth.

They reached Sky-god's town and went and told Sky-god what had happened, saying, "A subject of yours, whom you sent, slept at my house, and took Aso, and she conceived by him."

Sky-god said, "All my subjects are roofing the houses; go and point out the one you mean."

They went off, and the spider was sitting on a ridge-pole.

Aso said, "There he is."

And Ananse ran and sat on the middle.

Again, Aso said, "There he is."

Then Ananse fell down from where he was sitting.

Now, that day was Friday.

Ananse said, "I, who was Sky-god's soul, you have taken your hand and pointed it at me, so that I have fallen down and got red earth on me."

Immediately, the attendants seized Akwasi-the-jealous-one and made him sacrifice a sheep. When Akwasi-the-jealous-one had finished sacrificing the sheep, he said to Sky-god, "Here is the woman, let Ananse take her."

So Ananse took Aso, but as for the infant, they killed it, cut it into pieces, and scattered them about.

That is how jealousy came among the people.

This, my story, which I have related, if it be sweet, or if it be not sweet, some you may take as true, and the rest you may praise me for telling of it.

2

Akenda Mbani[12]

Apinji (Gabon)[13]

Redjioua, a king, had a daughter called Arondo, and she was very beautiful.

Redjioua said, "A man may give me slaves, goods, or ivory to marry my daughter, but he will not get her. I want only a man who will agree that when Arondo falls ill, he will fall ill also, and that when Arondo dies, he will die, also."

Time went on, and, as people knew this, no one came to ask for Arondo in marriage.

But, one day, a man called Akenda Mbani[14] came, and he said to Redjioua, "I have come to marry Arondo, your daughter. I come because I will agree that when Arondo dies, I will die, also." So Akenda Mbani married Arondo.

Akenda Mbani was a great hunter, and, after he had married Arondo, he went hunting and killed two wild boars. When he returned, he said, "I have killed two boars and bring you one."

Redjioua said, "Go and fetch the other."

Akenda Mbani said, "My father gave me a law that I must never go twice to the same place."

Another day, he went hunting again, and he killed two antelopes. When he returned, he said to Redjioua, "Father, I have killed two antelopes, and I bring you one."

The king said, "Please, my son-in-law, go and fetch the other."

He answered, "You know I cannot go twice to the same place."

Another time, he went hunting again, and he killed two bongos.[15]

Then Redjioua, who saw that all the other animals were being lost, said, "Please, my son-in-law, show the people the place where the other bongo is."

Akenda Mbani said, "If I do so, I am afraid I shall die."

In the evening of the same day, a canoe from the Oroungou country came with goods and remained on the river side.

Akenda Mbani said to his wife, "Let us go and meet the Oroungou people."

They saw them and then took a box full of goods and went back to their own house.

The people of the village traded with the Oroungou, and, when the Oroungou wanted to go back, they came to Akenda Mbani, and he trusted them with ten slaves and many bunches of plantains, mats, and fowls. Then the Oroungou left.

Months passed; then one day Arondo said to her husband, "We have never opened the box that came with the Oroungou. Let us see what is in it." They opened it and saw cloth.

Then Arondo said, "Husband, cut me two fathoms of it, for I like it."

They left the room. Arondo seated herself on the bed and Akenda Mbani on a stool, and then Arondo suddenly said, "Husband, I begin to have a headache."

Akenda Mbani said, "Ah, ah, Arondo, do you want me to die?" and he looked Arondo steadily in the face. He tied a bandage around her head and did the same to his own.

Arondo began to cry as her headache became worse, and when the people of the village heard her cry they all came around her.

Redjioua came and said, "Do not cry, my daughter. You will not die."

Then Arondo said, "Father, why do you say I shall not die? for, if you fear death, you may be sure it will come."

She had hardly said these words than she expired.

Then all the people mourned, and Redjioua said, "Now my daughter is dead, so Akenda Mbani must die also."

The place where people are buried is called Djimai. The villages went there and dug a place for the two corpses, which were buried together. Redjioua had a slave buried with Arondo, along with a tusk of an elephant, rings, mats, plates, and the bed on which Akenda Mbani and Arondo had slept. The cutlass, the hunting bag, and the spear of Akenda Mbani were also buried.

Then the people said, "Let us cover the things with sand and make a little mound."

When Agambouai, the speaker of the village, heard of this, he said to Redjioua, "There are leopards here."

Redjioua said, "Do not have a mound over my child's burial place, lest the leopards come and scratch the ground and eat the corpse of my child."

The people said, "Then let us build a deeper hole," and they took away Arondo and Akenda Mbani and placed both on stools. Then they dug and dug and put back the things that were to be buried with Arondo, then laid her in her place.

Then they came to Akenda Mbani, who awoke and said, "I never go twice to the same place. You put me in the tomb and you took me away from it, though all of you knew that I never go to the same place again."

When Redjioua heard of this, he became very angry and said, "You knew that Akenda Mbani never goes twice to the same place. Why did you remove him?"

Then he ordered the people to catch Agambouai and cut his head off.

3

The Cock[16]

Arabic (Egypt)[17]

There was once a man who had a thousand piastres, but he was afraid to go into business because of his money. Then he went away, not wanting to give anything to other people lest he should become poorer.

A neighbor of theirs, a woman, said to his wife, "You had better buy some spring chickens. They will soon grow into fowls, and you can sell each fowl for two piastres and a half or perhaps three piastres, and so you will make a good profit."

The wife replied, "Very well, when my husband comes, I will tell him of it."

When her husband came in, she said to him, "You had better buy some spring chickens so that we may make a good profit out of them. At present, ten spring chickens cost a piastre, but after a while when they grow big we can sell them for two and a half piastres each and so make a good deal."

Her husband replied, "Very good, you are a clever woman."

So he gave his wife a thousand piastres, and she bought spring chickens with five hundred of them and corn with the other five hundred. She put the chickens into a court and crushed the corn and threw it to the chickens and shut the door upon them.

But a kite came and picked out some of the chickens; a weasel came and carried off some others.

After a little time, the man and his wife went to see the chickens. They found only one of them left.

Then the man said to his wife, "Cook the cock, and we will dine off it." His wife killed the cock and cooked it.

When her husband came, he said to her, "Who can dine off a thousand piastres? It can only be the sultan. If I should make such a dinner, everyone would say, 'This fellow is mad, no one dines for a thousand piastres except the sultan.'"

So he took the cock in a dish and took the bread and went to the palace of the sultan.

The porter said to him, "Hello, where are you going, good sir?"

He replied, "I am going to the sultan to give him the cock."

The porter said, "If the sultan is favorable to you, what will you give me?"

He replied, "I will give you a quarter."

He said, "Very well, go!"

He reached the second gate, and the second porter asked him, "Where are you going?"

He answered, "I have a present for the sultan."

The porter said, "If the sultan grants you a favor, what will you give me?"

He replied, "I will give you a quarter."

So the other said, "Very good, go!"

He reached the third gate, and the porter asked, "Where are you going?"

He replied, "I have a present for the sultan."

The porter said, "If the sultan grants you a favor, what will you give me?"

He answered, "I will give you a quarter."

He said, "Very good, pass on."

He reached the fourth gate, and the porter asked him, "Where are you going, good sir?"

He replied, "I have a present for the sultan."

He asked, "If the sultan grants you a favor, what will you give me?"

He replied, "I will give you a quarter."

The porter said, "Very good, pass on."

The fellow entered the palace and found the sultan and the vizier and the sultan's children, sitting there. He made obeisance to the sultan.

The sultan asked him, "What have you got, good sir?"

He answered, "I have a present for you."

The sultan said, "A present? Of what sort is it?"

He answered, "Food."

The sultan said, "All right, I have not yet eaten."

They placed the food in the middle of them and sat down to eat.

The sultan said to the fellow, "Display the food!"

He replied, "Your servant!" and took the cock, broke its head, and gave it to the sultan, saying, "The head! you shall take the head." And he gave the neck to the vizier, saying, "The neck! you shall have the neck!" And he gave the children the wings and said to them, "The wings! and you shall take the wings."

The sultan exclaimed, "What is this, vizier?"

The vizier replied, "The head includes all the people. Therefore, you take the head."

The sultan was greatly pleased with the fellow and said, "Ask what I shall give you!"

He answered, "I want eight hundreds blows with the kurbash."

The sultan said, "My man, think of something else!"

He said, "No, I want eight hundred blows with the kurbash."

When they were going to give him the eight hundred lashes, he cried, "Wait a little! I have a partner!"

They went to the first gate. He said to them, "Give the Nubian two hundred!"

When they had given the fellow two hundred blows, they went to the second gate. He told them to give the porter of that gate another two hundred.

Next, they came to the third gate, and he told them to give the porter of it another two hundred.

They went to the fourth gate, and he told them to give the porter another two hundred.

The sultan asked, "What is the meaning of this, good sir?"

He replied, "Your majesty, when I came, the fellow said to me, 'If the sultan grants you a favor, what will you give me?' I answered, I would give a quarter. Each of the porters asked the same question, and I made the same reply, 'I will give you a quarter.' So if your honor wishes to give me anything, each will take a quarter, and I shall have nothing. Now each has taken a quarter, and I have had nothing."

The sultan laughed greatly. He was pleased with the fellow and gave him plenty of *bakshîsh*.

So he went back to his house and was happy.

He had a neighbor, a woman. When she saw that he had received plenty of *bakshîsh*, she said to her husband, "Come, I will prepare two cocks, and do you give them to the sultan so that he may give you plenty of money as he has done to our neighbor."

He replied, "Very well."

She prepared for him four cocks and a little bread, and he took the meat and the bread and went to the palace.

As soon as the porter saw him, he said nothing out of fear, so the fellow passed from the first gate to the last.

He found the sultan and the vizier and the children, sitting, and he made obeisance.

The sultan asked, "What have you got, good sir?"

He answered, "I have a present for you."

The sultan asked, "What is the present?"

He said, "Food."

The sultan said, "Very well, I have not yet eaten."

He put the food in the midst of them, and they sat down to eat.

The sultan said to him, "Display the food!"

The fellow gave a cock to each.

The sultan said, "Good sir, why is there nothing for yourself?"

He replied, "The wise man eats of the sauce."

The vizier said to the sultan, "This fellow is a fool: he makes us fools and himself the wise man."

The sultan grew angry with the man and said, "He must be beaten well."

Then they beat him and turned him out of the palace.

4

Tale of a Lantern[18]

Arabic (Morocco)[19]

There was once a man, a rich merchant of Fez, who had a very beautiful wife to whom he was greatly devoted. He gave her all that her heart desired and never allowed another woman, whether white or black, to share her place in his life.

One day, while they two were sitting over the evening meal, he drew from his bag a pair of very beautifully wrought silver bracelets and gave them to her, saying, "See if these will fit your arms, beloved, for this afternoon my fellow merchants refused to buy them from the auctioneer, saying, 'No woman has wrists small enough to slip them on,' and I knew in my heart that my Fatumah would find them a world too large."

And Fatumah, smiling, slipped the bracelets on with ease, for surely they fitted her as though they had been made to measure.

Then Fatumah said, "Oh, my lord, grant me one request."

He said, "It is granted, on my head be it."

And Fatumah said, "Should it please the Almighty that I should die before my lord, will my lord promise that he will marry again the one whom these bracelets, his munificent gift, will fit?"

And the merchant promised.

"No," she said, "but you must swear to it, and Dada here shall be witness."

And he swore a solemn oath, and Dada, the old black woman who had been Fatumah's nurse, was witness.

Shortly after, it was decreed that Fatumah give birth to a daughter and die.

But the baby lived, and it was given the name Shumshen N'har,[20] and the old Dada cared for her and brought her up, even as the daughters of sultans are brought up.

And she grew daily more beautiful, so that she surpassed even the loveliness of her mother. And her father regarded her as the apple of his eye.

Now, when Shumshen N'har had reached the age of fourteen, the relations and friends of her father spoke to him very seriously, saying, "It is necessary that you should marry again, Tajur.[21] Your daughter is growing up, and she ought to have a husband found for her. And who could arrange for her wedding as fittingly as her stepmother would? Would you leave such an important matter to Dada? Moreover, when your daughter is married, your house will be empty, and you will require more than ever a wife to cherish you and care for your welfare."

The merchant saw that they spoke the truth, and he said, "It is well; I shall wed."

That evening, when Dada stood before him to give an account of her stewardship that day and to hear his wishes, he told her what his friends' advice was and that he had determined to follow it.

Dada said, "Has my lord forgotten the oath that he swore to Lilla Fatumah, on whose soul be peace?"

The merchant said, "No, prepare the bracelets, so that when I hear of a suitable bride, you make take them to her and see if they will fit her arms. If they do, we will know that she is the wife Allah has destined for me. And, if not, we shall seek further."

Dada kissed his hand, and said, "On my head be it."

Soon after, the merchant told Dada, "Go to the house of such a one. I hear he seeks a husband for his daughter. Maybe she is the one who will do for me."

And Dada did as her lord commanded, but it was in vain. When the young woman tried to put the bracelets on, they stuck on her thumb bone, though she pushed until her hand was as white as milk.

And this happened many times, so that Dada grew weary of going from house to house with the bracelets. All who saw the bracelets marveled at their beauty and at the smallness of the wrists for which they had been made.

When Dada had returned from her tenth or twelfth effort, it was late in the evening, and she put down her *haik*[22] and the handkerchief containing the bracelets in one corner of the kitchen while she hastened to prepare the evening meal.

And Lilla Shumsen N'har entered the kitchen to speak with her and to help her.

She said, "I shall fold your *haik* for you, Dada, and put it away so that it does not get soiled."

When she lifted the *haik*, she saw the handkerchief knotted in a parcel.

She said, "What has Dada here?" and she opened the handkerchief. When she saw the bracelets, she admired them exceedingly and examined them carefully. Then she tried them on, for she thought they must be a pair prepared for her by her father. The bracelets slid onto her wrists and rested on her arms as though they had been made to her measure.

Then Shumshen N'har clapped her hands and called to her servant, saying, "See, Dada, how beautiful these bracelets are and how well they fit me. Did my father buy them for me?"

And Dada came with haste and looked and fell on the floor in a swoon, for she feared greatly.

Shumshen N'har called the other maids, and they poured water on Dada's face and rubbed her hands until she revived, but she would not tell them what ailed her. But she groaned heavily, and then the voice of her master was heard.

Shumshen N'har ran to her own apartments with the bracelets forgotten on her arms, for she feared she knew not what.

And that night, when the household was quiet, Dada stood before her master and recounted to him what had happened.

The merchant was greatly perplexed, and the next day he called all his chief friends and the learned men and the *kadi* and laid everything before them. For a long time, they talked and wondered and sought a way out of this difficulty.

But they found none.

Then the *kadi* said to the merchant, "My son, seeing that you have sworn this solemn oath to your wife, on whose soul the Almighty have mercy, before witnesses that you will marry the woman whom these bracelets fit, and seeing that these bracelets fit only your daughter, Shumshen N'har, though you have tried them on other young women, it seems to be that you must marry her. And if it does not please the All-Wise One to open a door of escape for you before the wedding, you can divorce her the day after the marriage ceremony and perhaps may thereby accomplish what is written in the Book of Fate."

And the merchant bowed his head and agreed to what the *kadi* said.

A wedding day was appointed, and the merchant went and lived in another house belonging to him, leaving his former home to Shumshen N'har and Dada. Dada set about preparing for the marriage, but with tears and lamentations as though she were preparing for a funeral.

As for Shumshen N'har, she shut herself in her own room and would see no one. She prayed day and night with tears that death might release her.

And it happened one evening, as Dada was bargaining in the courtyard with a Jew, a jeweler, about various ornaments of gold that he was preparing, that the moans of Shumshen N'har struck on his ear, and he inquired as to the reason of her grief.

Dada recounted to him the story.

And the Jew, being a charitable man, and having daughters of his own, was moved with pity for Shumshen N'har. He said to Dada, "This is truly a sad tale that you have related to me. May it please the Almighty to intervene and avert the evil." He added, "Wallah, my tongue cleaves to my throat with wonder and pity. Give me, please, a drink of water to steady me before I go out into the streets."

Dada went to find a cup.

While she was gone, the jeweler whispered at the door of Shumshen N'har's room, "Lilla, don't be afraid; I shall help you, God willing."

She said, "The blessing of Mulai Dris rest on you, charitable man."

Then the Jew said with haste, "I will send a large lantern for you to see. Hide yourself in it, and I will get you away from this place." But before he could say more, Dada returned with the water.

And the Jew left, promising to send all the ornaments of gold with his apprentice so that Dada might show them to her master before she paid for them.

The next morning, the apprentice of the Jew came, and he brought with him a most beautiful lantern made of silver inlaid with gold and colored glass, and so large that it had to be carried by two men.

The apprentice said, "My master has made this lantern for the son of the sultan who is about to be wed to the daughter of his uncle, Lilla Ameenah. It is to be carried in front of the *amareeyah*.[23] My master has sent it for your master to see so that if it pleases him, another may be made for his wedding."

Dada said, "But my lord does not live here, and I cannot carry this great lantern, as I can these jewels, from this house to the place where he lives so that he might see it."

The apprentice said, "Let it remain here a little while, for I have paid and dismissed the porters who brought it. I will go quickly to my master and ask him whether he is willing that I should hire two other porters and carry it to where your master now lives."

Dada said, "But it is Friday and about eleven o'clock. If you go now, my lord will be at the mosque. Come back this evening."

The boy replied, "I will come back at Dehhor,[24] so that your lord may have time to see it and decide before sunset."

And he went off, leaving the lantern in the courtyard covered with a sheet.

Shumshen N'har watched from the little window in her door until she saw that Dada and the other women were busied elsewhere; then she ran and entered the lantern, seating herself among the candlesticks and shutting the door after her.

No sooner had she entered the lantern than there came a knocking at the house door, and one of the slave children went to it. There was the jeweler himself and his apprentice and two porters, and the jeweler told how he had come to take the lantern away, for a message had come from the sultan's house that it should be sent there immediately.

The two porters lifted the lantern, and the Jew was instructing them how to carry it to his shop in the Mellah, when another messenger came from the sultan's wife regarding the lantern. He said, "Take it at once to the palace."

"But my lord," said the Jew, "I have something yet to do to the door. At present, it will not open or shut properly, so I have locked it, and the wife of our blessed lord, the sultan, will not be able to see the interior."

"What matter, dog," said the sultan's slave rudely. "Our lady wishes to see it now, and as to the door, you can adjust it tomorrow or the next day."

So the jeweler had to let the lantern be carried into the palace with its precious burden.

By the time the porters arrived with the lantern, the sultan's wife had lost all desire to see it, so the slave had it placed in a corner of the apartment of the prince for whose wedding it had been ordered and left it there, draped with its sheet.

Now the prince, whose name was Abd-el-Kebir, had after the morning prayers gone for a long ride outside Fez, and he returned to the palace late that evening. He was so weary with his exertions that he ordered his people to bring him some supper into his room and then to leave him at rest.

After partaking of the meal, he threw himself on a couch and fell asleep.

Meanwhile, Shumshen N'har had remained all day concealed in the lantern, scarcely daring to breathe, until, overcome by weariness, she too slept.

When she awoke, it was about midnight, and she was consumed with hunger. Emboldened by the quiet that reigned around, she opened the door of the lantern and peered out. She saw that she was in a lofty, spacious room, sumptuously furnished, and lit by a large lamp that hung in the center of an arch. Beneath this lamp was a small table with a tray and food, and in the recess beyond, on a divan, lay a most beautiful youth, fast asleep.

At first, overcome by fear and bashfulness, Shumshen N'har retreated into her lantern, but her hunger was too much for her.

"After all," she said, "this youth seems too sound asleep to awake easily, and the food is not too near to him. I will creep out, making less noise than a mouse, and assuage my hunger. Then I'll return before he sees me."

So she stole to the side of the table and began eating with fear and trembling.

But gradually curiosity made her creep closer to where he lay so that she might the better see his features, and their beauty was such that she forgot all but bent over closer and closer, and he, feeling that someone approached him, awoke suddenly.

At first, these glorious creatures gaze speechlessly at each other, and then with a cry Shumshen N'har tried to flee. But Mulai Abd-el-Kebir seized her caftan and implored her in earnest tones to fear nothing but to recount to him how it was that she was there.

His honeyed words prevailed on Shumshen N'har so that her fear departed, and she told the prince all her tale.

Mulai Abd-el-Kebir comforted her, and made her eat food and rest on his divan. And he said, "I will devise a way for you to escape from this dreadful thing that your people wish to do to you. In the meantime, you must remain hidden in your lantern in this room. No one shall know that you are here until I can find some other place where you will be safe."

And Shumshen N'har and the prince talked together until the morning light peeped in at the window.

Then she returned into her lantern and lay on some cushions that he had placed there. Then Mulai Abd-el-Kebir called his slaves and said, "Let no one enter this room when I am out, and this evening place food here just as you did last night."

And so it went on for three days. Every evening, when the palace was quiet, Shumshen N'har emerged from her lantern and ate with the prince and spent the whole night in conversation with him. And the heart of Abd-el-Kebir was filled with love for her, for her beauty was great, and he swore to her by a great oath that he would save her from her father and that he would marry her. In token, he gave her his ring, which was a diamond set in silver.

And Shumshen N'har loved him with a love greater even than that which he had for her.

On the fourth day, Prince Abd-el-Kebir went with his young men and his kaids to hunt gazelle.

While he was away, his sister, the Lilla Heber, said to her favorite slaves, "Mesoda, I will go to my brother's apartments this morning, because the

air there is cooler than in mine, and I know that he will not return until
evening."

Mesoda said, "It is well."

And the two went to the door of Mula Abd-el-Kebir's rooms. The slave
who was stationed there tried to stop them, saying, "Sidna said no one is
to enter here."

But Mesoda chided him, saying, "Don't you know that it is his own
sister, the Lilla Heber, who wishes to enter?"

And the slave was afraid and let them pass.

Lilla Heber was very pleased with her brother's room. It was much
cooler than in the woman's court, and the windows opened into a small
court full of flowers, and from them one could see the roofs of all Fez.
Moreover, the room was filled with beautiful and strange things, and Lilla
Heber and Mesoda amused themselves examining them all.

Then Mesoda lifted the sheet off the lantern, and said, "Look at this
splendid lantern, oh Lilla. It is for the wedding of your noble brother and
the Lilla Ameenah."

Lilla Heber said, "It is truly a magnificent thing, and how large it is.
I believe I could enter it."

And she tried to open it, and Mesoda helped her. At last, they managed to open it, and there lay on some cushions a young woman asleep,
even more lovely than a day in Yum-er-'Rbia. And when Lilla Heber saw
her, her anger was great and her jealousy was kindled, and she said to
Mesoda, "Roll this evil thing in a mattress and bear her to the baker's
and have her burned in the oven. Say that the mattress is infested with
lice."

Mesoda did as the princess commanded, stuffing a handkerchief into
Shumshen N'har's mouth, and she gave a piece of gold to the slave at the
door so that he might not tell Mulai Abd-el-Kebir who had entered the
rooms.

And Shumshen N'har, rolled in the mattress and bound about with
cords, was taken to the chief oven, and the master of the oven was told
to bake the bale thoroughly, in order to kill the vermin.

But, thanks be to God, the baker's wife saw the bale, and when her husband told her that it was from the sultan's palace she said, "I will examine
it before we put it into the oven, for it may have gold or silk embroideries
on it that may spoil with the heat. And also I may be able to get rid of the
vermin in some other manner."

When she cut the cords and the mattress fell open, there lay within neither gold nor silver nor noisome insects but a fair and slim young woman

with a face like the silver moon and hair that covered her as though with a garment.

The baker's wife took her into her own room and gave her reviving drinks until she opened her eyes, and then Shumshen N'har told her all her tale, and the baker's wife recounted how Lilla Heber's slaves had brought her to the oven in a mattress.

Then the baker's wife consulted with her husband, and they agreed to keep Shumshen N'har hidden from all people, and they clothed her in poor clothes, like those of their own daughter, whose name was Aisha. And Shumshen N'har lived with these good people and assisted them in their labors. Aisha was never tired of hearing her adventures and made Shumshen N'har show her the bracelets that had been the cause of all her woe.

And Aisha tried them on, and they fit her as if they had been made for her, for she was also a pretty young woman and graceful, though not fit to be compared with Shumshen N'har.

But the ring of Mulai Abd-el-Kebir Shumshen N'har showed to no one, and of his promise to wed her she said nothing. But in her heart she dwelled on these things, and when Aisha and her parents slept, she lay awake and wept and thought of the beauty and goodness of Mulai Abd-el-Kebira. And she prayed to Allah and our patron Mulai Drees to keep him from ill and to restore her to him.

Meanwhile, in the palace of the sultan there reigned woe and sorrow and distress, for Mulai Abd-el-Kebir, the favorite of the ruler, had fallen sick and shut himself up in his rooms. He would see no one and would eat no food, but he lamented day and night.

And no one knew the cause of his suffering.

His mother and father rose up to comfort him, but he would have none of them.

His sister, Lilla Heber, said, "Let it be. When he is wedded to his cousin, Ameenah, all will be cured." And she advised her brother to have the wedding.

But when Lilla Heber's words were repeated to Mulai Abd-el-Kebir, he cursed her most dreadfully, and he swore he would never marry Lilla Ameenah—no, not if all women died and only she were left. And the sultan was greatly perplexed.

But the sultan's wife, she who was mother of Abd-el-Kebir, said, "What does this talk of brides and weddings matter? If my son does not eat, he will die." And she caused it to be cried through the streets of Fez that all women versed in cookery might prepare a dish of food that would be placed before the prince, Mulai Abd-el-Kebir, so that he might perhaps be tempted to partake of it and thus eat and live. Moreover, the wife of the sultan promised a rich reward to her whose cookery would tempt her beloved son to eat.

On the first day, many dishes were brought to the rooms of Mulai Abd-el-Kebir, and he glanced at them, but with loathing, and would not touch so much as a grain of *kuskusoo.*

On the second day, this is what happened. That evening, the baker recounted to his wife how the prince had fallen ill and how all the women of Fez were vying with each other to make delicacies for him, so that his oven—yes, and every other oven—was filled with *tajjins.*[25]

Shumshen N'har heard what he said, and when he had returned to his oven, she said to his wife, "Oh my mother, let me also try, to see if I can tempt the prince to eat."

And she got *kuskusoo,* and some fat chickens and onions and vegetable marrows and spices and eggs and dates and raisins, and many other things. And she made a most succulent dish of *kuskusoo,* and the outside she orna- mented most lavishly. On it, she wrote "Bismillah" and "Long life to our lord" in cinnamon, and under that she wrote the word "Shumshen N'har," and inside the *kuskusoo,* right in the middle, she hid the diamond ring.[26]

And on the third day, as the slaves passed before the couch of Abd-el- Kebir, carrying the various dishes so that he might see them, he caught sight of the *kuskusoo* that Shumshen N'har had prepared. And he read what she had written on it. He beckoned to the slave who had carried it to place it before him. And the prince sat up and plunged his hand into the dish.

And he felt the ring. And he drew his hand out and ate.

Then he said, "This is good *kuskuskoo.* Find out who brought it."

They said, "My lord, my lord's baker brought it, and his daughter cooked it."

Lilla Heber's slave was standing nearby, and she heard and trembled and fled to her mistress. And Mulai Abd-el-Kebir got up, mounted his horse, and went down to the house where the baker lived.

The baker's wife brought a veiled Shumshen N'har out to him, and she spoke to him. He knew her voice. She told him all that had happened to her and how she had found a substitute to be her father's bride—Aisha, the baker's daughter.

Mulai Abd-el-Kebir took Shumshen N'har home to the palace and married her with great rejoicing. And the lantern was carried before her *amareeyah* by two porters.

Lilla Ameenah was married to Mulai Abd-el-Kebir's brother, Mulai Abd-el-Wahed, and Lilla Heber was sent by the sultan to Tafilet as a wife for the governor, and Mesoda and her slave accompanied her. As for the Jew, the charitable jeweler, there was a rich recompense.

And Shumshen N'har and Mulai Abd-el-Kebir's love was blessed by many children, and they lived for many years in prosperity and happiness.

Noplani Gxavu, a Xhosa storyteller, October 28, 1975

5

The Favored Daughter[27]

Batanga (Mpongwe) (Cameroon)[28]

Ra-Mborakinda lived in his town with his women and sons and daughters and servants. Among his women were Ngwekonde, his chief wife, and Ngwe-lĕgĕ, whom he neglected. But Ngwe-lĕgĕ had a beautiful daughter named Ilâmbe, much beloved by him. Ra-Mborakinda prized this daughter so much that he left everything to her direction.

One day he wished to start on a journey, intending to stay a long time. He had, in his anxiety for her safety, a rule that she should not go out of her house to walk far, lest she get into trouble. When he was arranging to go, he gave her all the keys and directions of everything into her hands. He said to her, "As I shall be away a long time, I leave all cloth and other goods for you to give out as you may see the people need."

Ilâmbe consented to do this work, and Ra-Mborakinda went away. After he had been away for quite a while, and she thought it time to give out cloth and whatever was required for the women, she was very careful not to show partiality to her friends, not even to give more to her mother. So if she gave, for instance, two cloths to her mother, she would give as many as five to Ngwekonde, and to all the others what she thought they needed. Yet Ngwekonde was not satisfied. Even though she had been given more than the others, her heart was planning mischief to Ilâmbe.

So Ngwekonde made up her mind, "I will know what I shall do some day," for she was jealous that the petted daughter had been put into authority over her.

One day the people saw Ilâmbe walking on the premises, and they remembered that she was going out of the bounds her father had assigned her.

They called, "Ilâmbe, Ilâmbe! Where are you going?"

She replied, "I'm going for a walk."

Soon they all seemed to forget to observe where she had gone, for Ngwekonde by her sorcery had caused Ilâmbe's head to be confused and had made the people forget to watch her.

Soon after Ilâmbe had gone out of the town into the forest, Ngwekonde also followed to go after her, without the people seeing her go. Ilâmbe went aimlessly, with Ngwekonde behind her.

Then, when they were far from the town, Ngwekonde said, "Yes, I've got you now!—you, with your pride because you are the beloved daughter! Do not think that you will again see your father and mother."

So she seized and dragged Ilâmbe to the foot of a big tree, tied her to it, and began to give her a severe beating.

Ilâmbe pleaded and said, "Ah, Ngwekonde! Please, what have I done? In what have I wronged you?"

But Ngwekonde only replied, "No mercy for you!" and then tied her hands fast to the tree. Then Ngwekonde returned to the town.

Soon after Ngwekonde had gone, Ilâmbe longed to get back to the town, for she feared the forest. She began to try to loosen the knots. She tried and tried, but the knots were hard.

Darkness came, and she was very much afraid. Finally, after long effort, she got the cords loosened, but she was weak and faint with hunger. She thought, "When I started on the walk, it was at random, and when I came to my senses, when Ngwekonde dragged me to the tree, I did not know in what direction we came, and now I do not know the direction back to the town."

So she began to walk in any direction. As she went on and on, at last she happened down a path. She said to herself, "This path, even if it does not lead to any town, may lead me to where people are." She went on and on, and after a while, by daylight, she saw that the view ahead opened. By that, she knew that she was getting near to some clearing and perhaps to some village.

Following the path, she came straight to a hamlet, but she was afraid to enter it. She thought, "Perhaps the owners of this place are enemies of my father, and they may beat me, just as Ngwekonde did. I must hide." So she remained for a while on the outskirts and then slowly and gradually crept from tree to tree on one side of the path, lest someone should see her. When she was close to the hamlet, she peeped through the bushes to see whether she could recognize anyone, for she feared strangers. She saw no one at all and went on into the street and entered a large house, and she began to look around her. She saw no person, only goods and food. After she had examined this large house, she went into a smaller one, which was the kitchen where the cooking was done. She exclaimed to herself, "Ah, it is not very late, and I am very hungry. I will try to cook something. And I must be quick, lest the owners come and find me and kill me."

So she started to work. She took of different kinds of food, and dried fish, and firewood, and began rapidly to cook. After the pot had boiled, she took out a little of its contents and began to eat hurriedly. As to the remainder of the food, she went to the larger house and got clean dishes, put the food into them, and set them on the table.

Then she went out of the hamlet and hid herself in the bushes near by. Soon after she had hidden herself there, the owners of the house came. They were carpenters. They entered their house, and on the table was food that was still warm.

They exclaimed, "Who has done us this good thing?"

They looked all through the house and into the kitchen, but no person was there. Then they looked outside, in the back yard, and no person was there.

They said, "Perhaps some other day we shall find out."

So they went into the house, took their seats at the table, and began to eat. As they ate, they shouted, "You who have done this, if you are a man or a woman, come out and show yourself!"

But there was no reply. Ilâmbe had heard them but remained quiet.

So they said to themselves, "Never mind. Tomorrow we will by artifice find out this person, whether it be a man or a woman. If it be a man, we will take him for a brother in our work. If it be a woman, then none of us shall marry her. She shall be our sister."

At night, she did not enter the town but remained hidden near.

Next morning, the carpenters said among themselves, "We go to our work, but one of us must return early, as if unexpectedly, and perhaps we can find out this person."

And they went to their work, but one returned early.

In the interval, Ilâmbe was busy with her work of cooking. She made the food and put it on the table. As she was passing from house to house, the man who had been watching came softly behind her and seized her.

She began to scream, and beg, "Please, please let me go!"

He said, "Do not fear. You have done no wrong. Be quiet."

Then he asked her questions, and she told her story. So Ilâmbe was quieted, and she completed the arranging of food on the table. Not long after that, the other men came, and the first man told them of Ilâmbe.

They said to her, "Remain quiet. You are our sister. We will take good care of you."

The next day, off at their place of work, they began to buy nice things for her. And they dressed her in fine clothes.

But they warned her, "One thing we must tell you. Be very careful.

Sometimes there is a certain big bird that comes here and picks up people and kills them. When it comes, people have to remain in their houses and shut their doors and windows." They also told her that the usual time of the coming of the bird was at noon.

On another day, they went away to their work, as usual. When they returned, Ilâmbe made their food, and they went into the house to eat it.

And the bird came at an unusual hour, and it killed Ilâmbe.

When the men came from the house where they had been eating, they found her dead. They mourned for her. When they had made a coffin and placed her in it, they refrained from burying it, for the body looked so lifelike and did not decay.

So they kept it suspended in the air, and daily they went to look at her face.

6

The African[29]

Berber (Algeria)[30]

BY MESSOUD BEN EL HADJ

Once there was a man who had seven wives and seven mares, but the wives had no children and the mares no foals.

So he asked advice, and a wise man said, "Go to a forest and get seven sticks. Break a stick on every mare. Go to market and buy seven apples. Give every one of your wives an apple."

He did so, and the seven mares had foals and his seven wives had children. Five had noble sons, one had a blind girl, and one had an African boy.

One day, the six boys were riding out of the town, and the five said, "Let us get rid of the African boy."

So they turned him away from them, and he returned crying to his father.

One day, the blind sister called to them and said, "Choose, my brothers, the one who is strong among you, and he will go to the house of the daughter of the chief of the Christians and bring me back her soap. Then I shall wash my eyes with it and recover my sight."

They all said, "We are ready."

All six started together, but again the five wished to get rid of the African. So they struck him.

At this place was a large stone, and the road divided.

The African said, "I will leave a feather under this stone. If one of us returns by this road, he will take out the feather and burn it."

The five went by one road, and the African by the other.

The five went along the road until they saw a castle. They went in to pass the night. There were women in the castle who welcomed them and said, "This is our custom. Each one of you will choose a woman, and if in the morning she is asleep on his lap he will marry her. But if he is asleep on her lap, she will take all his possessions."

Each brother took a woman, but after a little the women went out, each saying, "I shall change my clothes," and another woman came. She said, "I will go and put kohl on my eyes," and another came, so that the men became tired and slept. Then the women took all their possessions and turned them out. They walked until they found a Mozabite,[31] so they stopped and worked for him.

The African went along the road until he came to some corn. He let his horse eat the corn. A ghoul appeared, and the African fought with him and killed him. He took away the ghoul's flesh and continued his journey.

Then the African found a large, blind vulture. The vulture had seven young ones who were always looking for food for their father, but never found enough to satisfy him. The African gave the vulture the ghoul's flesh and satisfied him.

The vulture said, "You have satisfied me. What do you want?"

The African said, "I want to cross the sea and return."

The vulture said, "Sit down until I call to you."

The African went and filled his bag again with the ghoul's flesh and sat down until the children of the vulture came back.

The first one who returned said, "Open your mouth, father."

The old vulture said, "Put the results of your hunting there. I am satisfied."

All seven children of the vulture brought food, and the old vulture said to all, "I am satisfied." Then the old vulture said, "Choose the strongest one among you to take this Negro across the sea and to come back with him."

The eldest young vulture said he would do it in a year, and all offered to do it in less time. The youngest said, "I will take him in the morning and return with him in the afternoon."

So they started.

Every time the young vulture flapped his wings, the African sitting on his back threw him a piece of ghoul's flesh.

And so they crossed the sea.

The African went to a Jew and said, "Make me a golden cock. I will get inside it, and it will walk by itself."

The Jew did so, and the African went to the house of the daughter of the chief of the Christians. In the house, he found the daughter of the chief of the Christians asleep. Her custom was to sleep for a month and to be awake for a month.

The African changed rings with her and changed soap with her, then got on the vulture and returned to his horse, which he found as fat as a fish.

So he mounted and rode to the stone.

The African found that the feather was still under the stone, so he knew that his brothers had not returned. He said, "The road that has eaten my brothers will eat me also." So he went along that road until he saw some smoke, and then he saw that his brothers were there, working and making charcoal. They knew him, but he did not know them because their faces were blackened with charcoal.

They said to him, "What are you looking for?"

He answered, "I am looking for my brothers."

They wept and embraced him, and said, "We are your brothers."

Then they told him what had happened to them.

The African told the Mozabite that he must release his brothers or he would kill him. So the Mozabite let them go, and then the African went with his brothers to the castle of the women.

The women welcomed them as before and proposed the same conditions.

Then the African chose a woman, but when she wanted to change her clothes he said, "Here are some." And when she wanted to put kohl on her eyes, he said, "Here is some." And so, when the morning came, the woman was asleep on his lap.

So each man took a woman, and the men took the women's money and their clothes and went along the road until they were thirsty.

They found a well, but no one would go down it until the African said, "I will go down."

They let him down with a rope, and they all drank. Then they cut the rope and left the African in the well. They quarreled about his horse, but the horse remained at the well.

Then they returned to their father the sultan, who said to them, "Where is your brother?"

They replied, "We do not know. We got rid of him the first day."

A mueddin went up a minaret to call to prayer and saw the horse and thought it was thirsty. So he went with a rope to the well and saw the African in the well but was unable to pull him out. So he tied the rope to the horse, which pulled him out. Then the mueddin took the African to his house.

The daughter of the chief of the Christians then came to the sultan's place and said, "Where is your son the African?"

The sultan said, "I do not know. He went with his brothers. His brothers have returned, but he has not returned."

The daughter of the chief of the Christians said to the brothers, "Where is your brother the African?"

They said, "We do not know."

So she cut off all their heads.

Then she said to the sultan, "If you do not tell me where your son the African is, I will cut off your head, too. You have three days to find him."

The sultan sent a crier, who said, "He who has found my son or has seen him, I will give half my money."

Then the mueddin said to the sultan, "Here he is, with me."

The daughter of the chief of the Christians rejoiced and said to the African, "You will go with me."

And the African said, "You must cover the ground from here to your house with silk, so that my horse can walk on it."

So she took him to her house, and he stopped and worked for her and her father.

7

Dschemil and Dschemila[32]

Berber (Libya)[33]

There was once a man whose name Dschemil, and he had a cousin who was called Dschemila. They had been betrothed by their parents when they were children, and now Dschemil thought that the time had come for them to be married. He went two or three days' journey to the nearest big town to buy furniture for the new house.

While he was away, Dschemila and her friends set off to the neighboring woods to pick up sticks, and as she gathered them she found an iron mortar lying on the ground. She placed it on her bundle of sticks, but the mortar would not stay still, and whenever she raised the bundle to put it on her shoulders, it slipped off sideways. At length, she saw that the only way to carry the mortar was to tie it in the very middle of her bundle, and she had just unfastened her sticks when she heard her companions' voices.

"Dschemila, what are you doing? It is almost dark, and if you mean to come with us you must be quick!"

But Dschemila only replied, "You had better go back without me, for I am not going to leave my mortar behind, if I stay here until midnight."

"Do as you like," said the young women and started on their walk home.

The night soon fell, and at the last ray of light the mortar suddenly became an ogre, who threw Dschemila on her back, and carried her off into a desert place, a whole month's distance from her home town. Here he shut her into a castle and told her not to fear, as her life was safe.

Then he went back to his wife, leaving Dschemila weeping over the fate that she had brought upon herself.

Meanwhile, the other young women had reached home, and Dschemila's mother came out to look for her daughter.

"What have you done with her?" she asked anxiously.

"We had to leave her in the wood," they replied, "for she had picked up an iron mortar and could not manage to carry it."

So the old woman set off at once for the forest, calling to her daughter as she hurried along.

"Do go home," cried the townspeople when they heard her. "We will go and look for your daughter. You are only a woman, and this is a task that needs strong men."

But she answered, "Yes, go. But I shall go with you! Perhaps it is only her corpse that we shall find after all. She has most likely been stung by asps or eaten by wild beasts."

The men, seeing that her heart was bent on it, said no more, but they told one of the young women she must come with them and show them the place where they had left Dschemila. They found the bundle of wood lying where she had dropped it, but the young woman was nowhere to be seen.

"Dschemila! Dschemila!" they cried.

But nobody answered.

"If we make a fire, perhaps she will see it," said one of the men.

And they lit a fire and then went, one this way and one that, through the forest, to look for her, whispering to each other that if she had been killed by a lion they would be sure to find some trace of it. Or if she had fallen asleep, the sound of their voices would awaken her. Or if a snake had bitten her, they would at least come on her corpse.

All night, they searched, and when morning broke and they knew no more than before what had become of the young woman, they grew weary and said to the mother, "It is no use. Let us go home. Nothing has happened to your daughter, except that she has run away with a man."

"Yes, I will come," she said, "but I must first look in the river. Perhaps someone has thrown her in there."

But the young woman was not in the river.

For four days, the mother and father waited and watched for their child to come back. Then they gave up hope and said to each other, "What is to be done? What are we to say to the man to whom Dschemila is betrothed? Let us kill a goat and bury its head in the grave, and when the man returns we must tell him that Dschemila is dead."

Very soon, the bridegroom came back, bringing with him carpets and soft cushions for the house of his bride. And as he entered the town, Dschemila's father met him, saying, "Greetings to you. She is dead."

At these words, the young man broke into loud cries, and it was some time before he could speak. Then he turned to one in the crowd that had gathered around him and asked, "Where have they buried her?"

"Come to the churchyard with me," he said, and the young man went with him, carrying some of the beautiful things he had brought. These he laid on the grass, and then he began to weep again. All day he stayed there, and at nightfall he gathered up his things and carried them to his own house.

But when the day dawned, he took them in his arms and returned to the grave, where he remained as long as it was light, playing softly on his flute.

And this he did daily for six months.

One morning, a man who was wandering through the desert, having lost his way, came upon a lonely castle. The sun was very hot, and the man was very tired, so he said to himself, "I will rest a little in the shadow of this castle."

He stretched himself out comfortably and was almost asleep when he heard a voice calling to him softly. "Are you a ghost," the voice said, "or a man?"

He looked up and saw a young woman learning out of a window, and he answered, "I am a man, and a better one, too, than your father or your grandfather."

"May all good luck be with you," she said, "but what has brought you into this land of ogres and horrors?"

"Does an ogre really live in this castle?" he asked.

"Certainly he does," replied the young woman, "and as night is not far off he will be here soon. So, dear friend, depart quickly, lest he return and snap you up for supper."

"But I am so thirsty!" said the man. "Be kind, and give me something to drink, or else I shall die! Surely, even in this desert, there must be some spring."

"Well, I have noticed that whenever the ogre brings back water, he always comes from that side, so if you follow the same direction you may find some."

The man jumped up at once and was about to start, when the young woman spoke again: "Tell me, where are you going?"

"Why do you want to know?"

"I have an errand for you, but tell me first whether you're going east or west."

"I am traveling to Damascus."

"Then do this for me. As you pass through our village, ask for a man called Dschemil, and say to him, 'Dschemila greets you from the castle that lies far away and is rocked by the wind. In my grave lies only a goat. So take heart.'"

The man promised and went his way, until he came to a spring of water. He drank a great draught and then lay on the bank and slept quietly.

When he woke, he said to himself, "The young woman did a good deed when she told me where to find water. A few hours more and I should have been dead. So I will do her bidding and seek out her home town and the man for whom the message was given."

For a whole month he traveled, until at last he reached the town where Dschemil dwelled, and, as luck would have it, there was the young man sitting before his door with his beard unshaven and his shaggy hair hanging over his eyes.

"Welcome, stranger," said Dschemil, as the man stopped. "Where have you come from?"

"I come from the west, and go toward the east," he answered.

"Well, stop with us a while, and rest and eat," said Dschemil.

The man entered, and food was set before him. He sat down with the father of the young woman and her brothers. Only Dschemil himself was absent, squatting on the threshold.

"Why do you not eat, too?" asked the stranger.

But one of the young men whispered hastily, "Leave him alone. Take no notice. It is only at night that he ever eats."

So the stranger went on silently eating his food.

Suddenly, one of Dschemil's brothers called out, "Dschemil, bring us some water!"

And the stranger remembered his message and said, "Is there a man here named Dschemil? I lost my way in the desert and came to a castle, and a young woman looked out of the window and—"

"Be quiet," they cried, fearing that Dschemil might hear.

But Dschemil had heard, and he came forward and said, "What did you see? Tell me truly, or I will cut off your head this instant!"

"My lord," replied the stranger, "as I was wandering, hot and tired, through the desert, I saw near me a great castle, and I said aloud, 'I will rest a little in its shadow.' And a young woman looked out of a window and said, 'Are you a ghost or a man?' And I answered, 'I am a man, and a better one, too, than your father or your grandfather.' And I was thirsty and asked for water, but she had none to give me, and I felt as if I were going to die. Then she told me that the ogre in whose castle she dwelled brought in water always from the same side and that if I too went that way, most likely I would come to a spring. But before I departed, she begged me to go to her home town, and if I met a man called Dschemil I was to say to him, 'Dschemila greets you, from the castle that lies far away and is rocked by the wind. In my grave lies only a goat. So take heart.'"

Then Dschemil turned to his family and said, "Is this true? And is Dschemila not dead at all but simply stolen from her home?"

"No, no," they said, "his story is a pack of lies. Dschemila is really dead. Everybody knows it."

"That I shall see for myself," said Dschemil, and, snatching up a spade, he hurried off to the grave where the goat's head lay buried.

They said, "Then hear what happened. When you were away, she went with the other young women to the forest to gather wood. And there she found an iron mortar, which she wished to bring home. But she could not carry it, and she would not leave it. So the other young women returned without her, and as night had come, we all set out to look for her but found nothing. And we said, 'The bridegroom will be here tomorrow, and when he learns that she is lost, he will set out to seek her, and we shall lose him, too. Let us kill a goat and bury it in her grave and tell him that she is dead.' Now you know, so do as you will. Only, if you go to seek her, take with you this man with whom she has spoken. He can show you the way."

"Yes, that is the best plan," said Dschemil. "Give me food and hand me my sword, and we'll set out at once."

But the stranger said, "I am not going to waste a whole month, leading you to the castle! If it were only a day or two's journey, I would not mind. But a month—no!"

"Come with me then for three days," said Dschemil, "and put me on the right road, and I will reward you richly."

"Very well," said the stranger, "so let it be."

For three days, they traveled from sunrise to sunset; then the stranger said, "Dschemil?"

"Yes," he said.

"Go straight on until you reach a spring, then go on a little farther, and soon you will see the castle standing before you."

"So I will," said Dschemil.

"Farewell, then," said the stranger, and he turned back the way he had come.

"It was twenty-six days before Dschemil caught sight of a green spot rising out of the sandy desert, and he knew that the spring was near at last. He quickened his steps and soon was kneeling by the side of the spring, drinking thirstily of the bubbling water.

Then he lay down on the cool grass and began to think. "If the man was right, the castle must be somewhere about. I had better sleep here tonight, and tomorrow I shall be able to see where it is."

So he slept long and peacefully.

When he awoke, the sun was high, and he jumped up and washed his face and hands in the spring before continuing his journey. He had not walked far, when the castle suddenly appeared before him, though a moment before not a trace of it could be seen.

"How am I to get in?" he thought. "I dare not knock, lest the ogre hear me. Perhaps it would be best for me to climb up the wall and wait to see what will happen."

So he did, and after sitting on the top for about an hour, a window above him opened, and a voice said, "Dschemil!"

He looked up, and, at the sight of Dschemila, whom he had so long believed to be dead, he began to weep.

"Dear cousin," she whispered, "what has brought you here?"

"My grief at losing you."

"Go away at once. If the ogre comes back, he will kill you."

"I swear by your head, queen of my heart, that I have not found you only to lose you again! If I must die—well, I must."

"What can I do for you?"

"Anything you like."

"If I let down a cord, can you make it fast under your arms and climb up?"

"Of course I can," he said.

So Dschemila lowered the cord, and Dschemil tied it around him and climbed up to her window. Then they embraced each other tenderly and burst into tears of joy.

"But what shall I do when the ogre returns?" she asked.

"Trust me," he said.

Now, there was a chest in the room, in which Dschemila kept her clothes. She made Dschemil get into it and lie at the bottom and told him to keep very still.

He was hidden just in time, for the lid was hardly closed when the ogre's heavy tread was heard on the stairs. He flung open the door, bringing men's flesh for himself and lamb's flesh for the young woman.

"I smell the smell of a man!" he thundered. "What is he doing here?"

"How could any one have come to this desert place?" asked the girl, bursting into tears.

"Do not cry," said the ogre. "Perhaps a raven has dropped some scraps from its claws."

"Yes, I was forgetting," she said. "One did drop some bones about."

"Well, burn them to powder," said the ogre, "so that I may swallow it."

So the young woman took some bones and burned them and gave them to the ogre, saying, "Here is the powder. Swallow it."

When he had swallowed the powder, the ogre stretched himself out and went to sleep.

In a little while, the man's flesh, which the young woman was cooking for the ogre's supper, called out,

"Hist! Hist!
A man lies in the kist!"

And the lamb's flesh answered,

"He is your brother,
And cousin of the other."

The ogre moved sleepily and asked, "What did the meat say, Dschemila?"

"Only that I must be sure to add salt."

"Well, add salt."

"Yes, I have done so," she said.

The ogre was soon sound asleep again, when the man's flesh called out a second time:

"Hist! Hist!
A man lies in the kist!"

And the lamb's flesh answered,

"He is your brother,
And cousin of the other."

"What did it say, Dschemila?" asked the ogre.

"Only that I must add pepper."

"Well, add pepper."

"Yes, I have done so," she said.

The ogre had had a long day's hunting and could not keep himself awake. In a moment, his eyes were tightly shut, and then the man's flesh called out for the third time:

"Hist! Hist!
A man lies in the kist!"

And the lamb's flesh answered,

"He is your brother,
And cousin of the other."

"What did it say, Dschemila?" asked the ogre.

"Only that it was ready and that I had better take it off the fire."

"Then if it is ready, bring it to me, and I will eat it."

So she brought it to him, and while he was eating she supped off the lamb's flesh herself and managed to put some aside for her cousin.

When the ogre had finished and had washed his hands, he said to Dschemila, "Make my bed; I'm tired."

So she made his bed, putting a nice soft pillow for his head, and tucked him in.

"Father," she said suddenly.

"Well, what is it?"

"Dear father, if you are really asleep, why are your eyes always open?"

"Why do you ask that, Dschemila? Do you want to deal treacherously with me?"

"No, of course not, father. How could I? And what would be the use of it?"

"Well, why do you want to know?"

"Because last night I woke up and saw the whole place shining in a red light, which frightened me."

"That happens when I am fast asleep."

"And what is the good of the pin you always keep here so carefully?"

"If I throw that pin in front of me, it turns into an iron mountain."

"And this darning needle?"

"That becomes a sea."

"And this hatchet?"

"That becomes a thorn hedge, which no one can pass through. But why do you ask all these questions? I am sure you have something in your head."

"I just wanted to know. And how could anyone find me out here?" and she began to cry.

"Oh, don't cry. I was only in fun," said the ogre.

He was soon asleep again, and a yellow light shone through the castle.

"Come quick!" called Dschemil. "We must fly now while the ogre is asleep."

"Not yet," she said. "There is a yellow light shining. I don't think he is asleep."

So they waited for an hour.

Then Dschemil whispered again, "Wake up! There is no time to lose!"

"Let me see if he is asleep," she said, and she peeped in and saw a red light shining. Then she stole back to her cousin and asked, "But how are we to get out?"

"Get the rope, and I will let you down."

She fetched the rope, the hatchet, and the pin and the needles and said, "Take them. Put them in the pocket of your cloak, and be sure not to lose them."

Dschemil put them carefully in his pocket. He tied the rope around her and let her down over the wall.

"Are you safe?" he asked.

"Yes, quite."

"Then untie the rope, so that I may draw it up."

Dschemila did as she was told, and in a few minutes he stood beside her.

Now, all this time the ogre was asleep and had heard nothing.

Then his dog came to him and said, "Sleeper, are you having pleasant dreams? Dschemila has forsaken you and run away."

The ogre got out of bed, gave the dog a kick, then went back again and slept until morning.

When it grew light, he rose, and called, "Dschemila! Dschemila!" but he heard only the echo of his own voice.

He dressed himself quickly, buckled on his sword, and whistled to his dog. And he followed the road that he knew the fugitives must have taken.

"Cousin," said Dschemila suddenly, turning around as she spoke.

"What is it?" he said.

"The ogre is coming after us. I saw him."

"But where is he? I don't see him."

"Over there. He looks only about as tall as a needle."

They both began to run as fast as they could, while the ogre and his dog kept drawing always nearer. A few more steps, and he would be by their side.

Then Dschemila threw the pin behind her.

In a moment, it became an iron mountain between them and their enemy.

"We will break it down, my dog and I!" cried the ogre in a rage, and they dashed at the mountain until they had forced a path through.

And they came nearer and nearer.

"Cousin!" said Dschemila suddenly.

"What is it?"

"The ogre is coming after us with his dog!"

"You go on in front then," he said, and they both ran on as fast as they could, while the ogre and the dog always drew nearer and nearer.

"They are close!" cried the young woman, glancing behind. "You must throw the pin."

So Dschemil took the hatchet from the cloak and threw it behind him, and a dense thicket of thorns sprang up around them, which the ogre and his dog could not pass through.

"I will get through it somehow, if I burrow underground," the ogre cried, and very soon he and his dog were on the other side.

"Cousin," said Dschemila, "they are close to us now."

"Go in front, and fear nothing," replied Dschemil.

So she ran on a little way and then stopped.

"He is only a few yards away now," she said, and Dschemil flung the needle on the ground. It turned into a lake.

"I will drink, and my dog will drink, until it is dry!" shrieked the ogre, and the dog drank so much that it burst and died. But the ogre did not stop for that, and soon the whole lake was nearly dry. Then he exclaimed, "Dschemila, let your head become a donkey's head, and your hair fur!"

When it was done, Dschemil looked at her in horror and said, "She is really a donkey, and not a woman at all!"

And he left her and went home.

For two days, poor Dschemila wandered about alone, weeping bitterly.

When her cousin drew near his home town, he began to think over his conduct and to feel ashamed of himself.

"Perhaps by this time she has changed back to her proper self," he said to himself. "I will go and see."

So he made all the haste he could, and at last he saw her seated on a rock, trying to keep off the wolves who longed to have her for dinner.

He drove them off and said, "Get up, dear cousin, you have had a narrow escape."

Dschemila stood up and said, "Bravo, my friend. You persuaded me to fly with you and then left me helplessly to my fate."

"Shall I tell you the truth?" he asked.

"Tell it."

"I thought you were a witch, and I was afraid of you."

"Did you not see me before my transformation? And did you not watch it happen under your very eyes, when the ogre bewitched me?"

"What shall I do?" said Dschemil. "If I take you into the town, everyone will laugh and say, 'Is that a new kind of toy you have got? It has hands like a woman, feet like a woman, the body of a woman, but its head is the head of an ass, and its hair is fur.'"

"Well, what do you mean to do with me?" asked Dschemila. "Better take me home to my mother by night and tell no one anything about it."

"So I will," he said.

They waited where they were until it was nearly dark; then Dschemil brought his cousin home.

"Is that Dschemil?" asked the mother when he knocked softly.

"Yes, it is."

"And have you found her?"

"Yes, and I have brought her to you."

"Oh, where is she? Let me see her!" cried the mother.

"Here, behind me," said Dschemil.

But when the poor woman caught sight of her daughter, she shrieked, and exclaimed, "Are you making fun of me? When did I ever give birth to an ass?"

"Hush!" said Dschemil. "It is not necessary to let the whole world know. If you will look at her body, you will see two scars on it."

"Mother," sobbed Dschemila, "do you really not know your own daughter?"

"Yes, of course I know her."

"Where are her two scars then?"

"On her thigh is a scar from the bite of a dog, and on her breast is the mark of a burn, where she pulled a lamp over her when she was little."

"Then look at me and see if I am not your daughter," said Dschemila, throwing off her clothes and showing her two scars.

And at the sight, her mother embraced her, weeping. "Dear daughter," she cried, "what evil fate has befallen you?"

"It was the ogre who carried me off first and then bewitched me," answered Dschemila.

"But what is to be done with you?" asked her mother.

"Hide me away, and tell no one anything about me. And you, dear cousin, say nothing to the neighbors, and if they should put questions, you can answer that I have not yet been found."

"So I will," he said.

Then he and her mother took her upstairs and hid her in a cupboard, where she stayed a whole month, going out to walk only when all the world was asleep.

Meanwhile, Dschemil had returned to his own home, where his father and mother, his brothers and neighbors, greeted him joyfully.

"When did you come back," they asked, "and have you found Dschemila?"

"No, I searched the whole world for her and heard nothing of her."

"Did you part company with the man who started with you?"

"Yes. After three days, he got so weak and useless that he could not go on. It must be a month since he reached his home again. I went on and visited every castle and looked in every house. But there were no signs of her, so I gave it up."

They said, "We told you before that it was no good. An ogre or ogress must have snapped her up, and how can you expect to find her?"

"I loved her too much to be still," he said.

But his friends did not understand, and soon they spoke to him again about it.

"We will seek a wife for you. There are plenty of young women prettier than Dschemila."

"Perhaps, but I do not want them."

"But what will you do with all the cushions and carpets and beautiful things you bought for your house?"

"They can stay in the chests."

"But the moths will eat them! For a few weeks, it is of no consequence, but after a year or two they will be useless."

"And if they have to lie there ten years, I will have Dschemila, and her only, for my wife. For a month, or even two months, I will rest here quietly. Then I will go and seek her again."

"You are quite mad! Is she the only young woman in the world? There are plenty of others better worth having than she is."

"If there are, I have not seen them. And why do you make all this fuss? Every man knows his own business best."

"Why, it is you who are making all the fuss yourself—"

But Dschemil turned and went into the house, because he did not want to quarrel.

Three months later, a Jew who was traveling across the desert came to the castle and laid himself down under the well to rest.

In the evening, the ogre saw him there and said, "Jew, what are you doing here? Have you anything to sell?"

"I have only some clothes," said the Jew, who was in mortal terror of the ogre.

"Oh, don't be afraid of me," said the ogre, laughing. "I shall not eat you. Indeed, I mean to go a bit of the way with you myself."

"I am ready, gracious sir," replied the Jew, rising to his feet.

"Well, go straight on until you reach a town, and in that town you will find a young woman called Dschemila and a young man called Dschemil. Take this mirror and this comb with you and say to Dschemila, 'Your father, the ogre, greets you and begs you to look at your face in this mirror, and it will appear as it was before. And you should comb your hair with this comb, and it will be as formerly.' If you do not carry out my orders, I will eat you the next time we meet."

"I will obey you punctually," cried the Jew.

After thirty days, the Jew entered the gate of the town and sat down in the first street he came to, hungry, thirsty, and very tired.

By chance, Dschemil happened to pass by, and, seeing a man sitting there, full in the glare of the sun, he stopped, and said, "Get up at once, Jew. You will have a sunstroke if you sit in such a place."

"Ah, good sir," replied the Jew, "for a whole month I have been traveling, and I am too tired to move."

"Which way did you come?" asked Dschemil.

"From out there," answered the Jew, pointing behind him.

"And you have been traveling for a month, you say? Well, did you see anything remarkable?"

"Yes, good sir. I saw a castle and lay down to rest under its shadow. And an ogre woke me and told me to come to this town, where I should find a young man called Dschemil and a young woman called Dschemila."

"My name is Dschemil. What does the ogre want with me?"

"He gave me some presents for Dschemila. How can I see her?"

"Come with me, and you shall give them into her own hands."

So the two went together to the house of Dschemila's uncle, and Dschemil led the Jew into his aunt's room.

"Aunt," he said, "this Jew who is with me has come from the ogre and has brought with him, as presents, a mirror and a comb that the ogre has sent her."

"But it may be only some wicked trick on the part of the ogre," she said.

"I don't think so," said the young man. "Give her the things."

The young woman was called, and she came out of her hiding place. She went up to the Jew, saying, "Where have you come from, Jew?"

"From your father, the ogre."

"And what errand did he send you on?"

"He told me I was to give you this mirror and this comb and to say, 'Look in this mirror, and comb your hair with this comb, and both will become as they were formerly.'"

Dschemila took the mirror and looked into it and combed her hair with the comb.

And she had no longer an ass's head but the face of a beautiful woman.

Great was the joy of both mother and cousin at this wonderful sight, and the news that Dschemila had returned soon spread, and the neighbors came flocking in with greetings.

"When did you come back?"

"My cousin brought me."

"But he told us he could not find you."

"I did that on purpose," said Dschemil. "I did not want everyone to know."

Then he turned to his father and his mother, his brothers and his sisters-in-law, and said, "We must set to work at once, for the wedding will be today."

A beautiful litter was prepared to carry the bride to her new home, but she shrank back, saying, "I am afraid, lest the ogre carry me off again."

"How can the ogre get at you when we are all here?" they said. "There are two thousand of us, altogether, and every man has his sword."

"He will manage it somehow," said Dschemila. ""He is a powerful king."

"She is right," said an old man. "Take away the litter, and let her go on foot if she is afraid."

"But it is absurd!" exclaimed the others. "How can the ogre get hold of her?"

"I will not go," said Dschemila. "You do not know that monster. I do."

While they were disputing, the bridegroom arrived.

"Let her alone. She shall stay in her father's house. After all, I can live here, and the wedding feast shall be made ready."

So they were married at last, and they died without having had a single quarrel.

8

Half-a-Cock[34]

Berber (Morocco)[35]

In times past, there was a man who had two wives, and one was wise and one was foolish. They owned a cock in common.

One day, they quarreled about the cock, cut it in two, and each took half. The foolish wife cooked her part. The wise one let her part live, and it walked on one foot and had only one wing.

Some days passed thus.

Then the half-a-cock got up early and started on his pilgrimage. At the middle of the day, he was tired and went toward a brook to rest.

A jackal came there to drink. Half-a-Cock jumped on his back, stole one of his hairs, which he put under his wing.

And then he resumed his journey. He proceeded until evening and stopped under a tree to pass the night there. He had not rested long when he saw a lion pass near the tree where he was lying. As soon as he saw the lion, he jumped on his back and stole one of his hairs, which he put with that of the jackal.

The next morning, he got up early and took up his journey again. Arriving at the middle of a forest, he met a boar and said, "Give me a hair from your back, as the king of the animals and the trickiest of them have done—the jackal and the lion."

The boar answered, "As these two personages so important among the animals have done this, I will also give you what you request."

He plucked a hair from his back and gave it to Half-a-Cock.

Half-a-Cock went on his way and arrived at the palace of a king. He began to crow and to say, "Tomorrow, the king will die, and I will take his wife."

Hearing these words, the king gave to his servants the command to seize Half-a-Cock and cast him into the middle of the sheep and goat-pen to be trampled upon and killed by them so that the king might get rid of his crowing. The servants seized him and cast him into the pen to perish.

When he got there, Half-a-Cock took from under his wing the jackal's hair and burned it in the fire.

As soon as it was near the fire, the jackal came and said, "Why are you burning my hair? As soon as I smelled it, I came running."

Half-a-Cock replied, "You see the situation I am in. Get me out of it."

"That's an easy matter," said the jackal and immediately blew in order to summon his brothers. They gathered around him, and he gave them this command: "My brothers, save me from Half-a-Cock, for he has a hair from my back that he put in the fire. I don't want to burn. Take Half-a-Cock out of the sheep-pen, and you will be able to take my hair from his hands."

At once, the jackals rushed to the pen, strangled everything that was there, and rescued Half-a-Cock.

The next day, the king found his stables deserted and his animals killed. He looked for Half-a-Cock, but in vain.

The next day at the supper hour, Half-a-Cock began to crow as he did the first time. The king called his servants and said to them, "Seize Half-a-Cock and cast him into the cattle-yard so that he may be crushed under the feet of the cattle."

The servants caught Half-a-Cock and threw him into the middle of the cow-pen. As soon as he got there, he took the lion's hair and put it into the fire. The lion came, roaring, and said, "Why do you burn my hair? I smelled from my cave the odor of burning hair and came running to learn the motive of your action."

Half-a-Cock answered, "You see my situation. Help me out of it."

The lion went out and roared, calling his brothers. They came in great haste and said to him, "Why do you call now?"

"Take Half-a-Cock from the ox-yard, for he has one of my hairs, which he can put into the fire. If you don't rescue Half-a-Cock, he will burn the hair, and I don't want to smell the odor of burning hair while I am alive."

His brothers obeyed. They at once killed all the cattle in the pen.

The king saw that his animals were all dead, and he fell into such a rage that he nearly strangled. He looked for Half-a-Cock, to kill him with his own hands. He searched for a long time without finding him and finally went home to rest.

At sunset, Half-a-Cock came to his usual place and crowed as on the former occasions.

The king called his servants and said to them, "This time, when you have caught Half-a-Cock, put him in a house and shut all the doors until morning. I will kill him myself."

The servants seized him immediately and put him in the treasure-room.

When Half-a-Cock got there, he saw money under his feet. He waited until he had nothing to fear from the masters of the house, who were all sound asleep, and then he took from under his wing the hair of the boar. He started a fire and placed the boar's hair in it.

At once, the boar came running, shaking the earth. He thrust his head against the wall. The wall shook, and half of it fell down. Going to Half-a-Cock, the boar said, "Why are you burning my hair at this moment?"

"Pardon me, you see the situation that I am in, without counting what awaits me in the morning, for the king is going to kill me with his own hands if you don't get me out of this prison."

The boar replied, "That is easy. Don't fear, I will open the door so that you may go out. In fact, you have stayed here long enough. Get up, go and take money enough for you and your children."

Half-a-Cock obeyed. He rolled in the gold, took all that stuck to his wing and his foot, and swallowed as much as he could hold. He took the road he had followed the first day, and when he had arrived near the house he called the mistress and said, "Strike now, don't be afraid to kill me."

His mistress began to strike and struck until Half-a-Cock called from beneath the mat, "Enough now. Roll the mat."

She obeyed and saw the earth all shining with gold.

At the time when Half-a-Cock returned from his pilgrimage, the two women, the foolish wife and the wise wife, owned a dog in common. The foolish one, seeing that her companion had received much money, said to her, "We will divide the dog between us."

The wise woman answered, "We can't do anything with it. Let it live; I will give you my half. Keep it for yourself. I have no need of it."

The foolish one said to the dog, "Go on a pilgrimage as Half-a-Cock did, and bring me some gold."

The dog started to carry out the commands of her mistress. She began her journey in the morning and came to a fountain. As she was thirsty, she started to drink. As she stopped, she saw in the middle of the fountain a yellow stone. She took it in her mouth and ran back home.

When she reached the house, she called her mistress and said to her, "Get ready the mats and the rods; you see that I have come back from the pilgrimage."

The foolish one prepared the mats, under which the dog ran as soon as she heard the voice of the mistress, and said, "Strike gently."

The woman seized the rods and struck with all the force possible.

For a long while, the dog cried out to her to stop the blows. But her mistress refused to stop until the animal was cold. Then she lighted up the mats and found the dog dead with the yellow stone in her mouth.

Nombulela Kholisile, a Xhosa storyteller, November 4, 1975

9

The Boy and the Girl[36]

Bulu (Cameroon)[37]

Once, there was a man who was a hunchback. When he went courting, he saw a woman who was also a hunchback. He said to the woman, "I wish to marry you, because you are a hunchback, even as I myself. Therefore, I wish to marry you."

The woman assented, and they were married.

The man happened to hear of a person who had the power to heal hunchbacks, so he arose to go to this man. As he was journeying on the road, he came upon a very old man, and he gave him some food. The man was offensive and ugly and dirty, but he nonetheless gave him of his food.

The old man said to him, "My young man, when you have reached the town and they cook food for you, then take the food to a house that is old and tumble-down; do not object, but go and eat there."

And the young man did that. When he reached the town, they cooked food for him, then took it to a bad-looking house. He went there and entered the house and began to eat the food.

Suddenly, he noticed a very old man lying there, and he took part of his food and gave it to the old man.

The old man asked him, "Who instructed you in this matter?"

He answered, "I myself."

Then the old man said, "This very night, if they come and ask you, 'Which do you prefer, a charm covered with the skin of the genet or a charm covered with the skin of a civet cat?' you reply, 'I prefer a charm covered with the skin of a genet.' And if they ask you, 'Which do you prefer to be, straight as an arrow or bent over?' you answer, 'Straight as an arrow.'"

When night had come, they showed him a house in which he was to sleep.

During the night, they came to him.

"Which do you prefer, a charm covered with the skin of the genet or a charm covered with the skin of a civet cat?"

He said, "I prefer a charm covered with the skin of a genet."

And they asked, "Which to do you prefer to be, straight as an arrow or bent over?"

And he said, "Straight as an arrow."

And thus he was healed.

He returned to his own town, a man healed completely.

When his wife saw this, she was very much grieved, because she and her husband had both been hunchbacks, but now her husband was a well man.

So the woman jumped up quickly and started to go.

But her husband called out to her, "Wait! I will instruct you as to what you should do."

But she replied, "No! Did you say anything to me at all, or even say goodbye, when you went away?"

So she went in great haste.

And when she came upon the old man lying by the roadside, she spat on the ground, and said, "What a horrid old thing this is!"

And the old man, in turn, said, "My youthful woman, go on to where you wish to go."

The woman said to him, "I see that you wish to offer me insult with your talk."

She left him lying there and went on her journey.

When she had come to the town, they cooked food for her, and they took the food to the house where the old man was staying.

She said, in her pride, "Am I of no account that they take food for me to such a horrible place?"

The people said to her, "We know of no better place where you can go to eat."

And the woman ate all the food herself. Not a bite did she give to the very old man.

When night came, they showed her a house to sleep in.

They came to her during the night and asked her, "Which do you prefer to be, straight as an arrow or bent over?"

She said, "Bent over."

They asked her, "Which do you prefer, a charm covered with the skin of a genet or one covered with the skin of a civet cat?"

She replied, "A charm covered with the skin of a civet cat."

And the hunch on her back became even worse than the one she had previously borne.

When she returned home to her husband, he said to her, "I will never live in marriage with you again."

Thus did the woman go went from bad to worse. Upon whom rests the blame for this affair? Is it upon the woman herself or her husband? Thus did the woman go from bad to worse.

10

Mbewa and Nkerma[38]

Bura (Nigeria)[39]

For many years Mbewa and Nkerma were happy together. Nothing had ever come between them to separate them. Neither of them thought that anything could ever happen that would make them fight.

Mbewa was raised by Heduma Ntsukwa and was like a son to him. Nkerma was a very near relative of Heduma Ntsukwa. The mother of Heduma Ntsukwa was a Miziwi. When Heduma Ntsukwa died, half of his property would go to Nkerma and the other half to Mbewa, because they both belonged to the same family as Heduma Ntsukwa. Because of these things, Mbewa and Nkerma could not be enemies, for they both sprouted from the same person.

There was a brother of Nkerma whose name was Bardi Dawi. This Bardi Dawi dug up a peanut farm near to the farm of the slaves of Heduma Ntsukwa. Each dug up his own farm and planted peanuts. When the peanuts grew, thieves came to steal them. The slaves of Heduma Ntsukwa had to guard the farms and keep the thieves from coming and stealing peanuts. When the peanuts were ready to be dug, each of them dug his own peanuts and spread them out to dry. When the peanuts were dry, each began to carry his peanuts home.

As they carried peanuts, the slaves of Heduma Ntsukwa insisted that they should have some of Bardi Dawi's peanuts as wages for keeping the thieves away. They declared that some peanuts must be given to them or there would be trouble.

While this talk was going on, Bardi Dawi was not there. He had gone to the house with a load of peanuts.

There was a woman there whose name was Yangasa Kwapiya. She guarded the peanuts.

She said to Bardi Dawi, "The slaves said that you must give them some peanuts. Or do you think that they are your slaves and will guard your peanuts for nothing?"

Bardi Dawi said, "Well, if they are going to ask and ask by force, I will not give them any peanuts, not even a few. Did they farm peanuts for me? Or are they showing off because they are slaves?"

Bardi Dawi and his wife gathered up their peanuts in baskets as if to take them home.

But here came the slaves of Heduma Ntsukwa, and Yangasa Kwapiya told them everything that Bardi Dawi had said. This made the slaves very angry, and they wanted to fight Bardi Dawi because he had cursed them.

They came after him with a fighting knife. They struck and stabbed. Yaska cut and gashed Bardi Dawi and received deep wounds from him before those who were near could get them separated. Both men's wounds caused great, foul ulcers, and they had to take them to men who knew ulcer medicine.

But Dawi's ulcer got worse. It was on his head, and before many days he died.

All the people cried, "Heduma Ntsukwa must run with all his people to prevent a feud."

Already, destruction had been caused by his slaves. In one night, Heduma with all his close kin fled. But all the Miziwi came out to follow the feud. They swore that if they found any member of the family of Heduma Ntsukwa, they would kill him for Bardi Dawi. They hunted and hunted, but they could find no one to kill in revenge.

For a time, everything was quiet, but the feud was not dead.

After a time, Heduma Ntsukwa sent a message to Nkerma, saying, "It was a slave who killed one of you; it is not as if one of us had killed one of you. I beg you to let me pay you cloth or a horse or anything you say, and let us be done with this awful thing."

Nkerma sent to Heduma Ntsukwa in reply, "Tell him that I will not receive cloth or anything else in lieu of a choice young man like Dawi. Nothing will end this feud but the life of a man, man for man."

When Heduma heard this, he was very sad and did not know what to do. He knew that the day Nkerma met one of his family, that person would be killed.

Heduma sent another message, begging Nkerma to take wealth instead of life in lieu of Dawi, but Nkerma would have nothing of the kind.

Time went on, and Nkerma followed every rumor of the presence of a relative of Heduma.

One day, Nkerma and the younger brother of the man who was killed went to a town named Vido. On their way back, as they came into a little flat, they saw a young man by the name of Kadari Helka. He was one of the Heduma Ntsukwa family. He was a brother of Bwati who lived at Pechuroma. He was one of the finest young men in the whole country. Everything he did, he did with vigor. He worked hard, and wherever he went he was always chosen as the one who could not be surpassed.

In an instant, Nkerma and the brother of the deceased whipped out their arrows and shot him. When they had killed him, they went home satisfied because the young man whom they killed was very much like the one from their own family who had been killed.

The Miziwi then became friendly, because they said that the feud was dead.

But the family was not satisfied.

Their hearts still hurt them, for always before, when a slave killed a man, a life was not demanded but only wealth was required to settle it. This thing was not right.

Heduma Ntsukwa sent to Nkerma, telling him to flee with all of his people or one of them would be killed, because they had killed Bwati's brother without cause.

Nkerma replied, "We will not run; the feud is finished, man for man. Let me settle with you with wealth."

All knew that the feud was really finished.

One difficult thing remained. Mbewa did a foolish thing. Nkerma had a bull with the cattle of Pechuroma. The day Nkerma killed Kadari Helka, Mbewa caught Nkerma's bull and killed him out of a hot heart.

After a while, wealth was poured out, and the feud spirit was satisfied. When the palaver about the murder was finished, then there was no more palaver about the feud.

However, the palaver had not reached its proper end, because the bull that belonged to Nkerma had been killed by Mbewa. There was no reason for this killing. A bull's blood can never equal the blood of a man. Only man can satisfy for man. He had killed the bull for nothing—nothing more than a hot heart. Nkerma liked to remember that he had a bull at Pechuroma, but it was no more.

After a time, Nkerma sent a man to fetch his bull.

When the man whom Nkerma had sent reached Pechuroma, the people said, "Nkerma's bull is no more, for Mbewa killed it."

When the man returned and told Nkerma that Mbewa had killed his bull, Nkerma raged and said, "What is between Mbewa and me that would be sufficient reason for him to kill my bull? Am I in debt to him? Nothing can bring us together about a debt. Nothing but his bull, without argument, can satisfy me."

Another man was sent to Mbewa, but he would not give up his bull.

Time went on, and Nkerma learned that Mbewa had a big bull with the cattle of Pechuroma. But this bull was not the only bull in that herd; there were many bulls in that herd.

Nkerma wanted to know the particular bull so that he could catch it. He begged a young man by the name of Yero to ask which bull belonged to Mbewa. He offered him a large gown if he would find out which, beyond doubt, it was.

This Yero could go to that area freely, for he had no enemies there. One day, he wandered over to Pechuroma and saw the cattle. A boy by the name of Chamasu was herding them.

Yero stopped and visited with Chamasu, and said, "You have a lot of big bulls."

"Yes," said Chamasu, "but each has its owner."

Then Yero said, "That one with the great long horns, that is a nice one. Whose is that one?"

The herd boy said, "That one? Oh, that is Mbewa's."

Yero looked very closely to make sure that he saw some distinguishing marks on it.

When he returned home, Yero told Nkerma that he without doubt saw the bull. "I cannot be mistaken about it, because I looked at it very carefully."

Nkerma counseled with his men friends as to how to get this bull. They decided that one day when the Pechuroma cattle were near, they would drive them all home and separate this bull from the rest, then return the others to Pechuroma.

They watched and they waited, but they could not find a time when it was safe to try. They feared that if the Pechuroma people saw their cattle being taken, they would raise the war cry and come prepared to fight.

On a certain day, the people of Pechuroma heard that a political officer was coming with members of the ruling clan. At that time, when they heard of a political officer coming, they would run and hide all their belongings. They would send their children and their cattle and horses and goats to the next village, which happened to be Garkida, where Nkerma lived. This they would do until they could be brought back after the political officer had gone.

The people of Pechuroma thought that Nkerma did not know Mbewa's bull. But he had sent a spy long before to find out for him. And now, Nkerma and the Miziwi frightened the herd boys away and drive the cattle to where they could separate Mbewa's bull.

The herd boys ran to tell the people of Pechuroma that their cattle had been stolen. And shortly, all of them came running with their quivers full of poisoned arrows. But before they arrived, the bull had been separated and put with another herd, and the rest of the cattle had been brought to their owners.

Fight was in the air, but those who had hot hearts were kept apart. They wanted to fight Nkerma, but the hot hearts could not get close to him. After much palaver, all went home without more bloodshed.

There was nothing more between Mbewa and Nkerma.

Nophindile Thelekiso, a Xhosa storyteller, November 5, 1975

11

The Twin Brothers[40]

Fiote (Republic of Congo)[41]

A certain woman, after prolonged labor, gave birth to twins, both sons. And each one, as he was brought forth, came into the world with a valuable charm. One of the sons the mother called Luemba, the other Mavungu. And they were almost fully grown at their birth, so that Mavungu, the firstborn, wished to start upon his travels.

Now, about this time the daughter of Nzambi[42] was ready for marriage. The leopard came and offered himself in marriage, but Nzambi told him that he must speak to her daughter himself, as she should marry only the man of her choice. Then the leopard went to the girl and asked her to marry him, but she refused him.

And the gazelle, and the pig, and all created things that had breath, one after the other, asked the daughter in marriage, but she refused them all, saying that she did not love them.

And they were all very sad.

Mavungu heard of this girl and determined to marry her. So he called upon his charm and asked it to help him. Then he took some grass in his hands and changed one blade of grass into a horn, another into a knife, another into a gun, and so on until he was quite ready for the long journey.

Then he set out and traveled and traveled, until at last hunger overcame him. He asked his charm whether it was true that he was going to be allowed to starve. The charm hastened to place a sumptuous feast before him, and Mavungu ate and was satisfied.

"Oh, charm," said Mavungu, "are you going to leave these beautiful plates that I have used for the use of any commoner who might come along?"

The charm immediately caused all to disappear.

Then Mavungu traveled and traveled and had to ask his charm to arrange a place for him where he might sleep. And the charm saw to his comfort, so that he passed a peaceful night.

After many days' weary traveling, he at length arrived at Nzambi's town. And Nzambi's daughter saw Mavungu and at once fell in love with him. She ran to her mother and father and cried, "I have seen the man I love, and I shall die if I do not marry him."

Then Mavungu sought out Nzambi and told her that he had come to marry her daughter.

"Go and see her first," said Nzambi, "and if she will have you, you may marry her."

And when Mavungu and the daughter of Nzambi saw each other, they ran toward each other and loved one another.

They were led to a fine house. And while all the people in the town danced and sang for gladness, Mavungu and the daughter of Nzambi slept there.

In the morning, Mavungu noticed that the whole house was crowded with mirrors but that each mirror was covered so that the glass could not be seen.

He asked the daughter of Nzambi to uncover them so that he might see himself in them. She took him to one and opened it, and Mavungu immediately saw the perfect likeness of his home town.

She took him to another, and there he saw another town he knew.

And she took him to all the mirrors save one, and this one she refused to let him see.

"Why will you not let me look into that mirror?" asked Mavungu.

"Because that is the picture of the town from which no man who wanders there returns."

"Do let me see it!" urged Mavungu.

At last, the daughter of Nzambi yielded, and Mavungu looked hard at the reflected image of that terrible place.

"I must go there," he said.

"No, you will never return. Please don't go!" pleaded the daughter of Nzambi.

"Have no fear!" answered Mavungu. "My charm will protect me."

The daughter of Nzambi cried very much but could not move Mavungu from his purpose. Mavungu then left his newly married wife, mounted his horse, and set off for the town from whence no man returns.

He traveled and traveled, until at last, as he came near to the town, he met an old woman and asked her for fire to light his pipe.

"Tie up your horse first, and come and fetch it," she said.

Mavungu descended, and, having tied his horse up very securely, he went to the old woman for the fire.

And when he had come near her, she killed him, so that he disappeared entirely.

Now Luemba wondered at the long absence of his brother, Mavungu, and determined to follow him. So he took some grass and with the aid of his charm changed one blade into a horse, another into a knife, another into a gun, and so on until he was fully prepared for his journey.

Then he set out and after some days' journeying arrived at Nzambi's town.

Nzambi rushed out to meet him and, calling him Mavungu, embraced him.

"No," said Luemba, "my name is not Mavungu. I am his brother, Luemba."

"Nonsense!" answered Nzambi. "You are my son-in-law, Mavungu."

And immediately a great feast was prepared. Nzambi's daughter danced for joy and would not hear of his not being Mavungu.

Luemba was greatly troubled and did not know what to do, as he was now sure that Nzambi's daughter was Mavungu's wife.

When night came, Nzambi's daughter would sleep in Luemba's house. But he appealed to his charm, and it enclosed Nzambi's daughter in a room, lifting her out of Luemba's room for the night, bringing her back in the early morning.

And Luemba's curiosity was aroused by the many closed mirrors that hung about the walls, so he asked Nzambi's daughter to let him look into them. She showed him all excepting one, and this she told him was the one that reflected the town whence no man returns. Luemba insisted on looking into this one, and when he had seen the terrible picture he knew that his brother was there.

Luemba determined to leave Nzambi's town for the town whence no man returns, and so, after thanking them all for his kind reception, he set out.

They all wept loudly but were consoled by the fact that he had been there once already and returned safely, so he could of course return a second time.

Luemba traveled and traveled, until he also came to the place where the old woman was standing, and he asked her for fire.

She told him to tie up his horse and come to her to fetch it, but he tied his horse up only very lightly and then fell upon the old woman and killed her.

Then he sought his brother's bones and the bones of his horse. He put them together, then touched them with his charm.

And Mavungu and his horse came to life again.

Then, together, Mavungu and Luemba joined together the bones of hundreds of people and touched them with their charms so that they all lived again. Then they set off with all their followers to Nzambi's town.

Luemba told Mavungu how he had been mistaken for him by his mother-in-law and wife and how by the help of his charm he had saved his wife from dishonor. Mavungu thanked him and said it was well.

Then a quarrel broke out between the two brothers about the followers. Mavungu said they were his, because he was the elder. But Luemba said they belonged to him, because he had given Mavungu and them life.

Mavungu then fell upon Luemba and killed him. But Luemba's horse remained by his body.

Mavungu then went on his way to Nzambi's town and was magnificently welcomed.

Now Luemba's horse took his charm and touched Luemba's body so that he lived again. Then Luemba mounted his horse and sought his brother, Mavungu, and killed him.

When the town had heard the story, they all said that Luemba had done rightly.

12

Samba Gueladio Diegui[43]

Fuuta Jalon (Peuhl) (Guinea)[44]

This is the story of Samba Gueladio Diegui, Peuhl prince of Fouta.

Samba Gueladio Diegui was the son of Gueladio, king of Fouta. When Samba arrived at the age of adolescence, his father died. The brother of the dead king, Konkobo Moussa, took command of the country. Konkobo had eight sons. When they grew to manhood, he announced that he would divide Fouta among them, and each received his portion.

Samba remained with his mother, his griot,[45] named Sevi Malallaya, and a slave called Doungourou.

The griot, Sevi, came to Samba. He was weeping.

Samba asked him, "Why do you weep?"

"I weep," replied the griot, "because your father, Konkobo, has divided Fouta between his boys. And, as your father was no longer there, Konkobo has not kept a share for you."

Samba rose at once.

He went to his uncle and said to him, "Well, papa, and where is my share?"

"I am going to give something to you, too," Konkobo replied. "The first horse that you come across in the Fouta, take it. It is yours."

Samba returned. He went to his griot and said to him, "My papa has given me a share, too!"

"And what has he given you?"

"He has given me permission to take the first good horse that I find."

The griot said, "But that is nothing at all that he gives you! He has acted very badly toward you."

Samba went back to his uncle, Konkobo. "Papa," he said to him, "I don't want your present. It is not what I need. Give me what is due to me. I ask nothing else."

His uncle replied, "I saw a superb bull in Fouta. I saw a very pretty woman, too. Take them both. I make you a present of them."

Samba went again to Sevi, the griot. "Well," he said, "my papa has given me a beautiful Fouta woman and an ox. All that I can have if I choose to take it."

"That is worth nothing," said the griot. "It is like what he gave you before. If you find a beautiful woman who is married and you take her, her husband will kill you. You are a child, and you don't understand."

Samba went back once again. "Well, papa," he said, "I don't want what you offer me. What I want is my share of Fouta."

"If you really want it," said Konkobo, "you had better set about taking it. If not, so much the worse for you."

Samba went away. He saddled his mare, Oumoullatoma. He set out with his griot, Sevi Malallaya, and his slave, Doungourou, his mother, and the slaves destined for his wife. At that time, he was not yet married.

He said, "I am going to leave Fouta."

He went as far as a village called Tiabo. It was close to Bakel. He called the king of that country and said to him, "Tounka, I entrust to you my mother and the mother of my griot. You must provide for their needs and for those of my people until I return. Give them food and clothing. Lodge them well. Or else, when I return, if I find that they have lacked food or clothing, I will cut your head off."

After this, Samba and his griot crossed the river without further delay. They set out for a country the king of which was named Ellel Bildikri, to ask for warriors to help them in attacking Konkobo Moussa, Samba's uncle.

They marched for forty-five days through the forest before reaching the Peuhl country. I have forgotten the name of the king of this country.

As soon as he saw Samba, he said, "Here is a fine boy! He must be the son of a king."

He had oxen killed and sheep killed and presented them to Samba, saying, "All this is for you." He called his daughters and told them, "Go and visit Samba, who is leaving tomorrow. Talk to him and amuse him."

The young Peuhl girls stayed with Samba. They amused themselves together.

Presently, they left him.

"It is too hot," they said. "We are going to bathe."

When they had gone, Samba lay down on his bed to sleep. One of the young girls had taken off her gold necklace and had forgotten it on leaving. While Samba was sleeping, an ostrich came into the house and swallowed the necklace.

The young girls returned and woke Samba.

"I forgot my necklace a little while ago," one of them said. "Where is it?" They searched but could not find it.

Samba said, "Do you think I have stolen your necklace?"

"No," replied the young girl. "But all the same I was the last to leave, and there were only two of us in the house."

"Very well," Samba murmured.

The young girl went to her father.

"I left my gold necklace with this man who came here, and now I can't find it."

"Do you think he took it?"

"I don't know. There were only two of us in the house."

The king did not say what he thought about this. He only asked his daughter to return to Samba.

Meantime, Samba had examined the ground. He found the tracks of the ostrich's feet. So he went to the king, leaving the young girl in the house.

"I will give you a calabash full of gold," he said, "if you will sell me your ostrich."

"Agreed," said the king. "You can have it."

Samba immediately called some men and ordered them to kill the ostrich.

"When you have killed it," he said, "open its body and bring us whatever you find inside."

The men obeyed and returned to Samba in the presence of the king's daughter.

In the ostrich's stomach was the gold necklace.

Samba said to the young girl, "You accused me of stealing the necklace. I shall have you put in chains."

And the king left him free to act as he chose.

But the griot, Sevi, intervened. "You are wrong to act like this, Samba. We have left our own country to come here, and there are only five of us. Leave the king's daughter alone, and don't seek to make her captive."

Samba listened to his griot's advice. And the next day they set out again for the kingdom of Ellel Bildikri.

They marched fifteen days more in the forest, and they ran short of water.

"Samba," said the griot, "I can go no further! I am about to die."

Samba led Sevi to the shade of a tree and said to him and to the slave, Doungourou, "Wait for me here."

He mounted his mare, Oumoullatoma, went on his way for two hours, and at last reached a pool.

There, he saw a very tall bogy taking a bath.

The bogy turned toward him, and fire came out from all parts of his body.

Samba was not frightened. He looked him straight in the face.

Then the bogy made himself so tall that he touched the sky with his head.

"What are you doing now?" asked Samba calmly. "Are you trying to see whether I am afraid of you?"

"Never," said the bogy, "have I seen a man as brave as you are! Well, I am going to make you a present." And he gave him a gun. "Samba," he said, "do you know what the name of this gun is?"

"No," replied Samba. "I don't know it."

"It is called Boussalarbi," said the bogy. "If you so much as draw it from the holster, your enemy will fall dead."

Samba took the goat-skin from his shoulders. He went into the pool to get water, and when the skin was filled he put it on his mare's back.

"Good," he said. "Now I will see whether what the body told me is true or not."

He drew the gun from its holster, and the bogy fell dead.

This done, Samba returned to the spot where he had left his people, and he found his father, the griot who sang Samba's praises. He gave water to drink, both to the griot and to the slave.

The griot then said, "Well, Samba, what was that gun shot that I heard in the distance?"

"It was I who fired," replied Samba. And he told him about the adventure with the bogy and what he had done with him.

"That was wrong," replied the griot. "You did a very wrong thing. Someone makes you a present like that and you kill him. You have acted very unjustly."

"I did well," said Samba. "If I happened to pass that way, others might pass as well. I am not the only king's son. There are many kings' sons in Fouta, and many brave ones among them. They are all as daring as I. Today, the bogy gave this gun to me, and tomorrow he would have made the same present to someone else. Now he is through with making presents! No one else possesses a gun like mine. I am the only person to own such a marvelous thing."

After this, they decided to go further on. After several days, they reached the capital of Ellel Bildikri's country. It was a larger town than Saint-Louis. For nearly a year there, they had not drunk fresh water. A huge cayman lived in the river and prevented the inhabitants from taking any water. Every year, they gave up to the cayman a young girl, well dressed, with gold earrings, bracelets on her wrists and ankles, dressed like a king's daughter.[46] The cayman was very particular, and if he did not consider her well enough dressed, he refused the offering and forbade them to renew their yearly provisions of drinking water.

When Samba arrived, it was the last day of the year, and the inhabitants were preparing for the next day, when they would deliver a young girl to this cayman, Niabardi Dallo.

At about midnight, Samba stopped at the house of some slaves a little outside the village. He called the slave who was in the house and said, "Give me some water. I am thirsty."

The slave went inside. There was in her jar about as much water as would fill a small cup, and even this was putrid. Nonetheless, she brought it to Samba.

He took the water, smelled it, and, finding a bad odor, struck the woman, who fell down a few steps away.

"What!" he cried. "I ask for water, and you bring me filth like this!"

"Oh, my friend," the woman replied, "there is no more water in the country! Before we can have any more, we must sacrifice the king's daughter."

"Well, go," Samba ordered. "Show me the way to the river. I am going to water my mare at once."

The slave was terrified. "I am afraid to go to the river," she said. "Tomorrow, the king will see the tracks of my feet on the road, and he will ask, 'Why did you go there where I have forbidden anyone to go?'"

Samba grew angry. "If you refuse to take me," he threatened her, "you shall perish by my hand! Take the halter, Doungourou, and put it around Oumoullatoma's neck. And you, woman, walk in front of me."

The slave started out, leading the mare after him. The woman showed them the road. "It leads straight to the river," she said to Samba, who had pity on her fear, thanked her, and let her go back.

Samba walked until he reached the river. He ordered the slave to take off his clothes and go into the river with the mare to bathe her. The slave took off his garments and went into the water.

And immediately, from the middle of the river, Niabardi Dallo, the cayman, called to them.

"Who is there?" he cried.

"A newcomer," Samba replied.

"Well, newcomer, what are you doing here?"

"I am going to drink."

"If you have come to drink, drink alone, and don't let your horse drink!"

"The newcomer is going to water his mare," said Samba.

He drank, and with him his slave.

"Go back into the river, Doungourou."

The slave obeyed. The mare grazed the water with her hoof.

The cayman said, "Newcomer, if you want to know, you make me tired!"

Niabardi rose in the middle of the river, and all the water around him shone like fire.

"If what you see frightens you," cried Samba to Doungourou, "and if you let go of my mare, I will kill you as well as the cayman!"

After these words, the slave held tightly to the mare.

The cayman came toward them, opening his jaws widely, one above and one below, and fire spouted from his throat. When he was quite near, Samba fired at him.

The cayman was dead, and the whole river turned the color of blood.

Now that the cayman was killed, Samba filled his goat-skin bag with water. He put the bag on the mare, and they returned to the house to settle down and take some rest.

They gave some water to the slave whose house they were sharing.

The woman was amazed. "How did you get all that water?" she asked.

Samba said, "Your tongue is too long. As long as we give you water, all you have to do is drink it and not worry yourself about where it comes from."

After having killed the cayman, Samba had cut off a piece and brought it with him. He also left in the place of combat his bracelets and his sandal, for he knew very well that no one else would be able to put them on. Samba's feet were very small.

The next day, the king, Ellel Bildikri, gathered all the griots together to take the young girl to the cayman so he would allow the inhabitants to get their provision of water.

They fetched the young virgin and set her on a horse.

All the griots followed, singing.

"Ah, young girl, how brave you are!
The cayman has eaten your big sister!
He has eaten your other sister, too,
And yet, you are not afraid of him!
Now we shall have some water!"

Thus, the griots sang. They sang of the hundred victims whom the cayman had devoured.

Now, they reached the river. They led the young girl down. Formerly, the other young girls had waded a little way into the water, and then the cayman had come and snapped them up.

The girl they brought today went into the river and waded out until the water reached her chest. She climbed on the head of the cayman and stood there.

"The cayman is here," she said, "and I am standing on his head."

The people said, "The cayman is angry. You must have had relations with a man! You are no longer a virgin! Oh, what a misfortune! It is an evil day for us. You are a shameless girl!"

And they went at once to fetch another young girl.

The first one, however, defended herself indignantly. "You lie!" she cried. "No man has touched me since the day I was born! I have never shared a man's bed!"

The other young girl consented to be sacrificed to the cayman. She climbed up beside the first one. Now both of them were standing on the cayman's head.

And her father cried, "The cayman is dead!"

"Let everyone go into the river!" the king ordered. "We shall see whether it is true or not!"

Everyone went in, and they found it was really true.

"Well," said the king, "the first who says he has killed the cayman and can prove it shall have whatever he asks of me!"

There was a bunch of liars there who cried, "I killed him!"

"I came here last night!"

"The cayman tried to eat me, and I killed him!"

Each told his story, to prove to the king that he was the real slayer of the cayman and should have the reward.

A slave who was there picked up the bracelets and a sandal. "Here are the victor's bracelets," he said, "and here is his sandal. It is the man to whom these belong who has killed the cayman. It is he who will receive the reward!"

All came to try them on. But no one succeeded.

The captive woman then came forward. "There is a newcomer here," she said. "He is staying in my house. When he arrived, he asked for some water. I gave him some putrid water; it was all I had. When I gave it to him, he struck me. Then he went away, and stayed out for three hours. When he came back, he gave me some fresh water. You need only call him to find out. For my part, I am sure it was he who killed the cayman."

Then the king sent men to fetch the newcomer. They found Samba in bed. They gave him a slap to wake him up. Samba, furious at being disturbed in his sleep, kicked them.

Then the king sent another man to try and wake him.

"Let me have my sleep!" cried Samba. "If they send anyone else, I will kill him!"

The envoy returned. He told the king what had happened.

"Very well," said the king. "I will wait until he has had his sleep."

They waited two hours.

At last, Samba woke. He came to the river.

He saluted the king, and the king returned his salute. Then he offered him a seat beside him and told him to take his ease. Then, taking the bracelets and the sandal, he showed them to him.

"Do these belong to you?" he asked.

Samba took from his pocket the other sandal and put them both on.

"Well," said the king, "you shall come and stay with me." And he gave him a house, very large and lofty, a real palace.

The king sent men to fetch Samba's belongings, bringing his slaves and his mare. All were installed in the king's enclosure.

They killed quantities of sheep.

Samba stayed two months with the king, and he had young girls with him all the time.

At the end of this time, the king called his guest.

"With what intention did you come to this country?" he asked him. "Is there anything you want?"

Samba replied, "I want only fighting men."

The king called all his notables and said to them, "The slayer of the cayman asks us to give him some fighting men."

"To go all the way to Fouta!" they exclaimed. "How can we do that!"

"This man," the king went on, "has come all the way from Fouta. He has reached us here. He has killed the monster that prevented us from drinking, and all he asks in return is to have some fighting men. We cannot possibly refuse him."

"Well," replied the notables, "this is what we will do. There is a king called Birama N'Gourori. Let us send Samba Guenadio Diegui against this king, to take his flocks and make us a present of them. Then we will let him have some fighting men, and we will go with him into his country to make war."

The only objective of those who gave this advice was to get rid of Samba by false promises. They counted on his losing his life in the attack on Birama N'Gourori, for this king was very powerful.

To reach Birama N'Gourori's country, Samba had to cross at least eighteen deltas, and between each of these deltas there was eight days' march, and even more. Birama's flocks were guarded by three hundred shepherds all dressed in red trousers and jackets, with red caps on their heads, and they wore red boots, too. They were mounted on picked horses, white horses.

After crossing the marshes, Samba came to these shepherds.

He said to them, "I am going to take your cattle."

They replied, "You are crazy! Before you take the cattle, you will have to kill us all."

"Come on," Samba ordered. "March before me, and drive the cattle where I tell you."

The shepherds refused to obey him. They fell upon Samba, spear in hand. They struck him, but the spears glanced aside, for his charms were too powerful.

And it was he who killed them all, with the exception of one alone.

Samba took captive the one he had spared. He cut off his ears and said to him, "Now go to Birama N'Gourori and tell him that I have taken his herds."

The man went. He reached the large house belonging to Birama. The first person whom he asked to go and tell the king of the slaughter of his shepherds and the rape of his herds replied briefly, "No, I don't want to!"

That day, Birama was still asleep.

One of his wives, who was dressing her hair in the Peuhl fashion, said, "How can you tell such news to Birama?"

Then they gathered some hamond from the bushes. Hamond is a perfumed gum that the Wolof call *houmounguene* or *tiouraye.* The fumes were wafted to Birama, and he woke up.

He saw the griots all making music on their violins.

"What is it? What is all this about?" These were his first words as he woke up.

A man advanced, trembling. "A Peuhl came to your shepherds. He wanted to take your cattle—"

He had no time to finish before Birama killed him.

"Allah himself cannot steal my cattle!" cried the king in fury.

Another man drew near and told what had happened.

Birama killed him, also.

He killed three like this. All the rest ran away.

Then Birama's sister came in, bringing some curdled milk. She set it before him, saying, "This is all you have left to eat, now, since the Peuhl has taken your cattle. There is nothing else to give you."

King Birama straddled his horse. He rode off in a fury and overtook Samba Gueladio behind the village.

Samba stopped the cattle and waited for him quietly.

"Is it you who stole my cattle?"

"Yes, it was me. But I will leave you a few, if you like. The rest I shall keep for myself."

"You may do so, perhaps," said Birama, "but first you will have to kill me!"

Samba took out his pipe. He struck his flint, lit the pipe, and took several puffs. After which he said to Birama, "Well, take your time. Decide as you please."

That was how he talked to the king.

Birama thrust his spear firmly against Samba. The spear broke in two pieces. He quickly snatched another spear and thrust again. He struck with all his spears until there was only one left unbroken.

Then Samba struck in his turn. His spear also broke.

He jumped on his mare, and they both fought on horseback, while beneath them the horses bit and fought furiously.

At last, Samba won, and Birama ran away.

They reached Birama's place, which was made up of at least eight enclosures, each with its fate.

When Birama reached the first one, the men let him pass and fired on Samba. Until the smoke of their guns had dispersed, they thought Samba had fallen.

But not at all. They saw him still chasing their king.

At each gate, the same thing happened, until Birama and Samba reached the very middle of the houses.

"If it were not for your sister's protection, I would kill you," he said to the king, "but I am of her blood, and I cannot refuse her request when she has done me no wrong."

He returned to the herd, counted out three hundred cattle, and sent them back to the king, saying, "This is a present I make to Birama and his sister."

There remained as many again, as the price of his victory over Birama N'Gourori.

"You are a Peuhl like me," he said to the king, "so I cannot see you reduced to eating curdled milk."

And he departed, taking what he had kept of the herd.

He reached Ellel Bildikri's village. "Here are Birama N'Gourori's cattle," he said.

"That's good," said the king.

The notables came to the king. "This man has come here," they said. "He has killed Niabardi Dallo, and what's more he has captured all Birama's herds. Our grandmothers said that no one would ever succeed in taking them, yet he has done so! If we go out to war with him, he will have us all killed."

"Now you will be forced to give me some fighting men," Samba said to them.

The women of the country cried, "If our husbands are afraid to go with you, we, the women, will accompany you!"

Ellel Bildikri called Samba and promised him some men in a few day's time.

The village had four gates. Ellel Bildikri ordered some large tree trunks to be cut. They were to be used as steps of a staircase. When the wood was worn by the horse's feet, it should be taken as a sign that sufficient horsemen had passed.

By each stairway, Samba watched horses and horsemen passing for several days. At last he declared himself satisfied.

"Now let the foot soldiers come out!" he said.

And for several days more, he watched the foot soldiers pass.

"That is enough!" he said. "Now we have only to set out."

So Samba set out for Fouta. When he was quite near, he ordered his columns to continue their march beside the N'Guiguilone, following the river bank.

Samba went to see his mother, whom he had entrusted to Tounka.

There were a great many horses in the column.

On the day that Samba left to go to Tiyabo, in Fouta, Tounka said to himself, "Samba will certainly perish in the forest!"

And, having no more fear, he drove Samba's mother and her slaves away from the village.

The slaves took a waistcoat and made an awning with it, like the Moorish tents, and they put Samba's mother under the waistcoat to shelter her from the sun. Then they dispersed in the forest to look for a little millet, and each time they saw a man bringing home his crop, they followed him, to pick up whatever he let fall. They returned with what little they had been able to gather; with it, they made a couscous, and, adding some boiled leaves, gave it to Samba's mother to eat.

It was about two o'clock. Some of the slaves stayed with Samba's mother. Suddenly, they heard a griot.

He called out, "Ouldou Gueladio Diegui!—I am afraid of Samba, I respect him as my master!" His voice was loud and clear. It was that of Sevi.

Surely it was Samba coming!

The slaves cried, "It is a herald we hear! Undoubtedly, Samba is arriving!"

And Sevi's mother said, "Yes, I am sure that is my son singing."

But Samba's mother said sadly, "The griot is made to sing like that, for my son is lost. I shall never see my boy again!"

But at that very moment Samba's mare reached the river, and Samba himself crossed the water mounted on Oumoullatoma.

Then Tounka said to his men, "When Samba comes to ask for me, tell him I have been dead a long time."

Now Samba was with his mother. He found her outside the village.

"What does this mean?" he asked her.

"You see, my son, how Tounka has treated us since you went away."

Samba said simply, "All right!" He went to Tounka's house. He asked the people, "Where is Tounka? Go and bring him here."

"Tounka has been dead a long time."

"Take me to his grave. If he is dead, I am going to light a fire and burn him."

They took him a little way off. "Here is where Tounka is buried."

Samba called his men, ordered them to dig in the spot that was pointed out to them, and found nothing. "Bring him from his house," he said. "I want him!"

They dragged Tounka out into the middle of the village. Samba remained seated on his mare. He took a branch, and, stretching out his arm, said, "Pile up all your jewels, gold, hangings, and pieces of cloth until the heap is as high as my hand!"

They began to pile together gold, jewels, and cloths. When the heap was a yard high, Samba jumped from his horse on to the pile. He stamped down the cloths and said, "That is not enough! Bring more!"

They brought more, and Sevi began to squash the heap down again until Samba said, "That is enough!"

Then Samba addressed Tounka. "Another time, if I leave my mother with you, remember what I have just done, or wait until I catch you again!"

He took with him the waistcoats, the fabrics, and the gold and gave them to his mother and her people. Then he set out again on his way.

He went as far as Ouhoulde in Fouta. He passed and kept on his way until he rejoined his columns by the N'Guilguilone. From there, he sent a message to his uncle, Konkobo, telling him to be in readiness to fight him at Bilbaci.

Then he took up his position in front of the N'Guiguilone.

At that moment, his uncle was at Sadel, near Kayaedi. Samba went to him and saw that Konkobo was waiting with his army.

In those days, before a battle, they held a great war dance, and the war drum that the griots used was called Alamari. The dance that they danced was permitted only to brave men who had no fear. They also called the dance Alamari, and they danced it spear in hand.

The drum of which I speak was covered with the skin of a young girl. From where he stood, Samba heard the sound of the war drum.

"Well," he said, "I am going down there. I want to dance the Alamari!"

His griot, Sevi Malallaya, said, "Are you crazy? You must stay here until tomorrow."

But Samba said, "Say what you like, I don't care! I am going."

Samba crossed the river. He went as far as the war dance and joined the circle of lookers-on. He covered his head with his waist-cloth, hiding his face. He went and danced, spear in hand.

And each said to himself, "But that is Samba Gueladio Diegui!"

He never breathed a word. There he was, in the war dance.

He called his cousins, the sons of Konkobo Moussa, and said to them, "Come, let's go to your father's house. We will have a chat there together."

There was a slave there named Mahounde Gali, who had a bad eye.

His son asked him, "Papa, how can you go and fight tomorrow in that state?"

"Bring me a pound of capsicum," replied his father. He spread the capsicums on his bad eye and kept them there with a bandage. Then he lay down to rest, and when he took the bandage off his eye was all fiery red, and he said, "When Samba's army sees a man with an eye all fiery red like this, they will run away in terror!"

At six o'clock in the morning, Samba's columns and those of Konkobo began to fight. Samba remained lying down in Konkobo Moussa's house. He passed the night in joking with his cousins until sunrise.

At that moment, he said to them, "Bring me some water to wash myself." He said this in front of everyone.

Then he took his spear, and went out from the village. He crossed the columns of Konkobo Moussa. Then he went toward his own columns and overtook them.

He found his mare, tethered to a stake. He ordered her to be saddled, and his slave saddled her. He mounted and set off at a gallop.

He entered Konkobo's ranks. He drew his gun, Boussalarbi, from its holster, and at each shot he killed at least fifty warriors.

"What?" cried Konkobo's soldiers. "In the beginning of the battle, we thought Samba's men were in flight. But not at all! They are still holding their ground!"

Then, discouraged, they deserted their chief. You should have seen how they ran!

But Konkobo was not one to run away. When his horse fell dead, he took some earth and filled his trousers. If he wanted to run away now, he could not, because the earth was too heavy.

Samba killed all before him.

And now he was face to face with Konkobo, standing on his dead horse.

"Well, papa," he asked, "what has happened?"

"You see," replied Konkobo, "they have killed my horse."

Konkobo ran after one of Konkobo's horsemen. He killed him and brought the horse back. "Here, papa," he said. "Mount this horse and keep on fighting."

Konkobo got in the saddle again. He threw himself on Samba's columns. His second horse was struck and fell dead.

Samba came to him again.

"Well, papa?" he asked. "Have they killed another horse for you?"

He went and killed another of Konkobo's horsemen.

"Here, papa," he said to his uncle, "here is a new mount for you."

Samba thus replaced, at least eight times, the horses that were killed beneath his uncle. He killed Konkobo's boys; he slaughtered everyone.

Now he was lord of Fouta.

He took his uncle aside from the village, and said to him, "Stay here from now on. You shall beg charity from me."

After Samba died and they had buried him in the ground, a Peuhl passed near his grave and saw the ancient king's skull sticking out from the earth.

"Ah," he said, "there is a pig's head that thinks it isn't dead!"

He raised his staff and struck the skull with it.

The stick broke, and a flash of lightning pierced the Peuhl's eye and killed him.

The bambados of Fouta said, "Samba cannot die: it is he who killed the Peuhl!"

Sonina Medlane, a Xhosa storyteller, November 5, 1975

13

Fountinndouha[47]

Gourmanchéma (Gourma, Gourmantche, Gourmanti) (Niger)[48]

A man who was very jealous of his wife had retired to live some distance from the village, so there should be no possibility of her deceiving him.

Another man named Fountinndouha determined to possess this woman. So he chose a fine fat sheep from among his herd and went to the cautious husband.

The husband asked him the object of his journey.

"I am going to sell my sheep to the king of Outenou," Fountinndouha replied. "I want to see if I can't get fifteen cowries for it."

"Fifteen thousand cowries, you mean," cried the husband. "Or is it really only fifteen cowries?"

"I am asking fifteen cowries, yes."

The husband made haste to offer Fountinndouha the fifteen cowries and in return took the sheep, which he slaughtered. The seller helped him to skin it.

Evening fell before they had finished cutting the animal up. The wife cooked a lot of the meat and put plenty of fat with it. Fountinndouha ate with them, but for fear of giving himself diarrhoea he was careful not to take any of the fat. The husband, on the contrary, ate to excess. As a result, he was taken with violent diarrhoea.

When it was time to go to bed, he said to Fountinndouha, "As there is only one house here, you shall sleep near the door. My wife will sleep at the end of the house, and I between the two of you. But don't you try to take advantage of her while I am asleep."

Scarcely had they stretched out on the mats when the husband heard rumblings in his inside. He went out to run behind the bushes. Before he could get back, Fountinndouha had already taken advantage of the interval.

The husband returned, but, seized again with pains in his belly, he was obliged to run outside once more, and this happened seven times during the course of the night. At each of these departures, Fountinndouha rejoined his host's wife and employed his time conscientiously during the interval.

In the morning, he set out, thanking the husband and saying that he was going to the king of Outenou.

He came to the house of the blacksmith, to whom he gave a piece of iron with which to forge him a ring.

Meantime, the wife had told her husband what had happened and confessed to him that she had lain with Fountinndouha. Furious, both husband and wife dashed after Fountinndouha with the intention of avenging themselves upon him.

When the blacksmith had finished making the ring, it was about six o'clock. He held out the ring to Fountinndouha.

"Give it to your wife," said Fountinndouha. "I will pass by and get it tomorrow morning."

That same night, he went to the house of the blacksmith, who was away. He entered the house and said to the wife, "Your husband has given you to me. As a proof, he has given you my ring to keep for me."

He seduced the woman, took back his ring, and left.

The next morning, the first deceived husband came to the blacksmith to find out whether he had seen anything of a stranger.

"Fountinndouha just passed this way," said the workman. "He is a tall man. He slept here last night."

"That's quite right," said the blacksmith's wife. "What's more, he slept with me."

Then the two deceived husbands flung themselves on Fountinndouha's track.

Fountinndouha had by now reached the house of a husbandman, who gave him the best of welcomes and a calabash full of rice to eat.

At bedtime, Fountinndouha asked his host at what time he might leave without disturbing anyone.

The husbandman replied, "You have only to get up at the first cockcrow [literally, take the cock's throat]."

While everyone slept, Fountinndouha, taking this advice to the letter, entered the chicken yard and wrung the necks of all the fowls.

Next morning, the husbandman found all his poultry dead. At that same moment, the two deceived husbands arrived and asked whether he had seen Fountinndouha.

"We'll all three go after him," cried the husbandman. "He has killed all my fowls!"

"For our part," said the two husbands, "it's even worse than that! He has seduced our wives!"

All three hastened in pursuit of the rascal.

Fountinndouha had walked all night and all day. Toward evening, he found himself near the bank of a river where some griots,[49] wet through by the rain, had made their camp. These griots had lighted a big fire to dry and warm themselves.

Fountinndouha lay down in their midst.

When he saw that they were all asleep, he took their drums, big and little, and threw them on the fire. Then he ran away.

The next day, the three men who were after him fell in with the griots, who joined them in pursuit of the wicked joker.

In his flight, Fountinndouha reached a village where an old woman asked him why he was running so fast.

"Outenou," he said hastily, "has sent me as his courier to give orders that by sundown there shall not be a virgin left in any village."

The old woman, terrified for her daughters, said, "My son is away. Come, I beg of you, and do what is necessary that my daughters may satisfy Outenou's requirements!"

So Fountinndouha performed this kindness for all of the old woman's daughters.

When he had finished, she confided to him, "It is a long time since I myself knew the pleasures of youth. You might refresh my memory a little."

Fountinndouha could not refuse her this small service. He performed it conscientiously.

Then the old woman wanted to know his name.

"My name," he replied, "is Dinndinnma Sarbiari, meaning, I begin with the best and I end with the worst!"

Then he went on his way again.

When the old woman's son returned, she told him the whole affair.

He was very angry, and when the other victims of this rascal came to him for information, he joined them in their pursuit of Fountinndouha.

And Fountinndouha came at last to Outenou-Bado's house.

"King of kings," he said to him, "some people are coming to make complaint against me. Give judgment against them, and I will promise you three idiots as a present."

And Outenou promised to absolve him.

There arrived then the two husbands, the husbandman, the griots, and the brother of the erstwhile virgins.

Outenou heard the jealous husband first and accused him of stealing. What! He had the impudence to pay only fifteen cowries for a fat sheep?

He also dismissed the blacksmith for having given the ring to his wife after showing it to Fountinndouha.

He reprimanded the husbandman sharply for having told the prisoner to "take the neck of the cock," and also the griots for having not appreciated Fountinndouha's good intentions. Why had the latter thrown their wooden drums on the fire? To keep it burning! So what were they complaining about?

As for the daughters of the old woman, the latter did very badly to complain of a treatment that she herself had asked for, not only for them but for her own pleasure as well.

Outenou thus dismissed all the plaintiffs.

"Now," said Fountinndouha, "I am going to get the three idiots I promised you."

He went out and met a groom who was trying to carry on his head a bundle of fodder that he had just bound. The bundle was too heavy for him. And at each attempt he untied the cord and added fresh fodder to his bundle.

Fountinndouha advised him to decrease the amount. Then he told him to follow him with his load. The groom obeyed.

They came to a baobab tree. A man was throwing his stick into the branches to bring down the monkey-bread. Each time he threw it, the stick caught in a branch and remained hanging among the leaves. The man then climbed the tree, unhooked his stick, and came down again without thinking—simple as it was—to gather the fruit among which the stick was caught.

At the moment when this simpleton was up in the tree unhooking his stick, Fountinndouha called to him, "But gather the fruit this time!" The man took his advice and threw down the monkey-bread as well as the stick. He climbed down again, gathered up the fruit, and followed Fountinndouha, on his invitation.

The three came to a king. In the court, surrounded by houses, a big fire of straw was burning. The courtiers were gathered on the side from which the wind came so as not to get the smoke in their faces, while the king sat on the other side, in such a position that he was fast getting smoked like smoked meat. His nose was running, and the tears came from his eyes.

Fountinndouha took one of the courtiers by the hand and made him sit down in the king's place; then he led the king to the vacant spot.

Judging that this king was well fitted to form the third of his trio of imbeciles, he led him with the other two before Outenou, to whom he made a present of the three after having explained his reasons for considering them all three perfect idiots.

This done, he returned to his own village.

14

The Man and the Leopard[50]

Grebo (Liberia)[51]

A man once had for his personal friend a leopard.

As times became hard and the financial condition of the town more straitened, he moved his little family out on to an elevated tract of land nearly fifteen miles from every neighboring community. Though it seemed at first sight to be a rugged mountains region, there were to be seen many fertile parts dotted here and there with forest and yielding nice rich pastures. Here, all the wild deer and other herbivorous animals were found to repair every morning until midday, the time when they would retire under some large tree to wait until the cool of the day.

Having discovered the time of their grazing, the man placed a noose at the mouth of each of their paths. Before dawn, however, a convention was agreed to by the deer that they should all at daylight proceed to the pasture in one great body. The bushbuck was then made the leader.

Just before day, early in the morning, they all arose and went to the field. But when they arrived at the entrance to the road where the snare was, the bushbuck got caught. When the others saw the buck kicking and jumping and unable to get out, they all got frightened and ran.

When daylight came, the man went to his noose and, on approaching it, found it had caught a large buck. He took it to his wife and charged her that, as he was going for fire, should the leopard come before he got back, or in case she heard him clear his throat and say, "Ku ku!" she should hide the meat, for this was the sign of the leopard's coming.

He then went to the leopard's house, and the leopard asked him what luck he had had.

The man replied, "I got nothing."

But the leopard said, "I shall return with you, if for no other reason than the stroll."

When they reached the man's residence, the leopard passed quickly to the front premises, where the deer had been imperfectly concealed by the woman, and exclaimed, "Here I have found my buck!"

But the man said, "No! This is my buck, I just caught it in my noose." And he refused to give it up.

Finally, they all agreed to have it cooked and the whole eaten together. The bushbuck having now been cooked and dished into a large bowl, they again agreed that before eating each should be tied against a post and that he only should eat who of himself was able to break the string.

The leopard was then tightly tied with great cords against a tree, and in spite of all his force and strength the cords still held him firmly lashed to the tree.

But the man and his wife, having tied themselves with a thread, soon broke the strings and ate up all the meat. And when the meat had been eaten up, they washed the bowl with pepper and water and then dashed it in the leopard's face and left him there, tied against the tree.

But a rat passing by was hailed by the leopard and entreated to come and loose him. The mother rat consented, and she brought her two children to gnaw the strings. Then the leopard, having been freed, quickly seized her young ones and ate them up.

15

The Two Girls[52]

Hausa (Nigeria)[53]

One of two girls said to her sister, "I am more beautiful than you."

Her sister replied, "I am more beautiful than you."

The first girl said, "If you are more beautiful than I, come, let us go into the world. Let us see who gets the most goods."

Her sister said, "Very well."

When they got ready, they departed.

They came to a certain town, and they said to the people, "Which of us is the more beautiful? To the one whom you deem the more beautiful, you must give presents."

Some persons liked one of the sisters, some the other, so they gave them both presents in that town.

They departed and went to another town. When the sisters arrived there, the people again made them presents, and they passed on.

After they had gone on in this way, the younger sister had received much property.

They traveled through many countries and then returned home.

As they were returning home, they came to the shore of a lake. Their cows and their goats and everything they had received, they brought with them to that place, and they were drinking water. When they had drunk water and were satisfied, the younger sister began to draw water for herself.

The elder sister said to her, "Bring me water, that I may drink."

She said, "All right."

She went, took some water, and brought it to her sister.

Her elder sister said to her, "This water is not good. Your sheep and your goats and your cows have drunk; bring me something to drink, as well. I do not want to go myself. Bring me some water that is good."

She did this because she was jealous of her sister.

The younger sister went, and said, "From this?"

Her elder sister said, "Not from that. Go further."

She went to a deep place, and there she fell into the water and was lost. The elder sister took all the goods and carried them home.

When they asked her, "Where is your friend?" she said to them, "She is lost." When they asked her where, she said to them, "In the sea."

As they were sitting down, her younger brother went secretly to feed his sheep on the shore of the sea, and, singing the name of his sister, he said, "Come home." So he was there singing and calling the name of his sister. After waiting a little while, he saw his sister coming out of the water and walking toward him.

He saluted her.

She sat down, combing the hair of his head and anointing it with oil. Then she said to him, "I shall now go home."

He said to her, "To which house are you going?"

She said to him, "I am going into the water."

She went and fell into the water, and he saw her no more.

In the evening, he returned home and told the people, "I have seen my sister."

They said, "It is not true," and they did not believe him.

The next day he went, and on other days he sat down there feeding his flock and singing his song. She came out of the water and walked to him, saluting him, and he received her salutation. They sat down there the whole of the day.

In the evening, his younger sister went and fell again into the water, and he returned home.

Again, he told the people, "It is true, I have seen her." He said to them, "If you wish to see her, turn yourselves into sheep, and tomorrow we shall go, and you shall see her."

They said to him, "Very good."

When it began to dawn, they turned themselves into sheep and went to the feeding place. When they had gone to the field together with his mother and his father, after turning themselves into sheep, the younger brother came to the mouth of the sea and sat down, singing his song. She came out of the water and saluted him. They sat down, conversing together.

She said to him, "Before this, you did not have so many sheep."

He said to her, "I did have them."

She replied, "I do not believe it."

The sheep were eating the grass and looking at her.

In the evening, she said to him, "I am going home."

He said, "Very well."

She combed the hair of his head, anointed it with oil, and made him plaits, then went home.

He said to them, "Have you seen your daughter?"

They said, "Certainly, we have seen her. She combed the hair of your head and anointed it with oil. We saw her; certainly it was she."

They said, "How shall we manage to get her again?"

There was a certain man there, the son of a king. He said to them, "If I get her out of the water, will you give her to me in marriage?"

They said, "Yes, certainly, we will give her to you, to marry her."

He said, "Very good."

He turned himself into a leper. His whole face was not nice, and his hands were full of leprosy. The people did not know he did it on purpose.

He said to them, "When I have gone into the water, and you observe the water turning white, you must not rejoice. When you see the water turning black, you must scream, but not rejoice. When you see the water turning red, then rejoice."

They said, "Very good."

He took a razor and his knife and went into the water. After saluting the girl's husband, he said, "Are you well, king of the water?"

Dodo[54] answered, "Quite well."

He said to him, "Do you wish me to shave you?"

Dodo replied, "I wish it."

The man said, "Very good."

He pulled out his razor to shave Dodo, and the people noticed the water turning very white.

After waiting a little, they observed the water turning very red, so they began to rejoice, beating their drums and playing.

The man brought the girl out of the water. Her parents saw her and rejoiced with tears. The man took his wife, brought her to his house, and married her.

Whenever she prepared food, she would bring him his portion in a dish that was not nice or was dirty. She did not love him. She did not wash his plates after eating; she left them dirty. She gave him water to drink out of a calabash that was not clean.

On a certain day, he called the people together in the public court and told the people, "You see that this dish from which I eat my food is not nice, and from this calabash that is not clean I drink my water. My wife does not love me, because my body is not nice. Today, when I have gone to my house, I shall change my body."

They said, "We have seen them all."

He went, washed his hands, washed his whole body, and changed his body, and it looked fine. All his leprosy left him.

A certain woman ran, told this to the girl, and said, "Your husband, whom you do not love, has made himself very fine today. Go quickly, wash his dish and his drinking calabash, wash them well!"

She said, "Very good."

She rose, washed the dish, and washed the calabash, and washed them well. She cooked very good food and put it in the dish. She put it aside and waited a little while until it was dry.

Her husband came home and went into his house. He saw that his dish and his calabash had been washed, and he saw the good food in them.

He said to his wife, "As for me, I do not wish to eat from this dish that is clean; I do not wish to drink out of this calabash that is now clean. Give it to me in my dish that is dirty, so that I may eat it, and give it to me in my calabash that is not nice, so that I may drink. I do not want to eat from this clean dish and drink from this clean calabash unless you go and bring the tail of a young lion and wash the dish and the calabash with it. Then I shall eat and drink out of them."

She said, "Very well." She went into her room and sat down and said to herself, "How can I manage to get the tail of the child of a lion?"

She went and discussed this with another woman and said, "My husband will not drink from the calabash that is clean, nor will he eat from the dish that is clean. He says that I should go and bring the tail of the child of a lion, that I should wash the plate and the calabash with it, and only then will he eat and drink out of them."

The woman said to her, "This is what you have done to him; he now takes vengeance on you." The woman said, "I will help you. Go, prepare some corn, wash it. and leave the pure corn so that the flies may fall into it. Take the flies and boil them, then take them and go into the forest. When you have gone and seen the mother of the young lion, climb a tree and sit there. When the mother of the young lion opens her mouth, pour the flies into her mouth quickly, and you will get the tail of the child of the lion."

She said, "Very good."

She went into her house, took corn, soaked it, washed the corn, took the water of the corn, and put it aside. When the flies had got in, she took all the flies and boiled them; then she took them and went into the forest.

There, she met the mother of the young lions.

The mother of the young lions was plaiting the hair of a hyena. When she was tired, she opened her mouth. The woman, quickly taking some of the flies, passed them into the mouth of the mother of the young lions, and the mother of the young lions ate them.

Again, after waiting a little while, she opened the lion's mouth and poured the flies into it as before.

The mother of the young lions said to the hyena, "Go to your home. I am tired today."

The hyena did not know that the mother of the young lions felt sweet when she said that she was tired. The hyena went.

The mother of the young lions got up and looked up the tree, but she could not see anyone.

She said, "Who is up there in the tree?"

The woman answered, "It is I, a woman."

She said, "Why can you not come down?"

She answered, "If I come down, your children will eat me."

She said, "Oh, no, no, they will not eat you. Come down."

The young woman went down, took the remainder of the flies, and gave them to the mother of the young lions.

The mother of the young lions said, "What do you want, coming to this place?"

The woman said to her, "I want the tail of one of your children."

She said, "Very well, come, let me hide you so that they cannot see you when they come home."

She said, "Very good."

The woman went into the storeroom, and the mother of the young lions covered her over.

When she had covered her and the evening came, her children arrived and perceived the smell of a human being. They said, "Oh, mother! Today we perceive the smell of a human being!"

She said to them, "It is a lie. Where do you sense the smell of a human being?" She was crying and said, "You suppose that there is a smell of a human being, but I do not perceive it?"

The father of the young lions came home and said to her, "Sit down. Why are you crying?"

When they went to sleep, the mother of the young lions did not go to sleep but said to the woman, "Come out. Go, cut off the tail of the smallest of the young lions."

She said, "Very well."

Then the mother of the young lions said to her, "If you see that there is a light in the room, do not come in, because they are not yet asleep. But when you see that the room is very dark, go in, they will all be asleep."

She said, "Very good."

The woman, taking her little knife out of her pocket, went. But, seeing light in the room, she ran, came and hid herself, and said, "They are not asleep."

The young lions came to their mother's place, and said, "Mother, we have seen a human being!"

She said to them, "It is a lie!" She said, "Go, lie down again and sleep."

When they had gone and had fallen asleep, the woman came and saw that the room was dark. She went in, touched the little one, the youngest of the lion's children, and cut off its tail.

The mother of the young lions said to the woman, "Run quickly, and go to your town."

The woman said, "Very good."

She went running; she had got the tail of the young lion.

In the morning, one of the children of the lion got up and said, "I am rising with my tail erect."

The next one also got up, saying, "I rise with my tail erect."

When they had all got up with their tails, the youngest one got up and said, "I have left but the stump of a tail," for he got up without a tail. He said, "Who is it who has cut off the tail of the youngest of the lion's children?"

They took up their drums, they were drumming, saying, "Backwards! backwards! he who cut off the tail of the lion's child, let him come back!"

The woman turned back a very little way.

The mother of the young lions, seeing from a distance that the woman was turning back, said to her children, "Give me your drums. I myself will beat these drums." So now she was drumming and saying, "Forward! forward!" And the woman went forward, running.

She came to the town, bringing with her the tail of the young lion. She went into her house, washed the dish with the tail of the young lion, and washed the calabash with it. Then she dried them, put food in the dish, and poured water into the calabash. She brought the food to her husband and brought the water to her husband.

He put his hand in it and did eat his food. He was pleased.

From that day, the woman knew that her husband was the son of a king.

This is it, it is finished. The story of the two girls has come to an end.

A Xhosa storyteller, June 6, 1975

16

The Fleeing Girls and the Rock[55]

Herero (Namibia)[56]

A tale goes like this:

Girls were building houses in the river. And when they had built the houses, the kraals were removed to new pastures.[57]

As they were on the way, the children said, "He who has a burden, let him give it to his mother! He who has a burden, let him give it to his mother!"

And they spoke to their mothers: "Take the burdens; our hearts are attached to the houses."

And when they had returned to the forsaken kraal, they assembled in a house in the river.

Bergdamara, in the night, fell upon the door of the house, and they entered.

The favorite one,[58] the oldest girl, was hidden away by the other children. Her name was Onihova.

Now, the Bergdamara wanted to have all the children for wives, saying, "This one is mine!" "This one is mine!"

When they had finished, there remained a very old Bergdamara, and it happened that he saw this child who had been hidden away, the favorite one.

He said, "This one is mine!"

The Bergdamara chief said, "She is mine! I am the chief, the owner of the way.[59] How could she marry you, who are old?"

And they slept.

On the following day, they went hunting.

That old Bergdamara was left behind.

He said, "I lay myself cross-wise before the door. I'll take care of you." And he said to the children, "When I am not yet asleep, I say, *Graa! Graa!* And when I am asleep, I say, *Fuu! Fuu!*"

Now the children listened, to hear whether he was truly asleep.

He said, "*Graa! Graa!*"

They did not go out of the house.

But when he said, "*Fuu! Fuu!*" all the children who were wearing metal ornaments fastened them so that they did not make a noise.

Then they stepped over the old man and went outside. They took ashes and painted one another on their foreheads.[60] Then they lifted up a large stone, the seat of the chief,[61] and threw it on the head of the old Bergdamara. The brain came out.

Then they arose and departed. They followed the track of those who were trekking. As they were going along, they came to a large flat rock, which was like a large house.

There, the girl, the favorite, stood still, and said, "*Mbemburukire yena urumbu! Mbemburukire yena urumbu!*"[62]

The rock opened.

Then the child, the favorite girl, entered first with her younger sister.

Then all entered. Among them was one little, poor girl, whose name was Okahavandye.

When all were inside, the rock closed upon them.

In the interior of the rock, Onihova, the favorite girl, said to the others, "When the rock pinches, do not call names!"

The others consented, "Yes."

But one of them, Kahavandye, said to the others, "He is bad, yes, bad! bad! if he pinches people! Why, then, are we told not to call him names?"

They were silent.

The Bergdamara, in the meantime, were in the field, hunting, and they killed game. The Bergdamara chief sent meat to the children, thinking that they were hungry.

And the Bergdamara who were sent with the meat for the children found that the children had run away and that they had killed the old man. He went back to tell this to his master.

The Bergdamara left the meat, stood up, and followed the track of the children. And they followed the children until they reached the rock. At the rock, the track was lost, so they remained there, asking themselves, "Where has the track gone?"

Then it happened that the bell of the favorite child gave a sound in the interior of the rock.[63]

The Bergdamara said, "Ih! What was that? A little bird? An iron wire?"

They all asked themselves what it was, and some said, "It was a little bird!" and others said, "It was an iron wire."

Then they took their assegais, bows, and quivers, and laid these on top of the rock, and those who asserted that it was the sound of iron said, "You're lying!"

"Well, then, let us go back, let us leave our things here, then see whether we find them when we return or whether the children have taken them with them."

So the Bergdamara went back.

Then the favorite girl, Onihova, arose, and said, "*Mbemburukire yena urumbu!*"

And the rock opened.

Onihova came out with her younger sister, and then all the rest of the girls came out. Okahavandye was on the point of coming out among them all.

The others said, "Okahavandye, wait, that we may go out first. You go out after us."[64]

Now the others went out, and the rock closed.

And Okahavandye was left in the rock.

The other children picked up the assegais, bows, and quivers of the Bergdamara and proceeded on their way.

They implored the rock, "'*Mbemburukire yena urumbu!*' Have mercy! The child has spoken in her folly."[65]

But the rock did not open.

Now the children continued to follow the track of the trekking parties until they reached their kraals.

Then all the people cried over their favorite child, Onihova, who had nearly perished. And her father arranged a large festivity for her, and the children henceforth remained in their kraals.

In the meantime, Okahavandye remained behind, in the rock. She implored the rock, "*Mbemburukire yena urumbu!* I have spoken in my folly."

But the rock did not listen to that.

Then it happened that a lion had been walking about, and it came to the rock.

The lion said to the rock, "*Mbemburukire yena urumbu!*"

And the rock opened.

The child, Okahavandye, came out, and the lion chased the child who was following the tracks of the others. While the child was being pursued by the lion, she said, "I go to die at the side of my mother's house!"

And when the child was on the point of entering her mother's house, the lion took hold of her and killed her.

Now the Bergdamara had come back to the rock. When they saw that the children had taken their things with them, they followed the track for a little distance and then returned to the rock. They fought each other now, striking one another, and then they went home.

The story is finished.

17

The Old Woman[66]

Jindwi (Manyika) (Zimbabwe)[67]

There once lived an old woman who had four daughters and four sons with their two dogs. Her one knee was very large and looked as if it were swollen. She would walk about leaning on a staff.

Now, this old woman wished to have some place where she could stay, and in search of this she at last came to a chief.

When she had greeted him, he asked what she was seeking.

She begged of him to give her a place where she could live.

But the councillors whispered to the chief, "Look at her swollen knee. She is a cripple. What will you do with an old woman like her?"

He then told her that he could not keep her and that there was no place where she might live.

The old woman went on her way.

She walked and walked for many days and traveled very far, but each chief she asked refused to let her dwell in his land.

At last she came to a great chief and begged him to give her a place where she might live in peace.

His councillors said among themselves, "Look at her knee. That is the reason she is unable to find a place to dwell."

But the chief said to her, "I will ask my queens whether one of them will give you shelter."

When he spoke to the queens, the first excused herself, saying she had many children and that there was no room for the old woman.

The second one said that she had no food to spare.

Thus, they all made excuses, until at last one queen who was not beloved by the chief said, "Though I am poor and have little food to spare, the old woman may stay with me and share what I have. Let her come and live with me."

The chief agreed, and the old woman was taken to the queen's house.

Next morning, the queen gave two cobs of maize to the old woman, saying, "I have but little. This, you may have to eat while I am gone to my field for the day."

The old woman said, "Where are your pots, so that I may get them ready for your return?"

But the queen said, "No, no, you must not worry about them, for you are an old crippled woman."

But the old woman asked, "Where can I get fuel?"

But the queen answered, "No, no, you are not to fetch fuel. You are not able to walk about."

The old woman then begged her to point out the path leading to the field.

The queen said, "Do not walk to the field. It is far and you are a cripple, but this is the path. These wide tracks are made by the cattle coming to and going from the village."

And with that, she left.

When all the people had gone from the village, the old woman sat alone in the house.

And her four daughters and four sons with the two dogs came out of her knee.

Two of the young women quickly ground some rice in a mortar, and the other two fetched wood and water. The young men went off with the dogs to hunt, and later brought back a duiker. They prepared a tasty dish of rice and meat, and then all went back into the old woman's knee.

Then the old woman took a basketful of the food, and hobbled to the queen's field.

When the queen saw her, she was amazed, and said, "Since you find it so far to walk, why do you trouble to come so far?"

The old woman said, "I merely brought you a little food," and she handed the queen the basket.

When the queen saw what was in the basket, she cried, "Why, I only left you two cobs of maize, yet you bring me all this food!"

She ate of the tasty dish of rice and meat.

In the afternoon, they both returned home.

For many days, the old woman brought a basketful of food to the queen, who at last decided to tell her husband.

When the queen came to the chief, she said to him, "I have something to tell you. Please come to my house."

But, as he did not love her, he refused.

She begged, saying, "It is something concerning the old woman."

He became angry, and said, "Why will you worry me about her? You offered to shelter her."

But at last he came to the house, and she told him all that had happened.

He was amazed, and said, "Tomorrow, I shall come to the field and see for myself."

So next day he watched, and when he saw the old woman leave the village with her basket, he followed her. As she handed the basket to the queen, he appeared. She tried to take it back, but the queen held onto it.

The chief asked, "What is in the basket?"

The queen answered, "It contains some food that the old woman has brought to me, but as I have not yet washed my hands, I may not uncover it to give to you."

He, however, said, "Uncover it, that I may eat."

She did so, and he tasted the fine food that the old woman had brought.

Next day, the chief decided to watch the old woman and find out where she got the food. He hid himself, and when the people had gone from the village, he saw the young women and men come out of the old woman's knee, and he watched them prepare the food. The young women were very comely and the young men handsome and strong.

The chief ran toward the old woman.

When she saw him coming, she called to her children, who entered her knee and disappeared.

When he spoke to her, she said she had not seen anyone and that if there were any girls and boys about they must have entered the houses.

He went away but told one of his old councillors all he had seen.

The councillor said he would watch the old woman and catch the girls.

Next day, when all the people were gone from the village, the old woman thought she was alone. Her children came out of her knee and set about their usual tasks.

The councillor was watching, however, and when he saw them, he rushed out.

But no sooner had the old woman seen him than they all entered her knee and disappeared.

Now, the chief had fallen in love with the comely young women, and he wished to marry them. He spoke to his councillor and planned how to catch them.

The councillor advised him to get a large cloth and have some young men in readiness next day. This the chief did.

While the old woman lay down and her children were doing their usual tasks, the councillor crept up close to her. The children saw the young men running toward their mother. Then the councillor quickly covered the old woman with the cloth and caught hold of her.

She cried, "Let me go, let me go! I am but an old woman."

The chief ran up to her, saluted, spoke kindly to her, and said he wished to marry the young women and that no harm would come to her.

He begged hard, and at last she asked, "What will become of me and my sons?"

He replied, "You will stay here, and your sons will marry the chief's daughters."

In the end, she agreed.

The chief sent messengers to tell all the people—men, women, and children—to return to the village and that all the cattle were to be brought back.

When the people were assembled as the chief had ordered, it began to rain very hard. But the old woman's children went and danced in the rain until the sun had almost set.

Then she said, "Now they are fortified, for had they not gone out into the rain and danced, they all would surely have died." The chief married the old woman's daughters and gave princesses in marriage to her sons.

18

Thadhellala[68]

Kabyle (Tunisia)[69]

Thadhellala was a woman who had seven daughters and no son. She went to the city and there saw a shop rich in merchandise.

She went a little farther on and perceived at the door of a house a young girl of great beauty. She called the girl's parents and said, "I have my son to marry. Let me have your daughter for him."

They let her take the girl away.

She came back to the shop rich in merchandise and said to the man in charge of it, "I will gladly give you my daughter, but go first and consult your father."

The young man left a servant in his place and departed. Thadhellala sent the servant to buy some bread in another part of the city.

Along came a caravan of mules. Thadhellala packed all the contents of the shop on their backs and said to the muleteer, "I will go ahead. My son will come in a moment. Wait for him, and he will pay you."

And she went off with the mules and the treasures that she had packed on their backs.

Soon, the servant returned.

"Where is your mother?" asked the muleteer. "Hurry and pay me!"

"You tell me where she is, and I will make her give me back what she has stolen."

And they went before the justice.

Thadhellala pursued her way and met seven young students. She said to one of them, "A hundred francs and I will marry you."

The student gave them to her.

She made the same offer to the others, and each one took her word.

Arriving at a fork in the road, the first student said, "I will take you." The second one said, "I will take you." And so on to the last.

Thadhellala answered, "You shall have a race as far as that ridge over there, and the one who gets there first shall marry me."

The young men started.

Just then, a horseman came passing by. "Lend me your horse," she said to him.

The horseman jumped off.

Thadhellala mounted the horse and said, "You see that ridge? I will rejoin you there."

The scholars saw the man.

"Have you seen a woman?" they asked him. "She has stolen seven hundred francs from us."

"Haven't you seen her? She has stolen my horse!"

They went to complain to the sultan, who gave the command to arrest Thadhellala. A man promised to seize her. He found a comrade, and together they pursued Thadhellala, who had taken flight. Nearly overtaken by the man, she met an African who pulled teeth and said to him, "You see my son coming down there. Pull out his teeth."

When the other passed, the African pulled out his teeth. The poor toothless one seized the African and led him before the sultan to have him punished.

The African said to the sultan, "It was his mother who told me to pull them out for him."

"Sidi," said the accuser, "I was pursuing Thadhellala."

The sultan then sent soldiers in pursuit of the woman. They seized her and hung her up at the gates of the city. Seeing herself arrested, she sent a messenger to her relatives.

Then there came by a man who led a mule. Seeing her, he said, "How has this woman deserved to be hanged in this way?"

"Take pity on me," said Thadhellala. "Give me your mule, and I will show you a treasure." She sent him to a certain place where the pretended treasure was supposed to be hidden.

By this time, the brother-in-law of Thadhellala had arrived.

"Take away this mule," she said to him.

The searcher for treasures dug in the earth at many places and found nothing. He came back to Thadhellala and demanded his mule.

She began to weep and cry. The sentinel ran up, and Thadhellala brought a complain against this man. She was released, and he was hanged in her place.

She fled to a far city, the sultan of which had just died. According to the custom of that country, they took as king the person who happened to be at the gates of the city when the king died. Fate took Thadhellala there at the right time.

They conducted her to the palace, and she was proclaimed queen.

19

The Cunning Young Woman[70]

Kanuri (Sierra Leone)[71]

There was a man who had a beautiful daughter, and he saw that all the young men loved her on account of her beauty.

Now, two young men who were rivals arose one day and went to the young woman, saying, "We have come to you."

The young woman asked them, "What do you want of me?"

The two young men answered, "We love you; that is why we came to you."

The young woman arose, went to her father, and said to him, "Two young men have come to me."

The father got up, went to the two young men, and asked them, "What do you want, my sons, that you have come to me?"

The young men said to the young woman's father, "We are rivals of one another and have come to your daughter, because we wish her for a wife."

The young woman's father listened to what the young men said and replied, "Go, sleep at home tonight, and when you come again tomorrow you will see who will have my daughter for a wife."

The young men did what the young woman's father told them to do and went back to sleep at home.

But when it was day, the following morning, they arose and went again to the young woman's father, saying, "We are here. Because of what you said to us yesterday, we have come to you."

The young woman's father listened to the words of the young men and said to them, "Stop, wait for me, while I go and buy a piece of cloth at the market. Then, when I have brought it to you, you shall hear what I have to say."

The young men heeded the words of the young woman's father and waited while he arose, took money, and went to the market. He went to the place where cloth is sold, bought a piece of cloth, then came back with it to where the young men were waiting.

When he returned, he called his daughter, and when she had come, he said to the young men, "My sons, you are two, but the young woman is only one. To which of you should I give her, and to which of you shall I refuse her? Look at this piece of cloth. I will tear it into two pieces and give a piece to each of you. Whoever finishes sewing a dress first will be the husband of my daughter."

Each of the young men took a piece of cloth and got ready to sew, while the young woman's father looked at them.

Then the father called his daughter to the spot where the two men were, and when she had come, he took yarn and gave it to her, saying, "Look at this yarn. Twine it, and give it to these young men."

The young woman obeyed her father. She took the yarn and sat down by the young men.

But the young woman was cunning, and neither her father nor the young men knew it: she already knew whom she liked.

Her father went and sat down in his house and waited for the young men to sew the cloth, saying, "Whoever finishes sewing first, he shall be the young woman's husband."

The young woman began to twine the yarn, and the young men took their needles and began to sew. But the young woman was cunning: for the young man whom she liked, she twined short threads, and for the young man whom she disliked, she twined long threads. So the young men were sewing the cloth, and the young woman was twining yarn, and at noon she saw that they had not yet finished sewing the cloth. So she continued twining the yarn for them, and they went on sewing.

At about three o'clock in the afternoon, the young man who had short threads finished sewing the cloth, but the young man with the long threads had not yet finished.

Then the young woman's father arose and came to the young men. He said to them, "Have you sewn until now, and is the cloth not yet finished?"

The one young man got up, took his cloth, and said to the young woman's father, "My father, look, my part is finished."

The part of the other young man was not yet finished.

The young woman's father looked at them, and they looked at the young woman's father. Then the father said, "My sons, when you came to me, and both of you said that you wanted my only daughter, I would not be partial to either of you. Therefore, I brought you a piece of cloth, rent it into two pieces, gave them to you, called my daughter to twine thread for you, and said, 'Make these dresses!' You began to make them, and I said to you, 'He who has first finished the dress, he shall be the husband of my daughter.' Did you understand that?"

The young men answered, "Father, we understood what you said: the man who finished the dress would be the young woman's husband, and the man who did not make it would not be the young woman's husband."

It was the cunning young woman who decided the contest of the two young men. Her father did not know that his daughter, when she twined the thread, had made short threads for the man she liked, nor did he know that she had made long threads for the man she disliked.

He did not know that it was the young woman who had chosen her husband.

The young woman's father reasoned in reference to the young men, "If the man who first finishes sewing takes the young woman, he will work fast and maintain her, but were he to choose the young man who does not finish sewing—would he also work fast and maintain the young woman?"

So the two young men arose and went to their town. But only he who had first finished the dress took the young woman for his wife.

A Xhosa storyteller, June 9, 1975

20

The Little Wise Woman[72]

Khoikhoi (Southern Africa)[73]

A girl, it is said, went to seek onions. As she came to the place where the onions grew, she met some men, one of whom was half-blind, having only one eye. As she dug for the onions, the men helped her, digging also.

When her sack was full, they said to her, "Go, tell the other girls, so that many of you come here."

So she went home and told her companions, and early the next morning they set out.

But a little girl followed them.

The other girls said, "Let the little girl go back."

But her elder sister protested against this, saying, "She runs by herself; you need not put her into your awa-skin."

So they all went together, and when they reached the onion-ground, they began to dig.

Now the little girl saw traces of feet and said to the one who had guided them to this place, "Wonderful! Where did all these traces come from? Were you not alone here?"

The other replied, "I walked about and looked out, and that's why the foot prints are so many."

The child, however, did not believe that if the other girl had been alone the traces would be so many, and she felt uneasy, for she was a wise little woman. From time to time she rose from her work and looked about. Once, while doing this, she found by chance an anteater's hole. Still spying around, she saw some men, but they did not see her. She then returned and continued digging with the other girls, without, however, saying anything. But, in the midst of their work, she always rose and looked about her.

The others asked her, "Why do you always spy about and stop digging? What a girl!"

But she continued her work in silence. When she rose from it again, she saw the men approaching.

As they drew near, the one-eyed blew through a reed pipe the following air: "Today blood will flow, blood will flow, blood will flow!"

The little girl understood what was blown on the reed.

She said to the elder ones, while they were dancing, "Do you also understand the tune that is being blown on the reed?"

But they only said, "What a child she is!"

So she mixed in the dance with the others but managed while doing so to tie her sister's kaross-cloak to her own, and in this manner they danced on, until it became very noisy, and then they found an opportunity to slip away.

On their way out, the little sister asked, "Do you understand the reed—I mean what is blown on it?"

She answered, "I do not understand it."

Then the little girl explained to her that the tune on the reed said, "Today, blood will flow!"

While they walked along, the little girl let her elder sister go first, and she herself followed, walking backwards and carefully stepping in her sister's traces, so that they thereby left only one set of footmarks, and these going in a contrary direction. In this manner, they arrived at the anteater's hole.

But the men killed all those girls who had remained dancing with them. When the eldest of those who had escaped heard their wailing, she said, "Oh, my sisters!"

But the younger one answered her, "Do you think you would have lived if you had remained there?"

Now One-eye was the first to miss the sisters, and he said to the other men, "Where are the two handsome girls who danced with me?"

The others replied, "He lies. He has seen with his eye."[74]

But One-eye insisted that the two girls were truly missing.

Then they went to find their spoor, but the traces had been rendered indistinct enough to puzzle them.

When the men arrived at the anteater's hole, they could not see that the footmarks went further, so they spied into the hole but saw nothing.

Then One-eye also looked, and he saw the girls and cried, "There they sit!"

The others now looked again but still saw nothing, for the girls had covered themselves with cobwebs.

One of the men then took an assegai and, piercing through the upper part of the hole, hit the heel of the larger girl. But the little wise woman took hold of the assegai and wiped off the blood. The elder sister was about to cry, but the little one warned her not to.

When One-eye spied again, the little girl made big eyes at him.

He said, "There she sits!"

The others looked, too, but as they could see nothing. They said, "He has only seen with his eye."[75]

At last the men got thirsty and said to One-eye, "You stay here, and let us go to drink. When we have returned, you may go also."

When One-eye was left alone there, the little girl said, conjuring him,

"You dirty son of your father,
Are you there? Are you alone not thirsty?
Oh, you dirty child of your father!
Dirty child of your father!"

"I am indeed thirsty," said One-eye, and he went away.

Then the two girls came out of the hole, and the younger one took her elder sister on her back and walked on. As they were going over the bare, treeless plain, the men saw them and said, "There they are, far off!" and ran after them.

When they came near, the two girls turned themselves into thorn trees, called Wait-a-bit, and the beads that they wore became gum on the trees. Then men then ate of the gum and fell asleep. While they slept, the girls smeared gum over the men's eyes and went away, leaving them lying in the sun.

The girls were already near their kraal when One-eye awoke and said,

"Oh, the disgrace! Fie on you!
Our eyes are smeared over, fie on you, my brother!"

Then they removed the gum from their eyes and hunted the girls. But the girls reached home in safety and told their parents what had happened.

Then all lamented greatly, but they remained quietly at home and did not search for the other girls.

21

The Old Woman, Her Sons, and the Python[76]

Kikuyu (Kenya)[77]

A girl named Kasoni, on her way to get water for her father to drink, saw a large python basking in the sun near the path. The python had two mouths, and its hair was beautifully arranged like that of a warrior. Kasoni stood and admired it for some minutes.

The python, seeing the girl looking at it, said, "I am hungry. Will you give me enough food to satisfy my hunger?"

She replied, "Certainly I will. Follow me to my village, and I will give you as much as you can eat."

She then took up her water-gourd and proceeded in the direction of her home, followed by the python. Reaching the village, she took the python to a grain house and invited it to eat. The monster put its head inside the grain house and in a few minutes devoured all the contents.

She then took it to another store, which it soon finished.

Gradually it ate up all the grain in the village, but still it was not satisfied.

Kasoni then took it to the goat houses and told it to eat the goats if it wished. One by one, the goats were eaten, until none was left.

The python then started eating the men, women, and children of the village, until Kasoni was the only one left.

The monster asked her for more food, saying its hunger was not nearly satisfied.

She replied that the only people of her village still left in addition to herself were a bad-tempered old woman, the wife of the chief, and her two infant sons who lived in the forest, because the chief would not allow his wife near him.

"Well," said the python, "I will go and look for them but will first eat you," saying which it opened one of its huge mouths and swallowed her at a gulp. It then went to search for the old woman and her children in the forest.

The woman, who was sitting near her house, hearing a noise, looked up and saw the monster approaching. Seizing both her children in her arms, she fled and hid herself. The python searched for her for a long time but, not finding her, went back to its abode.

The old woman and her sons lived in the forest for many years, until the sons had grown into men.

They one day asked their mother why it was that they were alone in the world and had no relations. She then told them the story of how the python had eaten up everybody in her village, but they laughed at her and said such a thing was impossible.

A few years after she told them this story, she said to them one morning, "The time has now come for you to avenge the death of your father." She told them to bring their swords and, taking them to a path near the house, hid them in the bushes close to the path, placing each about one hundred yards from the other.

Having done this, she told them that she was going to call the monster who had destroyed their village and instructed the younger that when he saw the monster come along he was to allow it to pass and not to strike until he saw his brother jump from his hiding place and strike it. She told the elder brother that as soon as the monster's head came near to him, he was to rise at once and cut it off with his sword.

She then went to the river and sang,

"Evil one, you who ate up my people and still were not satisfied,
Come out of your resting place and I will give you a feast,
So plentiful is the food I have prepared that even you will hunger no
   more."

Hearing her voice, the python raised itself from the water and followed her. In a short time, they passed the hiding place of the younger brother and soon came to that of the elder. The elder brother at once jumped up and cut the monster's head off with one blow of his sword, and the younger brother at the same time rose and cut off its tail.

As soon as they had done this, they heard a babel of voices calling out to them to strike no more and to their amazement saw a large number of men, women, children, and goats emerge from the body of the dead python.

One old man, on seeing their mother, called her by name and asked her who these two bold warriors were who had rescued them from their enemy.

She told him that they were his two sons who were small children on the day that he had been eaten by the monster.

Great rejoicings took place, and the chief at once set the people to work to rebuild their village and to make a large house for his wife and one for each of his sons. All set to work with a good will, and in a short period the village was as flourishing as it had ever been, and the old woman and her sons were afterward treated with great respect.

22

Five Dead Men Attend a Dance[78]

Krio (Sierra Leone)[79]

One day, a big dance was held in a village. While this dance was going on, spirits from the forest came to attend. Dead people also came out of their graves to attend the dance.

There were five young women who lived in this village and who were very fond of men. Five dead men came to the dance in the village. They were very well dressed. They were so well dressed that people remarked that they had never seen anyone dressed in such clothes anywhere else in the world.

No sooner had the five dead men arrived that the five young women saw them and fell in love with them. They flirted with them all through the dance until it was time for the dance to end.

The dance ended, and people were getting ready to return to their homes.

The dance was over, and the five young women decided to accompany their boyfriends home. They left and were on their way.

But these men were dead persons.

The five young women accompanied their boyfriends. They had traveled for a little while when four of the women said, "We think we should return to our homes."

The dead men said, "Well, you can all go back now; you do not know where we are going. You can return now."

But the fifth young woman, the one who had not indicated that she would return with her four friends, a headstrong young woman, said, "Well, as for myself, I am not going back. I must know where my boyfriend is going."

Bop! Her four friends turned around and started to return home. They begged their friend to come with them, to return home with them. They begged and begged her, but this young woman replied, "I stick to what I say. I must see where you men are from, and the place where you eventually die will be the place where I will also die."

The dead men continued to head to the place that they were from. They had now reached their graves.

They said to the young woman, "Please, we plead with you. Go back."

They gave her a lot of things, money and clothes, begging her to return to her home, but she replied to her boyfriend, "I am not going back. The place where you die is where I am also going to die."

She remained there, standing.

Then one of the dead men approached his grave.

Another went to his grave.

They all did this, and they were standing, waiting for the girl to go. They did not want her to see where they were going.

So they begged her again to return to her home. They begged and begged, but she would not heed their advice.

She said, "The place where my boyfriend dies is where I will also die."

Well, there was a song that the dead men sang when they wanted to enter their graves. One of them lay down on his grave and he started to sing,

"I get up *tehteh*
I wriggle *tehteh*
I fall down *kpungbuju*
I stand up *yele o*
Maanya, I've gone."

Then his grave opened, and he went inside.

There were now four dead men remaining. These four dead men started to beg the young woman, "Please, we don't want to leave you here all by yourself."

The young woman replied, "The place where my boyfriend dies is where I will also die."

One of the dead men lay down on his grave. He sang the same song that the first dead man had sung:

"I get up *tehteh*
I wriggle *tehteh*
I fall down *kpungbuju*
I stand up *yele o*
Maanya, I've gone."

Then he disappeared into his grave.

Two of the remaining dead men lay on their graves. They sang the song:

"I get up *tehteh*
I wriggle *tehteh*
I fall down *kpungbuju*
I stand up *yele o*
Maanya, I've gone."

And then they disappeared into their graves.

It was now the turn of the fifth dead man. The woman was standing at his side. The dead man begged the woman. He said, "Please go back. We will return."

"The place where you are going, that is the place that I want to see," replied the woman.

The dead man lay on his grave, and sang the same song of the other dead men.

"I get up *tehteh*
I wriggle *tehteh*
I fall down *kpungbuju*
I stand up *yele o*
Maanya, I've gone."

Then he disappeared into the grave.

The young woman was now left alone. She had witnessed the five dead men disappear into their graves.

So she lay down on her boyfriend's grave and started to sing. She sang the song:

"I get up *tehteh*
I wriggle *tehteh*
I fall down *kpungbuju*
I stand up *yele o*
Maanya, I've gone,"

and then disappeared into the grave *fa*.

They were waiting for her inside the grave. When she disappeared, she found herself in another country, where there were people who had lots of wealth. It was from here that the wealth came to the people in the world of the living.

The woman met the dead men and said, "Well, I am here. You remember that I said that the place where my boyfriend dies is the place where I will also die. Well, here I am."

They took the young woman and started to travel. They traveled for some time, and then they said, "Will you do what we tell you?"

"Yes," replied the young woman.

"You will do it?" they asked again.

"Yes," replied the young woman.

They continued traveling. They approached an old woman who had a huge sore on her foot that I have never seen in this world. The sore gave off a stinking odor.

The dead men said to the young woman, "Well, wash this old woman's sore."

The young woman washed the old woman's sore, and she placed a bandage on it.

They left the old woman and continued walking. They came to a muddy pool of water. There was blood in the water.

The dead men said to her, "Drink this water."

She drank the water. They left and continued walking. They saw a huge heap of feces in which there were maggots.

The dead men said to her, "Eat this heap of feces."

She took the feces and ate it all.

Then they arrived at their town. It was a big town, and it was here that all the wealth was located. The young woman was there for three days.

On the fourth day, she said, "Well, I would like to return to my village."

"You want to go back?" they asked.

"Yes," she answered.

The dead men took some suitcases; there were three. One was dirty, and the other two were clean and shining. It was a very bright shine. It was in the dirty suitcase that all the wealth was packed. The suitcases that were shining contained all the animals, animals such as leopards, crocodiles, lions; anything that would devour a human was in the two shining suitcases.

The dead men said to the young woman, "Choose one suitcase out of the lot."

The young woman looked at them *pinnnnnnn*. She chose the dirty suitcase. She took it and left.

The dead men accompanied her part of the way. Then they left her and she returned to her home.

When her people saw her with this large suitcase, they were all very happy. They were happy to see the young woman. They opened the suit-case, and they found wealth in it. There was much money; there were many clothes. They saw all this and were pleased.

Now, the mother of this young woman had a mate, another wife of her husband. This mate also had a daughter.

It happened that there was another dance in the village. The dead men came to the dance, and the daughter of the mate fell in love with one of the dead men. She followed them to the place from which they came.

They pleaded with her, telling her that she must return, but she insisted that she would follow her boyfriend wherever he went.

She said, "I must go to the place that you are going. I won't be left here. The place at which my boyfriend dies is where I shall also die."

They went away. The dead men sang the song, and they disappeared, one after the other, into their graves. Then the young woman sang the song, and she disappeared into the grave of her boyfriend.

She arrived in another country. The dead men were waiting for her. They took her and started to travel.

They walked and walked until they reached an old woman who had a huge sore on her leg. The sore stank like the excrement of a hog.

The dead men said to her, "Wash this old woman's sore."

"Are you talking to me?" she asked, and asked impatiently: "Do you expect me to wash such a huge sore that gives off such a disgusting odor?"

They left and continued walking. They reached the heap of excrement, and the dead men said, "Eat this heap of feces."

"Do you expect someone like myself, who has become accustomed to eating rice, to eat such filth?" She rudely added, "Don't bother me with such nonsense."

They arrived at the town. The young woman stayed there for three days, and on the fourth day she said that she would like to return to her village.

The dead men again produced the three suitcases. There was the dirty suitcase, together with the two shining ones.

The dead men said, "Choose one from the lot."

Well, you know something? This young woman was a showgirl. She liked to make herself look very attractive. So she chose one of the shining suitcases. She placed it on her head and carried it away.

The dead men accompanied her part of the way home.

She arrived at her village. She was very happy, and so were her people. The friends of the other young woman, the one who had preceded her, said, "Well, look at this one. She has brought a shining suitcase. When you returned, you brought a dirty suitcase. See what your friend has brought! A brand-new suitcase!"

No sooner had the young woman arrived in the village when she called her mother, her father, her brothers, her sisters, and all her relatives. They went into a room in the house and locked the door of the room. She closed all the windows. Even where there was a small hole through which light entered the room, she stuffed the hole with a piece of cloth.

Then they opened the suitcase, and one of the crocodiles came out. The crocodile snapped the mother in two. With the third bite, it devoured the mother completely.

A leopard came out, followed by another one. They ate everyone inside the room.

Well, it was that young woman who brought all these problems into this world, things like the snake—she brought them into this country. That is the reason envy is not a good thing. You must not be envious of something a friend has—for you do not know how that friend has obtained what he has.

23

The Hole in the Tree[80]

Lamba (Zambia)[81]

A chief had daughters, and all of them except the youngest married.

When it came to the youngest one, she refused to marry, saying, "I want a man who can pass through a hole in the tree with a ball!"

The chief was astonished. He said, "Where shall I find such a person in this country?"

He called all the people. All gathered together and tried to pass through the hole, and they were baffled as to how to do that. Then that group returned home, and others came. And they tried to pass through the hole, and they too were baffled.

The child grew thin, and the chief remained sorrowful.

Others far off heard about this: "Over there is a chief's daughter; she wants a man who can pass through a hole in the tree."

Then two brothers and their brother-in-law, three people, got up to go there.

The little brother said, "I am going with you!"

They refused, "No, we don't want you to go with us."

Their brother-in-law said, "Let him come."

They said, "No, if he comes along, we shall beat him!"

So the youngest brother pretended to remain behind.

But when the elder brothers had risen, he too arose behind them, and he went along with them, hiding.

Their brother-in-law looked around and said, "Your little brother! We have come with him, friends!"

The brothers said, "Let's beat him!"

But the brother-in-law refused, saying, "No, he's only a youngster; he's not responsible."

He reached the house and sat down. And the brothers heeded the words of their brother-in-law and gave the youngest brother the basket of meal. He took it and carried it. And, as they set out, he remained behind with the basket of meal.

When he had traveled a little, he saw a huge bird rise up and turn to the west. He scooped up some meal and went and threw it on the place from which the bird had risen.

As they went on, he came to some black ants. And there, too, he scooped up some meal and threw it to the ground.

And they passed on.

He came to a stream; fish were swimming about. He scooped up some of that meal and threw it into the stream.

Then they reached the outskirts of the village.

They entered the village; they arrived and sat down.

Then a certain man went to the chief and said, "People have arrived over there."

He said, "How many are they?"

He said, "There are three adults and a child."

He said, "Show them to a house. What have they come for?"

"This business of your daughter."

They showed them to a house.

When morning dawned, the chief said, "Let those people who slept over there come."

The man went to call them, saying, "The chief calls for you. Let us go there, you three."

That youngster remained behind.

The three reached the chief. And he gave them a ball, saying, "Try now!"

One of the three went first. He threw the ball down, the ball bounced away, and when it reached the hole in the tree, he caught it in order to go through the hole. But he was foiled.

And the second tried, and he too was thwarted.

The third tried, and he too was disappointed.

The chief looked about and asked, "Are these the only people who came?"

Someone said, "The three of them came, and a youngster."

He said, "And the youngster, go and bring him."

They went and brought the youngster. He came with fear.

He reached the chief, and the chief said, "Give him the ball!"

He took it and threw it, and then he went after it. When the ball reached the hole in the tree, he caught it. And when he poked in his head, he went inside the hole with the ball. Again, he threw the ball down, and it caught on her[82] breasts.

Then the people were very glad, and they brought fine clothing.

But his brothers, when they saw that fine clothing, envied him and said,

"All right, we shall tell on him. They will drive him away. Or maybe we shall kill him."

When night came, both of the elder brothers went to his mother-in-law and said, "Wife of the chief!"

And she answered, "It is I."

They said, "That son-in-law whom you are about to marry has wisdom. If you say, 'If you were really a son-in-law, you would bring a baby this very day!' you will see that indeed he has brought it."

And the chief's wife answered, "Oh, you people! And where would be get a child from?"

They said, "It is true!"

Then the chief's wife accepted these words and went out. When she reached the courtyard of that son-in-law, she said, "If you were really a son-in-law, you would bring a child this very day!"

The youngster was astonished. He said, "Where am I to get a child from this very day?"

Then he went out, put on his little loincloth, and said, "I am leaving, my wife, for home!"

And his wife, when she saw her husband like that, wept.

Off he went. He arrived there at the river and crossed, and he arrived at that bird.

The bird asked him, "Where are you going, friend?"

He said, "I am going home. My mother-in-law is bothering me. She said to prove that I am a son-in-law I should bring a child this very day! And where am I to get it from?"

The bird heard and asked him, "Was it you who gave me the meal?"

He replied, "It was I, sir."

The bird said, "Stop here, and sit down."

He remained sitting as the bird rose and went westward.

When a short time had passed, he saw the bird coming with a baby. It gave the baby to him, saying, "Take it to your mother-in-law, and let her nurse it."

And he went to the village. When he reached the village, he gave the baby to his wife, saying, "Here is the child. Take it to your mother."

And she took the child to her mother, and her mother was greatly astonished. She said, "This person, where did he get the child from?"

And she took that child and went back to her house.

Those elder brothers of his came again and said, "Don't you see, wife of the chief, this person is a wise one! Now, you take some millet seed. Go and pour it out in the bush. And you will see that he has picked it up!"

The boy's mother-in-law agreed to do this. In the morning, she took a basket of millet; she arrived and poured it out. Then she went to her son-in-law and said, "If you were really a son-in-law, you would go and pick up the millet that I have spilled!"

And the child was again sad. He went out with his little loincloth. When he arrived at the place where the little black ants were, he saw a basket.

And the little black ants asked him, "Where are you going?"

He said, "I am going home. My mother-in-law has spilled millet seed, and she has told me to pick it up. Millet isn't picked up; it's difficult!"

The little ants said, "Is it you who gave us the meal?"

He answered, "It was I."

Then the little ants went in and called all their little mates and said, "That friend of ours, the one who gave us the meal, has come. His mother-in-law has spilled millet seed."

And they all came out, each of them picking up one seed. They put the seeds into the basket and gave it to him, saying, "Take this to your mother-in-law."

And he took the basket containing the millet seeds.

She was again astonished and said, "Indeed, this son-in-law of mine is wise!"

In the evening, his elder brothers again came and said, "Don't you see, wife of the chief, that this person is cunning? Even if you pour beads into the water, he will go and take them out."

And she agreed. She filled a basket brimful with tiny beads, and she arrived and poured them into the water. Then she returned and went and told her son-in-law.

And her son-in-law was very sad, and he went away.

He arrived there at the stream.

The fish asked him, "Where are you going, friend?"

He answered, "I am going home. My mother-in-law poured beads into the water here, and she wants me to pick them up."

The fish asked, "Was it you who gave us the meal?"

He said, "It was I."

Then the fish dived and told their companions down below. And they all picked up those beads and filled that basket.

The fish said, "Go now, friend."

And he went. He arrived and put the basket down and said to his wife, "Your mother is worrying me. Every day she sends me on improper errands."

And that child went and spoke to her mother.

Her mother said, "No, it is not my fault. His elder brothers tell me these things."

Then the wife went to her father and said, "Why does mother worry my husband like this?" She added, "She came first of all and said, 'To prove yourself a son-in-law, give birth to a child this very day!' My husband went and brought a child. She came back and said, 'If one really had a son-in-law, he would pick up millet seed!' He picked it up. And she poured beads in the water and again came to my husband and told him. And again he went, and he picked them up."

That chief was very angry. He said, "Call the chief's wife!"

And they went and called her.

When the chief's wife came, she denied it, saying, "No sir, his own elder brothers are telling on him."

The chief said, "Go and fetch those people!"

And they went and fetched them.

When those people came back to the chief, he bound them and sent men to take them back home. And they took them.

After a few days, the chief gathered goods together, and he said, "Take my son-in-law and his wife to their home."

And they arose with their people, and off they went.

They reached home, and they were very happy at home when they saw them. They swept out a house for him to enter.

In the evening, he portioned out goods to his uncles and mother.

When many days had passed at his home, he again arose to return to his wife's village.

They arrived at his wife's village.

24

The Jackal and the Little Antelope[83]

Luba (Democratic Republic of Congo)[84]

[T]he average Muluba. . . . [He] is a keen agriculturalist, he is the most musical of all the negroes, and he is a wonderful story-teller. The last two qualities have certainly been transmitted unto their descendants across the seas. I should not wonder if Uncle Remus had Luba blood in his veins; fabulists of his type are found in every village. They not only tell you the traditional stories, but can improvise on the spur of the moment a tale, which will explain anything to the smallest detail. They have a story ready to explain any occurrence, and the experienced bard will never miss the opportunity of doing so. Why? He receives no reward; it is just what Goethe called 'die Lust zum Fabuliren'—(the joy of spinning a yarn).[85]

The little antelope had been going apace. He had been buying up in the market everything that was good and dear, food, drink, and the most costly raiment. Then, as the moon rose, he invited his friends, and the drums were beating and the animals were dancing and singing until the first rays of the sun drove them home.

And the little antelope paid for everything.

One day, when after a night's debauchery the little antelope woke, he went to his money bag, but, turning it inside out and outside in, he could not find a single cowry in it to buy himself food to break his fast. There had been plenty, and now all was gone.

"What does it matter?" said the little antelope. "My friends are waiting for me to continue our revelry. I will ask them to lend me some money, and we shall again have a good time."

He found his friends at the appointed place, but when he mentioned that he wanted to borrow money they fled in great haste. Those who could run, ran; those who could fly, flew. The tortoise, who could neither run nor fly, drew back into its shell and shut its opening with a snap that sounded that a clap of thunder.

"Dear, dear," said the little antelope, "what am I to do now? My friends having treated me so shabbily, I will go to my old enemy, the jackal, and see what he will do for me."

Off he went and found the jackal in front of his house counting a big bag of cowries.

"Hundred and one, hundred and two. . . ."

The little antelope's mouth watered at the sight of the tremendous amount of money.

"Good morning, jackal," he said humbly. "I hope you are in good health and that your wife is in good health, and your children too!"

"Hm," said the jackal. "Hundred and ten, hundred and eleven. . . ."

"I came to ask you for a little service."

"Come another day . . . hundred and twenty. . . . I am busy today . . . hundred and twenty-one. . . ."

"Can I come tomorrow?"

"I am going to a wedding tomorrow . . . hundred and thirty . . . I have to clear a field the day after that . . . hundred and thirty-one . . . the next day there is a funeral . . . hundred and thirty-two . . . the next day. . . ."

"The next day you will have something else to do, I have no doubt. So we might just as well do the business now. I want to ask you a little favor."

"Ask away . . . hundred and forty . . . but I am afraid . . . hundred and forty-one . . . that I won't be able to oblige you . . . hundred and forty-two. . . ."

"How do you know? I have not yet told you what I want."

The jackal sneered. He had heard of the straits his old foe was in. "I just have a premonition . . . hundred and fifty. . . ."

"I want you to lend me a few cowries."

The jackal stopped counting. "Lend you money? If you want money, why don't you go to work instead of always seeking your pleasure, you good-for-nothing scamp? Then you will get all the money you want."

"I am itching to work," said the little antelope. "Work is a real passion with me."

"Well, then, why don't you?"

"Did you not tell me the other day that I must never give way to my passions?"

The jackal remembered having said something to that effect, but somehow it did not seem to fit in just now. He wondered why. So he grumbled, "Work ought to be a pleasure to honest people."

"Yes, yes," said the little antelope, "that is so. You have just told me that only good-for-nothing scamps always seek their pleasure."

The jackal, stupid as he was, saw now that the little antelope was making fun of him. The little antelope always did it. If only he could get his own back and play some trick on him. . . .

Suddenly, he thought of a hollow tree he had noticed the other day, and a fiendish idea occurred to him.

"I will lend you no money," he said, "because, first of all, I have none. Second, the little I own I want myself. And third, what I can spare is better in my money-bag than yours. But I will help you in another way. I know of a treasure. . . ."

"If you know of a treasure, why don't you fetch it yourself?" asked the little antelope, who was on his guard.

"Because it is in a hollow tree, and, hard as I tried, I could not squeeze through its entrance. You are small and slender, and I will push behind; you might get in."

This reassured the little antelope. Still, he was afraid that if he did manage to get the treasure, the jackal would rob him of it as soon as he had brought it out. So he thought it might be wise to offer him beforehand a big share of it; then he might he honest about the rest.

"I am willing," he said, "but as it is you who have found the treasure, you must take nine-tenths of it as your share."

"No, no, keep it all," said the jackal, who could be generous—when there was nothing to lose. He knew quite well that there was no treasure in the hollow tree.

Then there began the queerest bargaining the world has ever seen. Both wanted to give more and take less money, as if they were dealing in blows. At last, the little antelope, who was burning with the desire to handle the treasure, said, "Let us agree to this: each will have an equal share, and then we will add a little to it so that I shall have more than you and you shall have more than I." This seemed an equitable arrangement to the jackal, and he proposed starting at once on their treasure hunt.

Soon they came to the hollow tree. The hole was small, but the little antelope, having an empty stomach, and the jackal pushing with all his might from behind, at last went in. The white spot on his rump had not quite disappeared when the jackal gave a shout of joy and rolled a huge stone in front of the opening.

"Have you found anything, antelope?" he asked with malice.

"Not yet."

"I have. I have found a good dinner. Now I am going to make a roaring fire around this tree, and when you are roasted nice and brown, you must come and have dinner with me."

"Let me out, dear Jackal, let me out!" shouted the little antelope in anguish, having discovered too late that he had allowed himself to be tricked by that fool of a jackal.

"Not yet, my friend. I am too busy. Look at all the wood I have to pile up to roast you."

And he went on piling up wood while the little antelope retired to the deepest recess of the hollow, meditating how he could escape.

When the jackal had all the wood he wanted, he went to the tree and shouted, "Hello, antelope!" There came no answer. "Hello, antelope!" he shouted again. "Are you there?"

"No," answered the little antelope.

"What!" exclaimed the jackal furiously. "How dare you say that, you liar?"

"I am not a liar; I am not here."

"But are you sure of that?" asked the jackal anxiously.

"Well," giggled the little antelope, "who should know better than I? But if you doubt, have a look."

In all haste, the jackal removed the twigs and then the stone. As soon as he had done so, the little antelope threw some dirt into his eyes and, while he was trying to remove it, slipped out of the tree.

The blinded jackal was banging his head against the stone, against the tree, and tripping over the twigs, while the little antelope was running home as fast as he could. Some say that he stole the jackal's cowries, some say that he did not. But that is another story. . . .

Nokavala Ntshebe, a Xhosa storyteller, June 21, 1975

25

Andrianòro[86]

Malagasy (Madagascar)[87]

Once there was, it is said, a man named Andriambahòaka-in-the-midst-of-the-land, and this man had three children, one son and two daughters. The son's name was Andrianòro, and those of his two sisters were Ràmatòa and Rafàravàry.[88]

Andriambahòaka was rich and had large estates, and these two daughters of his were unmarried.

Then the son named Andrianòro said to his father and mother, "Get me a wife."

So his parents agreed to obtain a wife for their son.

But when they had fetched the wife for Andrianòro, he did not like her at all.

So his father said, "We will not again seek a wife for you. You yourself shall choose whom you like."

And, after some time, so the story goes, some one spoke to Andrianòro and said, "There is a most enchanting lake over there, with delightful sands and the water as clear as crystal. And there are three sisters whom we have seen swimming in that clear lake and whose beauty we have never seen the like of."

Then Andrianòro said, "I will capture one of them for my wife." Then he said to his subjects, "Where does the person most skilled in divination live?"

The people replied, "Go to Rànakòmbé; he is the most skilled diviner."

So Andrianòro went to Rànakòmbé and said, "Be so good as to divine for me, Rànakòmbé, for there is a person whom I wish for a wife in this lake. But if any one approaches the lake, then she flies away—it is said that her dwelling place is in heaven. So please give me good counsel as to what I should do to capture her."

Then Rànakòmbé answered, "Go to the lake and change into three very ripe lemons. Then, while the three sisters are playing, make them desire you. And when the three take you, then change again into a man, and then lay hold of one of the three sisters for your wife."

So when Andrianòro had come to the sand where the three sisters played, he changed into three lemons, according to Rànakòmbé's directions. And when the three sisters came there and saw the lemons, they were exceedingly astonished.

Then the youngest of the three said, "Come, let us take these lemons for ourselves."

But the eldest and the second one replied, "Don't let us touch these lemons; it is a snare, for from long ago there have been no such lemons here."

Then they flew away and went up into the sky.

So the lemons changed again, it is said, and became Andrianòro once more, and off he went afresh to Rànakòmbé to inquire what divination would enable him to obtain his wish.

And the divination worked by Rànakòmbé gave answer: "Change into bluish water in the middle of the lake, and when the three sisters swim there, lay hold of them."

So Andrianòro went away again.

But when the three sisters came again to swim, they were afraid to do so, saying, "That water is a snare, like the lemons we saw before."

And after a while, again, Andrianòro changed again in an instant into the seed of the *ànamàmy*[89] growing by the water side, but the sisters knew all about it.

So Andrianòro was perplexed and did not see what he could do, for he wished to obtain one of the three for a wife. And off he went again to Rànakòmbé to ask some more suitable counsel as to how he might obtain her.

Rànakòmbé said, "Change into an ant, and walk on the sand."

The three sisters came down from the sky again and sat on the sand; then Andrianòro caught one of them, the youngest, and said to her, "You are my wife, Ifàravàvy."

But she replied, "I am not your wife, Andrianòro."

Andrianòro said, "What is it that makes you unwilling to marry me?"

She answered, "There are many things about you that trouble me."

"What things are they?" he asked.

Ifàravàvy replied, "My parents live not here on the earth but in the skies, and you are of humankind here on the earth and are not able to live in heaven with father and mother, for if father speaks, the thunderbolt darts forth, and besides I do not drink *tòaka*,[90] for if spirits even touch my mouth I die."

Then Andrianòro said, "I can endure all that for my love to you, piece of my life."

Then she consented to be his wife.

When the pair went home to Andrianòro's house, they were met by a great many people, and both his subjects and his father and mother rejoiced. And Andrianòro made an exceedingly strong town, with seven enclosures, building them one within another,[91] and together with Andrianòro there lived also his younger sister, whom he loved best of the two.

After a long time, Andrianòro's wife said to him, "I should like to play with the horns of the *làloména*."[92]

He replied, "I will go to seek it, wherever it may be, so do not trouble yourself needlessly about it, my wife."

Then Andrianòro told his parents that he was going to seek the thing desired by his wife: "I am going, father and mother, to procure the horns of the *làloména*, and here is my wife to take care of, if you love me. And let my sister Rafàravàvy stay with her until I come, for if I do not find the horns of the *làloména* I shall not return."

Andrianòro's father and mother agreed to take good care of his wife and children until he returned. Then his dependents and servants pounded rice for the journey, for he was about to go. And when the rice was pounded, he went and took leave of his parents and his wife and sisters, saying, "May you live then until I come back. Do not grieve fruitlessly!"

Then Andrianòro set off with many of his people to seek the horns of the *làloména*.

After he had remained away a long time, his father and mother and eldest sister said, "Come, let us kill this woman, for it is because of her alone that Andrianòro has gone off to a country he does not know."

Her father-in-law said, "How shall we kill her?"

Her mother-in-law and sister-in-law said, "Give her spirits in a horn,[93] for that is what she told Andrianòro before they were married."

They went to buy *tòaka*, then put it in a horn.

But Rafàravàvy, Andrianóro's sister, was there with his wife, and they overheard the conspiracy to kill her.

The wife charged Rafàravàvy, saying, "When I am dead, say to the chief people, 'Bury her in the road by which Andrianòro will come.'"

"Yes," said Fafàravàvy, "but cannot I be substitute for what is to befall you, my relative, for what will it matter to me? for I will inform the chief people secretly."

The two sisters-in-law locked all the gates seven deep, and Andrianòro's parents and wife went and fetched the *tòaka*.

Soon the father called at the gateway, "Open the gate for me, my child, open the gate for me, for here is *tòaka* for you."

His daughter-in-law replied, "I do not drink *tòaka*, father, for if I drink it I will die, no matter if it is in a white horn or a black one."

Then her mother-in-law and her sister-in-law called at the gateway, and to the same effect, but Andrianòro's wife refused, as she had done before.

Then the three broke the gate where the wife and her sister Ràfàravàvy were, and they forced *tòaka* into Andrianòro's wife's mouth, and she died.

The sister then went to the chief people and said, "Bury her in the road by which Andrianòro will come, for that was the charge she left."

She was buried there, and there was a voice crying out for Andrianòro there in his wife's grave.

After some time, Andrianòro said to the people who went with him, "Come, let us return to the land of our ancestors, for I am longing to see my wife, for she appears to me constantly in dreams."

After a long journey, he got back to his house, and his sister Rafàravàvy chanced to be in the house weeping for sorrow for her brother's wife. When she stopped weeping, she told her brother about her father and mother killing his wife.

Andrianòro was in a swoon a long time before coming to his senses. And after he had lamented her a long time, he said, "Where did you bury my wife?"

His sister replied, "In the very road by which you came, we buried her."

Andrianòro then commanded his people to be gathered together at his wife's grave. Then they brought a quantity of red cloths to remove the corpse, and numbers of oxen to be killed as votive offerings, and dug open the grave. When it was uncovered and the cloths in which she was wrapped undone, Andrianòro's wife was alive again, and her face was exceedingly fair and fresh and tender as the young shoots of the banana.

Andrianòro swooned when he saw his wife alive again, but they blew on him, and he recovered from his fear. Then he told all the people to return to their homes. And Andrianòro was very happy, and he killed many oxen, all but those sacrificed for his wife, so that the people might eat.

Then he said to his father and mother and elder sister, "Go, depart you three, for I will not allow you to remain here. The populace also dislikes you because you killed their loved one and tried to destroy me, too. I therefore cast you forth, and if you will not depart I shall tell the people to kill you, for they dislike you and I hate you."

So the three departed and wandered in an unknown country.

After a little while, Andrianòro's wife said to him, "I will go now to father and mother in the sky, for it was you I waited for in the grave, because had I gone when your parents killed me, they could not have killed me by any means. But on account of your love for me and my love for you also, I waited for you, although I endured so much here. So now, let me go to visit father and mother in the sky."

But Andrianòro said, "I humble myself, feet and hands, do not go away."

But his wife said again, "Let me go, my lord, for my father and mother grieve for me, for the day is thundering and that is a sign of their grief."

Then Andrianòro said, "Let me go along with you, if you will not stay."

But his wife said, "Remain here, my lord, for father is obstinate, and when he speaks the thunderbolt darts forth. Not only that, the sky is no dwelling place for you, because you are of humankind here on earth. And there are spacious fields and giant trees, and if you cannot till the fields and fell the trees, father will kill you, for he will in no case suffer you to live. But if, on the other hand, you are able to accomplish it, he will give me to you afresh for your wife. And that is not all: there are also a thousand spades buried in a great lake, and if you are not able to obtain them you will be killed. Also, there are a thousand cows, and the mothers and the calves are exactly alike, but if you cannot distinguish which are the mothers you will be killed. Besides that, we three daughters and our mother are alike in appearance, but if you cannot tell which is our mother, then father will kill you. But if, on the contrary, Andrianòro, you can distinguish all these things, then father will give me to you for a wife, and you shall live and not die. So I beseech you, Andrianòro, do not go, but remain here. Anyway, your sister will be desolate if you leave her, my lord."

Then Andrianòro said, "I will nevertheless go with you."

So he went and bade farewell to his sister, who wept profusely.

Then, just before going away, Andrianòro went into the fields and called to all the beasts and the birds in the fields, "Oh, animals with black armpits! Oh, animals with black armpits! Help me, for I am in great distress!"

All the birds and beasts came to him, and Andrianòro killed oxen to feed the beasts and the birds. And he recounted to them what had befallen him, the things he was to do in the skies, the tests by which he was to know them. The beasts and birds gave him encouragement, telling him that they would accomplish the things that troubled him.

So Andrianòro and his wife went up to the sky. And when they arrived at the gate of heaven, Andrianòro wept for sorrow about his sister and called out, "Oh, this earth below us! this spacious earth! the earth where my dear Rafàravàvy lives!"

Then his sister also wept and replied to her brother's voice, "Oh, Andrianòro, do not forget me, your relative!"

Just as the gate of heaven was about to be opened, he was bidden again by his wife to return, for his difficulties were at hand.

"Besides, I grieve for you," she said, "so please return."

Then her father in the sky heard her words, and it thundered fearfully. And when Andrianòro would still not return to earth, his wife gave him this advice: "When you come in to father and mother, do not be persuaded to advance first, but remain there at the place where the firewood is stored, for they will kill you."

"Very well," he said.

And when he came in, his father-in-law said, "Come forward, my child."

Then the thunderbolt flashed out.

But Andrianòro was breathed upon for some time by his wife, and so he still lived.

"Go to that golden chair over there," said his father-in-law.

So he went to that part of the house.

"Give him rice in my plate," said his father-in-law.

But Andrianòro refused and ate from the plate of the servants.

The father-in-law was astonished and said, "Are you the husband of my daughter?"

"Yes," said Andrianòro.

Then he said, "If you, my lad, are indeed her husband, then go and do this work for me: cut down the trees over there that hide the sun, and fetch those thousand spades buried in the lake that is full of crocodiles, and also find which are the mothers that bore those thousand oxen, for the mothers and the offspring are alike. And also find out which is the mother among my wife and daughters. If you cannot accomplish all these things, you shall surely die, so do not hope to live. If, however, you can perform these tasks, and if you can cut down the trees, then you shall have my daughter to wife, and shall also have the wherewithal to live."

"Yes, my lord," replied Andrianòro.

Then he went off to call the beasts and the birds who had made a compact with him to help him: "Help me, oh beasts and birds!"

Then he went to work, and the beasts ploughed up the earth with their tusks, so that it was dug all over, and the trees were plucked up by the birds and uprooted by the beasts, so they were all felled. And the thousand spades were brought by the crocodiles until they were all fetched.

Then the great cattle-fly said, "Those that I bite on the nose are the mothers among those thousand cattle." And the little fly also said, "The woman on whose nose I settle is the mother, so pay close attention."

So Andrianòro asked his father-in-law to come out to look at the work that he had performed and also pointed out the mothers among the cattle and the mother among the four women.

The father-in-law was astonished, and he gave Andrianòro his daughter for his wife. And he gave a quantity of oxen and a number of slaves and much money to him and his wife.

So the pair returned to the husband's fatherland, and they all came in peace and safety to their house, but Andrianòro's sister Rafàravàvy had died of sorrow.

And these were the concluding words of the storytellers: It is not I who tell fictions,[94] but the people in former times related them. The heat of the sun tomorrow breaks the bald head; I break the bones, but you are those who suck them out.

26

The Hare, the Hyena,
and the Lioness's Cave[95]

Masai (Kenya)[96]

The hare once met the hyena and proposed that they go for a walk. They went for a walk together and then separated, after which the hare went to the lioness's cave and found it closed.

She cried out, "Stone, open!" and the stone rolled away from the mouth of the cave. She entered and said, "Stone, close!" and the stone returned to its place.

She then proceeded to the room where the lioness stored her fat; then she went to the room where the meat was kept.

Having had enough, she returned to the entrance, told the stone to open and, when she had passed out, to close once more.

Feeling hungry again later, she returned to the cave. On the road, she met the hyena, who asked her where she had come from and why her mouth was oily.

The hare denied that her mouth was oily, but as the hyena persisted in his statement, she told him to rub ashes on his mouth and it would become as beautiful as hers.

The hyena did as he was instructed, but no change took place in his appearance.

The hare next suggested washing it with water, and afterward with urine. But although the hyena tried both, his mouth remained as dry as before.

The hyena then said, "Please tell me where you go and feed."

At first, the hare refused to comply with his request, and said, "You are so foolish whenever you go anywhere and are sure to be caught."

But as the hyena would take no refusal, she consented to allow him to accompany her and told him about the lioness's cave. "There are," she said, "five rooms. In the first the ashes are kept. In the next, the bones. In the third, the tough meat. In the fourth, the tender meat. And in the last, the fat."

The hyena cried, "Get out of the way, take me there!"

And off they went.

When they arrived at the cave, the hare told the hyena that when he wanted the cave to open he must say, "Stone, open," and when he wanted it to shut, "Stone, close."

The hyena cried out, "Stone, open!" and the stone rolled aside. When they were inside, the hare said, "Stone, close," and it closed again.

The hyena at once started on the ashes, while the hare went to the room where the fat was kept. When the hare had had enough to eat, she returned to the entrance to the cave and said she was going away.

The hyena remonstrated with her, as he was not nearly satisfied.

After telling him how to get out of the cave, the hare went to the stone and said, "Stone, open," and again, when she was outside, "Stone, close."

When the hyena was alone, he went to the place where the bones were kept, after which he proceeded to the next room, where the tough meat was stored, and ate until he was satisfied. He then went to the entrance and said to the stone, "Stone, close," instead of "Stone, open." He repeated the words, "Stone, close," several times and could not understand why nothing happened.

At this juncture, the lioness, the owner of the cave, returned and said, "Stone, open!"

When the hyena heard her, he cried, "Ah! woe is me! That is what I wanted to say! Poor fellow that I am! Stone, open! Stone, open!"

The lioness entered and said, "Shall I eat you? Or shall I make you my servant?"

The hyena asked to be made her servant and was told to look after the lioness's cub. He was also given a bone and instructed to break it when the lioness had crossed four rivers.

The hyena counted the lioness's footsteps and, when he calculated that she had crossed the four rivers, broke the bone. A chip flew at the cub's head, fracturing its skull. Fearing that the lioness would kill him on her return, he searched for some hornets and stuffed one up each of the cub's nostrils so that it might be supposed that it had been stung to death.

The lioness returned to her cave a short while afterward and called to the hyena to bring her cub. The hyena prevaricated for some time, inventing several excuses for not doing as he was told. But the lioness was firm, and the hyena had to pick up the cub and bring it to its mother. The lioness at once saw that it was dead and told the hyena to take it outside.

While he was doing this, he ate one of the cub's legs.

A little later, he was again ordered to bring the cub to its mother and then to take it away once more.

He devoured another leg while carrying it away.

And when the lioness called out to him a third time to bring the cub to her, he said the birds had eaten two of its legs.

He then ate up the cub.

The lioness intended to punish the hyena for his misdeeds and, after tying him to a tree, went to get some sticks with which to beat him. As he was standing there, bound to the tree, some other hyenas bent on a raiding expedition passed close by, and one of them, seeing him, asked him why he had been tied up in this manner.

He replied that he was being punished for having refused to eat some oil that had some flies in it.

The other hyena suggested that they should exchange places, and, after untying the knots, he allowed himself to be bound to the tree instead, while the first hyena followed in the wake of the raiding party.

After a time, the lioness returned and commenced to flog the hyena, who cried out, "Stop, I will drink it now!"

"Drink what?" asked the lioness, and she started to flog him again.

"Oh! oh!" the hyena cried. "I will drink the oil with the flies in it."

The lioness then saw that this was not the hyena that had killed her cub.

The next morning, the hyenas, on their way back from their raid, passed the cave. The hyena that had killed the cub saw on the ground some strips of bark that the lioness had spread out in the sun to resemble meat.

"I will go to my master's kraal," he said, "for I see that there has been a kill."

When he reached the spot, however, he was seized by the lioness, who bound him to the tree once more and then beat him to death.

Then the lioness returned to her cave and said, "Stone, open." When the stone had rolled aside and she had entered, she said, "Stone, close," and it closed again.

A Zulu storyteller, 1975

27

Na Kimanaueze[97]

Mbundu (Angola)[98]

BY JELEMÍA DIA SABATELU, OF MALANGE

We often tell of na Nzuá of Kimanaueze kia Tumb' a Ndala, favorite of friends. Na Kimanaueze built, dwelt. His head wife conceived. She ate no meat, she ate no food, she wanted fish of the water. Na Kimanaueze would send his messenger, saying, "Go and catch fish in the Lukala, for my head wife who eats no meat."

The messenger took the net, and went to the Lukala.[99] He caught fish and brought them to the head wife. The head wife cooked the fish and ate.

They slept.

In the morning, she said, "What shall I eat? Messenger, take up the net, go and fish."

The messenger set out, arrived at the Lukala, and he caught fish. He returned with them and gave them to the head wife. She ate them all in one day.

The messenger said, "All the fish that I catch, you eat them in one day!"

He went fishing again and brought her fish again.

And so every day she ate no other food.

Every month, the same.

One day, the chief said, "Messenger, go fishing!"

He took up the net and arrived at the Lukala. He cast the net and waited a while. Then he pulled the net, and it was heavy. He pulled it again, another time. It refused to come.

The messenger said, "You who hold the net under the water, whether you are the river-genius or a crocodile, let go of my net! They sent me here; I didn't come of my own accord!"

He pulled the net, and it came up.

When he looked into the net, there was something in it, and he was afraid. He threw the net down and began to run.

The thing that was in the net said, "Don't run! Stand there!"

He stopped, and he pulled the net from the water and threw it on the land. The thing landed on dry land.

Fear again overwhelmed the messenger, and he trembled.

The thing said, "I am the lord of the land. I have come. Go home; fetch Kimanaueze kia Tumb' a Ndala and his head wife, who always send you to catch fish."

The messenger started off in haste; he arrived at home. He had left his loincloth by the water.

When he arrived at home, a crowd said, "Messenger, why are you walking about naked? Are you crazy?"

The messenger said, "Let me alone, please. Let me explain myself to the king!"

He arrived at the court. He sat on the ground, threw himself flat on his back, then bowed forward and touched the ground with his chin.

Na Kimanaueze said, "Explain yourself."

The messenger said, "Lord, when I left you, I arrived at the Lukala. I threw the net into the water, then waited a while. When I pulled the net, it was heavy. I said, 'You who are holding the net, whether you are the river-genius or a crocodile, let go of my net. I was sent here, I did not come of my own accord.' I pulled the net, and the river itself came ashore, Lukala himself. I began to run. He said, 'Do not run. Stand, please. Go and fetch your king and his queen, those who are wont to send you to catch fish. Let them come here, so that I may speak everything that is in my heart.' I, the messenger, that is what brought me here in haste. Lord, I have said it."

Na Kimanaueze said, "Very well. Queen, you shall dress. Let us go where we are sent for."

The queen dressed herself well. Na Kimanaueze, too, decked himself out well.

They set off with their prime minister and the messenger himself. They arrived at Lukala's and found him there, sitting on a chair.

Fear seized them.

Lukala said, "Don't be afraid. Approach, so that I may say what I want to say."

They sat on the ground.

Lukala said, "You, na Kimanaueze kia Tumb' a Ndala, favorite of friends, when you came to build in the land, you came to see me, the river. You settled in my land. Now, your wife is pregnant; she eats no food other than fish. Every day, she eats fish. At this rate, she will consume my people. Why? You, his prime minister, who came with him, the pregnancy that conceived the queen of Kimanaueze is finishing my people. Soon, when she gives birth to the child, if it is a girl she is to be my wife. Bring her to me. If it is a boy, he is to be my friend, my namesake. I, Lukala, have finished. I go."

Na Kimanaueze kia Tumb' a Ndala said, "Lord, very well. What should we do now?"

When he finished assenting, they looked to see where the river-genius had gone. But where he had gone, they did not know.

They got up and arrived at home. They lived on for some days. The messenger continued to catch fish.

Then the day came for the queen to give birth. She was restless. She gave birth to the child, and they went to announce it to the king: "The queen has given birth to a male child."

He said, "Very well."

He took a goat and gave it to the people who had assisted the queen.

They lived on for some days, bringing up the child.

The child grew up, and he came to marriageable age.

Lukala brought dreams in their sleep: "Bring me my friend. I will stay here with him. If you do not bring him, I shall kill him, he shall die."

They would awaken from their dreams after Lukala had spoken.

Na Kimanaueze said, "Head wife, what shall we do? My son, na Nzuá, the river says that it wants you."

When na Nzuá heard this, he was afraid. He said, "What shall I do? I, Nzuá dia Kimanaueze kia Tumb' a Ndala, where shall I flee?" He called a servant: "Put water in the trough for me."

The woman put water in the trough. Na Nzuá lay down in the trough; he stayed there for a while. He was thinking where to go. He got up from the trough and said, "What shall I do, father?"

His father said, "I don't know what I shall do. Come, I'll give you the things that belong to you. Enough. Go anywhere."

Na Kimanaueze took two slave-men and gave them to Na Nzuá, saying, "Take two male slaves." He took two riding-bulls; he took two mothers of goats and two mothers of swine. He said, "Your food to eat on the road, wherever you go. Soon, we shall see each other no more. Wherever you go, do not cross a river. All rivers, follow them up, go around by their springs."

The son assented.

He set out with the things that they gave him. He mounted a riding-bull; the slaves followed behind. They passed through the grass in the midst of the bushes.

First day, second day, third day, fourth day, they always went around the rivers.

On the beginning of the fifth day, they arrived in the middle of the bushes, na Nzuá riding his bull. When he appeared in the open circle of a tree,[100] when he looked about, he saw game, all the game that God made. There was no ferocious beast that was not there. Also, all insects that God made had gathered there, and they were thick. Also present were the beasts of the water and all the birds that God made.

What brought them together in one place was that they had killed a deer. Nobody was able so to divide the deer that all the beasts got a share.

When they saw na Nzuá, they said, "We are fortunate."

When na Nzuá arrived, he was afraid.

The beasts said, "Go on! We need someone to divide our deer for us. Now we are lucky!"

Na Nzuá said, "Oh, what shall I do, I, Nzuá dia Kimanaueze kia Tumb' a Ndala, the favorite of friends?"

The beasts said, "Don't be afraid! Get down from your bull."

He got down.

"Unsheathe your knife from your waist."

Our friend unsheathed the knife.

They said, "Divide this meat for us."

He said, "All this crowd, one deer. How can I divide it?"

They said, "Divide it well, so that all can eat."

He began to cut it in bits, and then he distributed the bits. The deer was finished, and not even a part of the crowd of beasts had received a piece.

The beasts said, "We are still looking. Divide it well, so that we receive equal portions."

He said, "The deer is finished. What shall I do?"

He had his male dog. He took it, killed it, and divided it.

Still not complete. Not even a part of the group has been given food.

He killed his bull, divided it. Not complete.

He killed his slave, divided, not complete.

He killed the second slave, divided, not complete.

The beasts said, "Na Nzuá, divide it so that all have equal portions. Let not one beast remain."

He took his other bull; he killed it.

The ants: he gave them only the hairs. The large beasts: he gave them only a little bone, tiny, small.

Still, some remained.

The beasts said, "Divide for us equally."

He said, "How shall I do that?"

His slaves and his bulls had been distributed. He remained with nothing more.

Himself alone, that is all.

The beasts said, "Sir, you have divided, we are satisfied. You alone remain."

The lion said, "Come here. Approach me, don't be afraid."

Na Nzuá approached the lion.

The lion said, "Open your mouth!"

Na Nzuá opened his mouth.

The lion spat into his mouth, saying, "Na Nzuá, on the day of your pressing distress, you shall say, 'Teleji! Small heap of debts.'"

The wolf said, "Come here!"

Nzuá arrived; he knelt on the ground.

The wolf said, "Open your mouth!"

He spat into his mouth, saying, "On the day of your pressing need, say, 'Teleji! Wolf of assegai, in the bush of the spirits.'"

Nzuá stood up.

The wild cat said, "Come here!"

He came and knelt down.

He said, "Open your mouth!"

He opened his mouth.

The wild cat said, "On the day that hardship presses you, say, 'Teleji! Wildcat of leopard.'"

The ant said, "Come here!"

Nzuá approached it; he sat on the ground.

The ant said, "Open your mouth! On the day that you are in need, say, 'Teleji! Little ant.'"

And the leopard said, "Come here!"

He came.

The leopard said, "Open your mouth."

He opened his mouth.

"On the day that misfortune grasps you, say, 'Teleji! Leopard.'"

The fox said, "Come here!"

He approached.

The fox said, "Open your mouth."

He opened his mouth.

"On the day that distress holds you, say, 'Teleji! Fox of jackal.'"

The hawk said, "Approach here!"

He approached; he opened his mouth.

The hawk spat into his mouth, saying, "On the day that you see hardship, say, 'Teleji! Hawk, the bird who caught a child, the friend began to play.'"

When the hawk finished speaking, the eagle said, "Come here!"

Nzuá came.

The eagle said, "On the day that distress grasps you, say, 'Teleji! Eagle, bird without a tail, the neighbor to the sky.'"

All the beasts did the same; all the insects did the same.

Then they said, "Go."

He took his staff; he went into the middle of the bushes, alone. He walked and walked; his feet hurt him.

He said, "What shall I do?"

He said, "Teleji! The bird who caught a child, the friend began to play."

He became a hawk.

He was in the sky, he was moving in the sky.

Hunger seized him. He arrived at a camp and said, "Teleji! Man, who is the last."

He became a man; he went to the camp.

He said, "What shall I eat?" He said, "Teleji! Wildcat of leopard."

He became a wild cat. He went to one side of a village that was a short distance away. He lurked for the fowls. When the fowls came to eat in the grass, he caught two cocks.

The people, when they heard the fowls shrieking, arose in haste. They arrived at the place and said, "It is a wildcat! Chase it!"

They chased it, and then they gave up.

He arrived there and said, "Teleji! Man, who was the last."

He became a man.

He tied the two cocks together and hung them on his staff.

He arrived at a camp. He found travelers there, and he sat on the ground.

The travelers said, "You, sir, where have you come from?"

He said, "I am going on to my brother. I was bringing him two cocks; they died on the road. Hunger grasped me, but I do not see anyone who might cook them for me."

The travelers said, "Give them to us. We will cook them for you."

They took the cocks and plucked them. Then they cooked them and gave them to na Nzuá. He ate, then slept.

Day shone, and he started again and walked. The noon heat set in. Hunger grasped him, and he said, "What shall I do?" He said, "Teleji! Wolf of assegai, in the land of the spirits."

He became a wolf.

He went into the grass, squatted down, and kept quiet.

Night came, and he went into the village, moving to the center of the village. Here, he found a sty of pigs, and he took out two sucklings. The pigs cried out.

The people were startled and said, "A wolf is catching the pigs! Chase him!"

They chased him and then gave up.

He went into the grass and slept.

Morning came. He said, "Teleji! Man, who was the last."

He became a man.

He bound the sucklings in the basket, which he had made in the grass, and he started out. He arrived at a camp and found travelers there.

They said, "You, sir, where have you come from?"

He answered, "I am going to my brother. I was bringing him two suckling pigs, but they died on the road from the heat. I do not see anyone who might cook them for me."

The travelers said, "Take them from him, and scrape them."

They took the pigs and scraped them. Then they cooked the meat of one of the pigs for him. He ate, then slept.

In the morning, he said, "Today, I cannot walk, my feet are hurting me. I will rest."

The travelers said, "We will rest, too. Tomorrow, we shall travel."

And so they passed the time. They took the meat of the pig outside and spread it on the roof of a camp house. A few village women came to sell food to the travelers.

When the women saw the pig's meat on the roof, they said, "Travelers, sell us a little pig's meat."

The travelers said, "It is not our meat. It belongs to another, to that man who is asleep there."

The women, saying nothing, departed. They went home and found the men. They told them, "We went to the camp and found pig's meat there. We thought, 'Our pigs, the wolves caught them during the night.' Maybe that man has stolen our hogs."

The men said, "Let's go. Show him to us."

The men took their guns and staves and spears and lances, saying, "We will beat him!"

They arrived in the camp, saying, "Where is the man who stole our pigs?"

The women said, "He is here!"

He said, "I, steal your pigs?"

They said, "This meat, where did you find it?"

And so they began to quarrel and to fight with him. Nzuá conquered them. They went home, called others, and an army was created.

They arrived again in the camp and said, "Come out!" The crowd said, "You have had a victory. Now, come out!"

Nzuá came out, and they began to fight. His arms became tired, and he said, "Teleji! Small heap of having debts."

And he became a young lion.

He roared, and the crowd of warriors scattered with haste. Some threw their guns into the grass, some fell on the path because they feared the lion.

The lion began to roar, and the travelers, too, scattered.

Nzuá remained alone.

He said, "Teleji! Man, who was the last."

And he became a man.

He said, "What shall I do? I will go, now!"

He entered the path, and arrived in the middle of the forest.

He thought, "My destination, Loanda:[101] I have not yet gone there. I have no kinsman there, no friend. What shall I do? At whose house shall I stop?"

He stood there, thinking. He said, "I am perplexed, I, Nzuá dia Kimanaueze kia Tumb' a Ndala. I have not seen the place to which I am going." He said, "Teleji! Hawk, the bird who caught a child, the friend began to play."

He became a hawk again. He was in the sky; he arrived in the city of Loanda. He circled the entire town in the sky.

He said, "Teleji! A little bird in the world."

He became a little bird.

The wings of this little bird were like gold, and so was its bill. In all the country, there was not a bird like this.

It flew over the house of the lord governor; it was circling in the sky.

Na Maria, the daughter of the lord governor, was in the veranda of the house, sewing clothes. She looked on the ground and saw the shadow of a little bird. It pleased her, and she turned her eyes upward and saw the little bird.

She said, "Oh, this dear little bird, how shall I catch it? The little bird is perfectly beautiful!" She took her white handkerchief and spread it on the ground. She knelt on one knee and recited the mass to it.

The little bird descended and lit on the handkerchief.

She caught it and said, "This little bird, where shall I keep it so that it doesn't die?"

She ordered a cage made of gold, and it arrived. She put the bird into the cage and kept the cage in her room. She put rice into the cage, and water.

Then she sent word to her father, the lord governor, who was upstairs: "I have a little bird here. You, my father, have never seen such a bird. Neither in Europe is there a bird like this, nor in Africa. I do not know where it came from."

Her father sent her word, saying, "Come with your little bird, so that I may see it."

She went upstairs with the little bird.

Her father looked at it, then said, "It's true, this little bird is not to be seen in the land."

Na Maria, the daughter of the lord governor, arose and went downstairs. The little bird refused to eat.

She put different foods, from Europe, into the cage, but the little bird would not eat.

She said, "How shall I treat this little bird? It will die."

Na Maria, the daughter of the lord governor, had her own habit of eating at noon and at the first cock-crow.[102] They would spread the table in her room. They placed the food on the table, and the girls would wait on her.

On this day, they put the food on the table. The little bird was in the same room.

In the middle of the night, the little bird said, "Teleji! Little ant!"

The bird became an ant. It crawled down; it picked up the crumbs of food that had fallen to the ground. It ate, and then it returned to its cage, saying, "Teleji! Little bird!"

He again became the bird.

Every day, it was the same.

On another day, he said, "Teleji! Little ant!"

He became an ant and got down on the ground.

He said, "Teleji! Man, who is the last."

And he became a man, elegantly dressed.

He sat at the table, eating the food.

Then he arose, saying, "Teleji! An ant."

He became an ant.

Having climbed into his cage, he said, "Teleji! Little bird."

He became a little bird, and he slept.

At the first cock-crow, na Maria got up and came to the table. There was no food.

She said, "Girls, where has the food gone?"

The girls said, "Mistress, we don't know!"

She beat them, saying, "You ate it!"

Day came; then another night came.

The girls said, "Today, we'll stay awake, so that we may catch the thief who yesterday caused us to be beaten."

In the middle of the night, the little bird said, "Teleji! Little ant."

It was transformed; the ant went down to the ground.

It said, "Teleji! Man!"

It became a handsome man.

He sat at the table, eating.

The girls saw him. Fear kept them from addressing him.

He finished eating and got up.

He said, "Teleji! Little ant."

The ant climbed into the cage and became the little bird.

It kept quiet.

The cock crowed, and na Maria got up. She came to the table, and the food was not there.

She said, "Girls, where has the food gone?"

She began to beat them.

The girls said, "Mistress, do not beat us unjustly. Wait, we'll tell you what happened. During the night, we saw a gentleman sitting at the table. He was eating. We could not question him, because we were afraid. Do not doubt this. Tomorrow, we'll awaken you, so that you too may see."

Na Maria assented.

They slept.

The day shone. They passed the day.

Night came down. They spread the table.

In the middle of the night, the little bird said, "Teleji! Little ant."

It became an ant. It got down to the ground.

It said, "Teleji! Man!"

He became a man, dressed elegantly, from head to foot.

He sat at the table, eating.

The girls saw him. They arose and went to tell na Maria: "Mistress, come, see the gentleman who is at the table!"

Na Maria arose. She went to the table and took him by the arm.

Na Nzuá dia Kimanaueze kia Tumb' a Ndala, favorite of friends, and na Maria: they saw each other, and they embraced.

They sat at the table and could only look at one another like this. Day dawned.

Na Nzuá wrote a letter to the lord governor.

The letter went to the lord governor, who opened it. The letter said, "I, na Nzuá dia Kimanaueze kia Tumb' a Ndala, favorite of friends, want to marry na Maria, daughter of the lord governor."

The lord governor returned a letter, saying, "Very well. I do not yet know his face. Tomorrow, let him come with my daughter herself. I must know the man."

The letter arrived at na Nzuá's. He opened it and read it.

He said, "Very well. I will sleep, and tomorrow we shall go."

They slept. The morning dawned.

Na Nzuá said, "Na Maria, dress, that we may go to your father."

They dressed, both of them, and they arrived upstairs. They were given chairs, and they sat down. The lord governor looked at na Nzuá; he looked at his daughter na Maria.

He asked her, "Na Maria, will you marry this man?"

Na Maria consented.

He asked the man, saying, "You, na Nzuá, do you want to marry my daughter? If you marry her, you shall do me service. If you do what I want you to do, it will please me."

He said, "You shall bring my daughter from Portugal. They carried her off to Portugal, and nobody can find her there. If you come with her, your payment shall be the governorship."

Na Nzuá agreed to do it.

The lord governor said, "After arriving in Portugal, if you see a young woman who is throwing ashes on a refuse heap, she is my daughter."

Na Nzuá set out. He said goodbye to his wife, "Stay well."

Na Maria said, "Go there."

When he started, na Nzuá said, "Teleji! Hawk."

He became a hawk; there he is in the sky.

He said, "Teleji! Eagle, bird without a tail, that is neighbor to the sky."

He became an eagle.

He arrived in Portugal, and he saw a young woman who was coming out of a house. She was going to a refuse heap to throw out ashes.

The young woman said, "What misery I have to see!"

Na Nzuá, who was in the sky, heard her. Now he knew, and he said, "It is she, the one they sent me for."

He said, "Teleji! Hawk."

He became a hawk.

He lowered his height, then lifted up the young woman.

People said, "Look! A bird is carrying off a person!"

He said, "Teleji! Eagle, the bird without a tail."

He became an eagle. He went with the young woman a great distance in the sky.

He arrived in Loanda.

He said, "Teleji! Man who is the last."

He became a man.

He entered the house of the lord governor and found his wife, na Maria. He said, "Is this your sister, for whom they sent me?"

Na Maria assented, saying, "It is she."

They slept.

When it dawned, he said, "I will go to the lord governor to hand him his daughter."

Na Nzuá and the young woman went, and they arrived upstairs. They found the lord governor there.

Na Nzuá said, "Your daughter is here; you sent me for her."

The lord governor said, "Well done. You have earned the dominion. Come to the governorship; take the glory that befits you."

And they lived together, na Nzuá dia Kimanaueze kia Tumb' a Ndala and na Maria, the daughter of the governor.

Thus far we heard it. If we want, we will tell more; if we will not, let us go to sleep!

Finished.

28

The Hyenas and the Sage[103]

Nandi (Kenya)[104]

The hyenas once all met together, and they decided to appoint a sage who would be able to advise them in all matters concerning the welfare of their country and who would divine future events and interpret omens and dreams. There was some discussion as to who should be invited to take up these important duties, and the choice eventually fell on the ground-hornbill.[105] A deputation was sent to him, and when he was informed what was required of him, he accepted. He thought it would be well to prophesy something at once, so he told the hyenas that there would be no more day and that if they required light other than that afforded by the moon, they would obtain it from his red gills.

The hyenas rejoiced at this good news and immediately set off to raid their enemy, man, who possessed a number of donkeys not far off.

They attacked the kraal in the middle of the night and killed several donkeys, which they proceeded to eat. Before they had satisfied their hunger, however, they were horrified to find that the sun was rising, just as it used to do before their sage told them there would be no more day. They at once saw that there was nothing left for them to do but to abandon their feast and make off as fast as they could.

But there was one old hyena with them who had difficulty walking, so they buried him under a mound of donkeys' dung and then fled to the woods.

They had scarcely left before the owner of the donkeys appeared on the scene, and when he saw what had happened, he called together his friends and decided to avenge himself on the raiders.

Just as he was leaving, he put his spear into the mound of donkeys' dung and stabbed the old hyena. He knew by this that it was the hyenas that had killed his donkeys during the night, so he followed their tracks to their lair in the woods, where he killed a large number of them.

Those that escaped met together that same evening and decided to depose their chief sage and to elect someone else in his place. The choice this time fell on the francolin, who was duly elected and who has ruled so wisely ever since that he has remained in power to the present day. If you listen in the fields in the evening, you will hear him calling to the hyenas to come out and feed, and again in the morning, long before the other birds are up, he is there warning them that it is time to go home.

The ground-hornbill, however, has never been forgiven, and whenever a hyena sees him he gives chase and drives him away.

A Swati storyteller, 1975

29

Kachirambe[106]

Nyanja (Malawi)[107]

Some young girls once said, "Come, let us go and pluck leaves for a relish with our porridge."

And when they were gathering them, one of the children saw the egg of a hyena and picked it up and put it in her basket. She said to her companions, "I have got all I want. I am going."

Her companions said, "When did you pluck the leaves, that you are off so soon?"

She said, "I filled my basket some time ago."

So her companions told her to go.

When she was gone, they saw a hyena. He came up to them and asked, "Who has taken my egg from here?"

They denied having done so, saying, "We do not know, but the one who has gone off, perhaps she took it."

And the hyena departed.

He came to where she lived and said, "Who has taken my egg?"

The mother of the girl replied, "But the child came in with an egg, and it's on the fire."

The hyena said, "Well, what am I to do?"

The woman replied, "Wait. When I have a child, you shall eat him."

The hyena said, "Yes."

Another day, when the mother went to the water, the hyena asked her if she had had the child, and the woman replied, "No, not yet."

Every day, the hyena asked the same thing, and then one day he said, "If you do not quickly have that child, you are the one I shall eat."

Then the woman saw a boil on her shin bone; it was all swollen and soft. It burst, and a child emerged. He had a bow and a quiver full of arrows, and a little gourd of medicine, and a knife and dogs.

And he said, "I have emerged, I, Kachirambe, the child born on a shin bone."

The mother of this Kachirambe was again asked by the hyena, when she went to the stream, if she had had the child.

And she replied, "Yes, and the child is very clever. You cannot catch him, but I myself shall deceive him for you. Let me tie you up in a bundle of grass; then I shall go and tell Kachirambe, 'Go and lift the bundle of grass that is there on the path.'"

Then Kachirambe went and, standing a long way off, said, "You bundle, get up so that I may more easily lift you."

And the bundle got up by itself.

Kachirambe said, "What bundle is it that gets up by itself? I have not seen such a one, and I do not intend to lift it."

And off he went to the village.

The hyena then came alone and told the woman that her child was a clever one indeed.

She told him that today she would deceive him over a falling stone trap for killing rats.

Then she said to Kachirambe, "Go, set a falling trap; the rats are finishing the baskets."

Kachirambe got a large flat stone and a forked stick, and the stick to lay across it, and bark string, and he got the little bit of stick that sets the trap and tied it on. Then he took the bait and put it in the trap.

In the evening, the hyena came to the trap and caused it to fall.

Kachirambe's mother called out, "Kachirambe, the trap has fallen."

Kachirambe said, "You trap, fall again, so that I'll know that a rat has been caught."

And the hyena was at the trap—heave, bang!

Kachirambe said, "What trap is it that falls twice? I have not yet seen one of that kind."

Then Kachirambe's mother told the hyena, "Go and wait at the bean tree, and I'll go and tell my child to go and pull beans."

So Kachirambe went and got his basket, then transformed himself into a fly.

The hyena kept looking out for him, saying, "I wonder if he will come."

He did not see a sign, and then Kachirambe had got all he wanted and returned to the village.

His mother was again astonished, saying, "Where did he get the beans when there is only one tree of them?" Then she said, "Today, I shall deceive him, telling him to go and bring firewood, and you, hyena, will corner him there."

She said to Kachirambe, "Go and get wood in the forest."

But that child had a dream that today he would go to his death. He took his bow and quiver and little medicine gourd, and his great big knife, and went off. He climbed into a tree and began to cut.

Then he saw that the hyena had come.

The hyena said, "You shall die today; you shall not escape. I shall eat you. Come down quickly from up there."

Kachirambe cut off a piece of wood and said, "While I am come down, you gape."

The hyena said, "Come down," and he gaped.

Kachirambe said, "Yes, I am coming."

He threw the lump of wood and it entered the mouth of the hyena, and it died. And Kachirambe's dogs, when they bit the hyena, also died.

Kachirambe came down and took his medicine; he scattered it over his dogs, and they got up.

When he went to the village, he shot an arrow and said, "What did I say to you that you send wild beasts against me to eat me?"

His mother begged pardon of him, saying, "Pardon, my child, my apologies suffice without the case being brought up for trial."[108]

30

The Girls Who Went to Have Teeth Made for Them[109]

Nyarwanda (Rwanda)[110]

I shall tell you a story, I shall stir you with a story.

Some young girls said to one another, "Come, let's go and have teeth made for us."

But one of the girls no longer had a mother. The wife of her father always hindered her, and she was therefore unable to go with them

The next day, for the last time, they went to the home of Imana[111] in order that he should make beautiful teeth for them.

So they went, and when they returned, they strutted in front of her, and she said nothing; she continued her work.

The cows returned, and they lit the fire, and she helped with the milking.

After she had helped with the milking, she served the food, she finished serving the food, she bathed, took the oil and anointed herself, and then departed.

In the night, she encountered a hyena.

It said to her, "You, girl! Where are you going?"

She said, "I intend to go where all the other girls went. The wife of my father prevented me from going with the others."

The hyena said, "Go in peace, child of Imana."

She went on and encountered a lion, which said to her, "You, young girl! Where are you going?"

She said, "I am going where all the young girls have gone, because the wife of my father prevented me from going with the others."

The lion said, "Go then, child of Imana."

She walked through the night, and then she encountered Imana, who asked her, "Oh young girl, where are you going?"

She said, "I have been living with the mother of my father, and she makes me do numerous jobs. This is why the others went to have teeth made and I was not able to come along. Now I have come thinking that you would make them for me."

Then he made for her teeth that surpassed in beauty those of the others.

He also created for her another body; he gave her a beautiful skin.

Then Imana asked her, "Show me the direction of your home," and he took her back to her home.

She said, "It's over there."

Imana then said, "When you arrive at your home, when you meet the others, you must not smile. Do not smile to your stepmother, do not smile to your father! Don't smile to anyone!"

Her stepmother saw her coming, and she cried out, "She has been stealing things at the capital city! These cows of her father, she has stolen them because she is dressed nicely and is so beautiful."

Her father asked her, "Where did you take these things from?"

She answered neither of them at all.

After two days, they asked to marry her, and she married.

She did not smile to her husband, and she did not smile to her beautiful sisters or to her stepmother.

And then, she gave birth to a boy.

The child grew up.

When he was herding the calves, his grandmother said to him, "Go! When your mother gives you milk, refuse it, insisting that she smile at you. Say, 'Smile at me, if you don't want me to cry or to die!'"

His mother refused to smile.

Then the child cried and died. He was buried.

Then, after a time, she bore another child, a boy.

This child grew up, and his grandmother pushed him, saying, "Go! When your mother gives you milk, refuse it, saying to her, 'Smile at me, so that I not cry and die.'"

But his mother refused to smile at him.

Then the child cried and died. And he was buried.

Now, she was left with her husband.

Soon, she gave birth to another child, a girl, and she nursed the child.

When the child was fully grown, her mother lifted her up one evening and went out to the prairie where they had thrown her children.

She removed the child from her back and said, "Oh, my father! Oh Imana, lord of Rwanda, seeing that I have never disobeyed you, will you not save this little child?"

Imana came and said to her, "Come here. See your children, smile at them, I have brought them back to life."

Then she smiled at them, and Imana made for her a new body and other teeth and said, "Go, smile at your husband, and all others."

He clothed her in beautiful things; he looked for cows to give to the children.

Then he brought them to their home, and he said to the husband, "Go and borrow four chairs."

He borrowed them, one for the husband, one for the wife, and each of the children sat on his. Imana sat in the center.

Then he said to this man, "Look at your children and your wife; live well together. She will smile at you, and she will also smile at her children. It was I who forbade her to smile, but then some malicious people pushed the children to make her smile, so that they not cry and die! Then they died and I resurrected them, and now here they are with your wife. Live well together."

Then he said, "Your mother, I am going to burn her in her house, because she did a bad thing. I leave you all these; enjoy them because you have done nothing wrong."

He went, and he burned her house.

He returned and said to the husband, "Sire children, multiply."

Then he departed.

That is the story of the woman and her husband.[112]

31

Ňwampfundla[113]

Ronga (Mozambique)[114]

BY SAMUEL MABIKA[115]

The lion is the chief of all the animals. He is the great chief of all the animals that are in the wild. He is chief even over the elephants, though they are bigger than he. There is no beast of them all that does not say, "Hail, king!" when they meet him on the path.

Now, as everybody knows, it is not good for a chief, even a little chief, to be alone. Everyone of them has his counselors and his servants. Is it not so?

Very well, the lion, who was the big chief of all the animals, had many servants. They were all servants of the lion, the chief of all the animals.

Now, Ňwampfundla, the hare, was the servant of the great chief, the lion. He went with him to all the places where he went. He did all things that his master, the lion, told him to do.

Now, one day, the lion said, "Let us go from this place. Let us pass through the lands to another place."

So all the animals who were the servants of the lion took their mats and the things that they wanted for the journey, and they went away from the kraal of the lion.

Now, they went all walking together. There were many of them. The servants of the lion were very many, for he was a great chief. By and by, they came to a very fruitful country, and soon before dark they came to a place where there was a big fruit tree. It had plenty of good fruit on it, so the attendants of the lion said to him, "Oh chief, here is a good place. Here is plenty of good fruit. Let us stop in this place. It is a good place for us to stop. Let us pass the night here. We can sleep here very nicely."

So their master, the lion, looked at the place, and when he saw the fruit tree he said, "Yes, your words are good. We will stop in this place. You must leave that fruit for me. That will be for me to eat, but you, my servants, may eat anything else that is in this place; only leave the fruit of this tree for me."

So they all put down the things that they were carrying and began to make ready to pass the night in that place.

Now, just before it got dark, just when all the animals were getting ready to sleep, the hare went to the counselors and said, "I have been thinking about something."

"Yes," they said, "what is it, oh Ňwampfundla the hare?"

"Well," said the hare, "I am not quiet in my mind about that tree with the fruit, which our master the lion says must only be for him."

"Oh! What about that? Everybody knows the will of our master. What then?"

"Well," said the hare, "I do not want to get into any trouble. Suppose somebody gets up in the night and steals the fruit of the tree? Things like that do happen sometimes, you know. If such a thing should happen, I know that you would say, 'Oh, it is Ňwampfundla the hare who has done this thing.'"

"Why should you think that?" said a counselor.

"Well, there is something in my mind that says it," said the hare. "But I have a good plan. Do you see that old wooden mortar that they use for stamping corn? I will tell you what to do. You had better cover me with that old mortar, and then I shall be safe inside it, and if anything happens in the night everyone will know that it cannot be I, for I shall be shut up in the mortar."

"Very well," said the counselor.

They laughed at the hare, but they took the mortar and turned it upside down and covered the hare with it so that he was quite shut up in the mortar. Then all the animals went to sleep, sleeping there on the plain, in the place where was the fruit tree.

Now, in the night, when all the animals were asleep, the hare lifted up the side of the mortar and looked out. He did it very quietly. He looked out on this side, and the other side, and on every side, but everything was still, for all the animals were asleep.

Then, when he saw that all were asleep, he came out of the mortar very quietly, and he went to a place where they had left a basket, and he took the basket. Then he stood still to listen. He could hear the breathing of the animals as they slept, but none moved; they were all asleep, for they had eaten much of the fruits of the other trees that the lion had given them, and they were all asleep.

So the hare climbed up the tree quietly, going up a little bit, and listening, and then going up another little bit and listening again. But there was no movement among the beasts; they were all fast asleep.

Then the hare came to the branches where the fruit was, and he began to eat the fruit as fast as he could, eating all the fruit, and putting the stones of the fruit into the basket that he had taken with him.

When he had eaten up all the fruit, the basket was full of stones. Then he came down quietly and went among the animals, walking very softly, until he came to the place where the elephant was. The elephant was fast asleep. So the hare hung the stones of the fruit that he had eaten in a bag behind the ears of the elephant.

Then he went back again into the mortar and covered himself up and went to sleep.

Now, early in the morning, all the animals awoke and warmed themselves in the sun. By and by, they heard the hare scratching inside the mortar, crying, "Can't you please open for me? I want to see the sunshine."

They said, "Oh, we have forgotten about you."

Then one of them lifted the mortar, and the hare came out.

The hare came and stood before the lion and said, "Good morning, my lord!" Then he looked up at the fruit tree and cried out, "Oh! I said last night that you must put me inside that mortar. Was it not true? Just look at that tree, the tree of our master the lion. Just look at it! Where is the fruit? It is all gone; someone has eaten it up! If I had not been shut up in the mortar all the night, you would think that I had done it!"

Then all the animals looked up at the tree and saw that all the fruit was eaten up, and they were very much afraid. And the lion was very angry, so angry that all the animals quaked.

The lion told all the animals to come together, and he tried to find out who had taken the fruit, but none of them could say who it was. The lion could not find out who had done it.

Then the hare came and stood just in front of the lion, and said, "Please, my master, may I speak?"

The lion said, "Speak!"

Then the hare said, "I will tell you a plan to find out the one who did this, the one who ate the fruit of our master during the night."

"Oh," said the lion, "what is your plan?"

"I will tell you," said the hare, "but first tell the animals to help me, and to do what I tell them."

Then the lion ordered all the animals to do what the hare might tell them to do, so that the one might be found who had eaten the fruit of the tree.

So they dug a big, long pit. Now, when the pit was finished, the hare said, "Now, let everybody jump over this place here. If we all do so, we shall find out who took the fruit of the tree, who ate the fruit of the tree of our master."

"Very well," said the lion." I myself, your master, will also jump."

So the lion jumped first. Nothing happened.

Then the hare jumped, and nothing happened.

After that, the leopard jumped. Nothing happened.

After him, all the animals jumped, and still nothing happened.

At last, the elephant was the only one left. The elephant jumped, and when he jumped the stones of the fruit of the tree fell down on the ground, falling from behind his ears.

Then the hare jumped up and said, "Look at this fellow! Look at the stones of the fruit that he has eaten! I told you we would find out who ate the fruit of that tree!"

The elephant said, "I do not know how these stones came here. I did not eat the fruit. How could I climb a tree to get the fruit?"

But the animals did not believe him. They all thought that he had eaten the fruit of the tree of their chief the lion.

Then the hare said, "What a shame for a big fellow like you to steal the things of the chief!"

The lion said, "Kill him!"

So they caught the elephant and killed him and gave the hare some of the flesh to carry to the chief's kraal.

While the animals, servants of the great chief the lion, were going away from the place of the tree, where the fruit of the lion had been stolen by the hare and the elephant had been killed because of the hare's trickery, Ňwampfundla the hare was carrying a large piece of the elephant's flesh.

Now, the hare, although he is very clever, is, as indeed you know, only a little animal. So as he was walking on the path carrying the flesh of the elephant, that piece of flesh became too heavy for him. He was very tired, for the flesh was too heavy on his shoulders. And, also, he began to be very sorry in his heart because of the elephant who had been killed because of him, although that elephant had not done any wrong. He was very sorry for the elephant that was dead.

So as he walked behind the other animals, carrying the heavy piece of flesh, he was crying, saying, "They have killed my friend, the elephant, but he did not eat the tree of our master, the lion."

Now the animals who were walking in front heard the hare crying and saying something, but they did not understand what he was saying, for they were far in front of him.

Then the lion stopped and cried out in a loud voice, "Hare, you hare, come near, and walk close to us; I do not want you to walk so far behind."

"Oh, my master," said the hare, "this piece of meat is too heavy for me. It is a very large piece, and I myself am not big. It is too heavy for me to carry. If I must carry it, I cannot walk fast enough to keep near you. It is too heavy for me."

So the lion gave the large piece of flesh to one of the other animals to carry; and gave the hare a little piece that he could carry better.

But soon the hare was walking a long way behind the other animals again, crying and saying, "They have killed my friend, the elephant. I weep for my friend, the elephant. They have killed him, although he had no fault. He did not eat the fruit of the tree of our master, the lion. It was I, the hare, who ate the fruit of that tree. The elephant had no fault."

Then the lion found that the hare was again walking a long way behind. He heard the hare talking, but he could not hear what he said, he was so far behind on the path.

So the lion again called to the hare, saying, "Come near, you hare. Why do you walk so far behind on the path? Come close, and walk near the other animals, my servants."

And the hare said, "Well, my master, I cannot walk as fast as the other animals, for this piece of meat is too heavy for me."

Then the chief gave him his assegais to carry, saying, "Hare, carry these assegais, they are not too heavy. Now, you must walk with the other animals. I cannot have you walking behind us on the path. Go before me."

So the hare walked on the path in front of the lion. As he was walking on the path in front of the lion, he kept on singing the song that he had made about the elephant, saying, "Oh, they killed my friend, the elephant, but he had done no wrong thing. They killed him, but he had not eaten the fruit of the tree of our chief. It was I, Ňwampfundla, the hare, who ate the tree of the chief."

Now the lion heard what the hare was singing, and he began to ask the hare about it.

"What!" said the lion. "Was it you who ate my tree?"

"Yes, chief," said the hare. "I am very sorry because you have killed my poor friend, the elephant, who had no fault at all. It was I myself, the hare, who ate the fruit of your tree."

"Is that so?" cried the lion. "Catch him, people!"

But when they tried to catch him, the hare quickly ran away. He ran away as fast as he could run, and all the animals ran after him, trying to catch him.

Soon the hare saw a hole in the ground, and he ran into it. The animals came to the hole, and they said to the lion, "Chief, the hare is here, in this hole in the ground. We saw him go into it."

"Oh," said the lion, "that's all right. We shall soon catch him now. Get him out of the hole."

So they went into the bush and cut a long stick with a hook at the end of it, and they came back and put the stick into the hole so as to pull out the hare who was in that hole.

They put in the stick, and as soon as they put it in, the hook caught hold of one of the hare's legs.

When he saw that the hook had caught his leg, the hare laughed and said to them, "Oh, you can do what you like. You will never catch me like this; you have only caught hold of a root. Pull as much as you like; you are only pulling at a root." He laughed at them and said, "Pull, pull, all of you. It is only a root."

They took the stick out, then put it in again, trying to get hold of the hare. This time, the hook caught in a root inside the hole. When he saw that the hook was fast round the root, the hare began to cry, weep, and ask for pardon. Now they thought that they had caught him, and the lion came to help them, and they all pulled with all their strength, all the animals, holding one another, until the hook at the end of the stick broke, and all the animals fell down on top of one another on their backs on the ground.

Now, the lion was very angry, and he told the hare all the things he would do to him when he caught him.

After that, they cut another stick, and the same things were done again. They caught the foot of the hare, and he laughed at them.

They thought, "We cannot have got hold of the hare, for he cannot laugh when we catch him."

So they tried again. This time, they caught a piece of root, and the hare cried out and wept, saying, "Oh, please, pardon me! I will come out if you will only stop pulling. My leg will break. Please stop pulling. You are hurting me very much."

Then all the animals came to that piece of stick, and they all pulled as hard as they could, and the hook broke, and they all of them fell backward again on the ground.

The lion became exceedingly angry. His first anger was nothing compared to this. He spoke, and all the animals trembled.

But the hare in the hole only laughed at them, saying, "Do what you like, you cannot catch me. I, the hare, am greater than you all." He did this until they got tired of him.

Then the lion said, "We will leave this miserable hare in the hole. He went into the hole, let him stop in it. Bring plenty of grass, and shut up the hole so that he cannot get out. Let him be made fast in the hole. That will teach him to try to play with me."

So they took some grass and shut up the hole and went away.

When they were gone, the hare tried to pull away the grass that was shutting the hole, but there was so much and the animals had put it in so tightly that he could not. He was shut in the hole.

By and by, the hare began to become very hungry in that hole. He had nothing to eat. He became hungrier and hungrier, until at last he ate one of his own ears. He was hungry and he had nothing to eat.

And later he became hungry again. He had nothing to eat, so this time he ate one of his legs. He was so hungry that he ate one of his legs.

Then he became very thirsty. His mouth and his throat were all hot and dry, and there was no water in that hole. There was nothing for him to drink. So he took one of his eyes, thinking that because the tears had come out of his eyes he would find some water in his eye to drink.

Then, when the hare had eaten his ear and his leg and his eye, there came a big storm of wind. And in this great storm of wind, the grass was blown out of the mouth of the hole in which the hare was.

Some Ṅwampfundla could see outside. He came out and looked around carefully, but there was nobody there. He could not see anybody. Then he went to a beehive that he found in a tree nearby and took some of the wax that was there and made two little horns of that wax and put them on his head, so that it appeared that he had two little horns growing on his head.

Then he went to the place where the king lived.

Now, when the king saw him, he called all the animals, and said to them, "Who is this strange person who comes here?"

They said, "Oh, chief, this seems to be that hare that went inside the hole and mocked you."

The hare said, "What, was that hare like me? I did not know that there was another hare like me. Was that hare lame in one foot? Was he blind in one eye? Was he without one ear? Had he two little horns growing on his head?"

The animals all said, "No, the hare that went into the hole was not like this one."

"No," said the hare, "I thought not. The fact is that I belong to a special society of hares. We are not like the ordinary hares that you see every day. We are a special kind of hare. We are all just like I am, with three legs and one ear and one eye. But know this, all of you, that I am cleverer than any other hare. I know how to run faster with three feet than anyone that you every saw, I can see farther than anyone else with one eye, I can hear better than anyone of you with one ear. I can wait upon chiefs better than anyone else can."

The lion was pleased to see a hare like that. He had never seen a hare of that society of hares before. He was very pleased to see this new kind of hare that could do all these things with fewer legs and ears and eyes than other people.

So the lion said, "Well, hare, you had better be my servant. If you can do all these things, you had better do them for me. You can be my servant."

So the hare became the servant of the lion again.

32

The Young Man Who Was Carried Off by a Lion[116]

San (Namibia)[117]

A young man of the early race was, while hunting, ascending a hill, and he became sleepy. While he sat looking around for game, he became sleepy. And he thought that he would lie down, for he was not a little sleepy. But what could have happened to him today, because he had not previously felt like this?[118]

So he lay down on account of it, and while he slept a lion came. It went to the water pit; because the noonday heat had killed it, it was thirsty. And it saw the man lying asleep.

And it took up the man.

And the man awakened, startled; he saw that it was a lion that had taken him up. He decided that he would not stir, for the lion would bite and kill him if he stirred. He wanted first to see what the lion intended to do, for it appeared to think that he was dead.

The lion carried him to a zwart-storm tree,[119] and it laid him in that tree. And the lion thought that it would continue to be thirsty if it ate the man. It therefore would go first to the water so that it might drink, and it would return afterward to eat, when it had drunk.

For it would continue to be thirsty if it ate. And it trod, pressing the man's head between the stems of the zwart-storm tree, and then it went back.

The man then turned his head a little.[120] And, because of that, the lion looked back. It had thought that it had trodden, firmly fixing the man's head. And the lion concluded that it had apparently not laid the man nicely, for the man fell over. So it again trod, pressing the man's head into the middle of the stems of the swart-storm tree. And it licked the man's eyes' tears.[121]

The man wept, and the lion therefore licked the man's eyes.

The man felt that a stick[122] was sharply piercing the hollow at the back

170

of his head, and he turned his head a little, looking steadfastly at the lion, he turned his head a little.

The lion looked to see why it was that the man seemed to have moved. And it licked the man's eyes' tears.

The lion decided to tread, thoroughly pressing down the man's head, so that it might determine whether it had not properly laid the man's head down, because it seemed that the man had stirred. And the man could see that the lion suspected that he was alive. So he did not stir, even though the stick was piercing him. The lion saw that it had apparently laid the man down properly, because the man did not stir. It went a few steps away, and it looked at the man while the man drew up his eyes: he looked through his eyelashes; he saw what the lion was doing.

And the lion went away, ascending the hill. Then it descended the hill on the other side, while the man gently turned his head because he wanted to see whether the lion had really gone away. And he saw that the lion appeared to have descended the hill on the other side, and he saw that the lion had again raised its head, standing there, peeking from behind the top of the hill,[123] because it appeared that the man might be alive. Therefore, it wanted to look again carefully. It seemed that the man had intended to rise, it thought that the man might have been feigning death. But it saw that the man was still lying down, and it decided to run quickly to the water so that it might drink, and then it could quickly come away from the water and then it could eat. It was hungry, and it was very thirsty: it intended first to go to drink, and then, when it had drunk, it would return and eat.

The man lay there, looking at the lion, at what the lion was doing, and he saw its head[124] turn away and disappear. It seemed now that the lion had indeed gone. And the man thought that he would first lie still so that he might see whether the lion would again come peeking. The lion was cunning; it intended to deceive the man, appearing as if it had actually gone away, while it watched to see if he would arise, for he seemed to have stirred. It did not understand why, after it had laid the man down properly, he had been falling over. That is why it decided to quickly run, then quickly return, so that it might make sure that the man still lay there.

The man saw that a long time had passed since the lion had again come back to peek at him, and it now appeared that it had gone completely. But the man decided to wait a little longer. Otherwise, he would startle the lion if the lion were still around. And he saw that a little time had passed, and he had not seen the lion. So it appeared to have really gone away.

And he behaved appropriately at the place where he lay. He did not immediately arise and flee. He got up and then sprang to a different place, hoping that the lion would not know where he had gone. When he fled, he ran in a zigzag direction,[125] desiring that the lion not be able to smell his footsteps, hoping that the lion would not know the place to which he had gone and would seek him elsewhere. That is why he ran in a zigzag direction, so that the lion would not smell his footsteps and the man would be able to go home. But the lion, when it came, would come to seek him, and he therefore would not run straight to his house. He knew that the lion, when it came back and missed him, would look for his footprints, that the lion would follow his spoor, seeking him, attempting to seize the man.

When he came out at the top of the hill, he called out to the people at home that he had just been "lifted up" while the sun stood high, he had been "lifted up." Therefore, the people must find many hartebeest skins and roll him up in them, for he had been "lifted up" while the sun was high. He thought that the lion would, when it returned from the place to which it had gone, come back and miss him, and it would then resolve to seek him, to track him down. Therefore, he wanted the people to roll him up in many hartebeest skins, so that the lion would not come and get him. They knew that the lion is a creature that acts in that way to the thing that it has killed: it does not leave that thing when it has not eaten it. The people must therefore take the hartebeest skins and roll him up in them, and also in mats: these are the things that the people should roll him up in, so that the lion would not be able to get him.

And the people did this. The people rolled him up in mats and also in hartebeest skins, which they rolled together with the mats. The man had asked them to do this, and they therefore rolled him up in hartebeest skin. They felt that he was their hearts' young man, and they did not wish the lion to eat him. They therefore intended to hide him well so that the lion would not get hold of him. He was a young man whom they did not only love a little, and they therefore did not want the lion to eat him. They said that they would cover the young man with the screen or shelter of the house so that the lion, when it came, when it came seeking the young man, would not seize him when it came seeking him.

The people went out to seek roots. They dug out roots, brought them home at noon, and they baked the roots. And an old San, as he went along getting wood for his wife so that she could make a fire over the roots, saw the lion as it came over the top of the hill, the same place which the young man had come over. He told the people about it, saying, "Do you see that hill over there, the top of that hill which the young man came over?"

The young man's mother said, "Do not allow the lion to come into the houses. You must shoot it dead before it gets to the houses."

The people slung on their quivers, and they went to meet the lion. They shot at the lion, but the lion would not die, although the people were shooting at it. Another old woman spoke, saying, "You must give a child to the lion, so that it might go away from us."

The lion answered, saying that it did not want a child. It wanted the person whose eyes' tears it had licked; he was the one it wanted.

Other people said, "In what manner are you shooting at the lion, that you could not manage to kill it?"

An old man said, "Can you not see that it must be a sorcerer? It will not die when we are shooting at it; it insists upon having the man whom it carried off."

The people threw children to the lion. But the lion did not want the children whom the people threw to it; it looked at them and left them alone.

The people were shooting at the lion while it sought the man, attempting to seize the man; the people were shooting at it.

The people said, "Bring assegais for us, we must kill the lion!"

The people were shooting at it; they were stabbing it with assegais, hoping to stab it to death. The people were not successful; the lion continued to seek the young man, saying that it wanted the young man whose tears it had licked. He was the one it wanted.

The lion scratched, tearing the houses of the people to pieces, seeking the young man.

The people said, "Can you not see that the lion will not eat the children whom we have given to it?"

Others said, "Can you not see that it is a sorcerer?"

And others said, "You must give a girl to the lion, to see if the lion will eat her and go away."

But the lion did not want the girl; it wanted only the man whom it had carried off; he was the one it wanted. And the people said that they did not know how to act toward the lion. In the morning, they had shot at the lion, but the lion would not die. It walked about while the people were shooting at it. They said, "We do not know how we should act toward the lion. Because of the man whom it carried off, the lion has refused the children we gave to it."

The people said, "Speak to the young man's mother about what is happening. Tell her that, although she loves the young man, even though he is the child of her heart, she must give him to the lion. She must see that the sun is about to set because the lion is threatening us; it will not leave us, insisting that it have the young man."

And the young man's mother said, "You may give my child to the lion. But you must not allow the lion to eat my child, you must not allow the lion to continue to walk about. You must kill it, then lay it on my child. It must die like my child. It must die and lie on my child."

When the young man's mother had spoken, the people took the young man out from the hartebeest skins in which they had rolled him, and they gave the young man to the lion.

And the lion bit the young man to death. While the lion was biting the young man, the people continued to shoot at it, to stab it. And it bit the young man to death.

And the lion spoke, it said to the people that now it would die, for it had seized the young man whom it had been seeking; it had seized him.

And the lion died while the man also lay dead. And the lion lay dead with the man.

A Swati storyteller, 1975

33

The Magic Mirror[126]

Sena (Mozambique)[127]

A long, long while ago, before ever the white men were seen in Sena, there lived a man called Gopáni-Kúfa. One day, as he was out hunting, he came upon a strange sight. An enormous python had caught an antelope and coiled itself around it. The antelope, striking out in despair with its horns, had pinned the python's neck to a tree, its horns sunk so deeply in the soft wood that neither creature could get away.

"Help!" cried the antelope. "I was doing no harm, yet I have been caught and would have been eaten, had I not defended myself."

"Help me," said the python, "for I am Insáto, king of all the reptiles, and will reward you well!"

Gopáni-Kúfa considered for a moment, then, stabbing the antelope with his assegai, he set the python free.

"I thank you," said the python. "Come back here with the new moon, when I shall have eaten the antelope, and I will reward you as I promised."

"Yes," said the dying antelope, "he will reward you, and your reward shall be your own undoing."

Gopáni-Kúfa went back to his kraal, and with the new moon he returned to the spot where he had saved the python.

Insáto was lying on the ground, still sleepy from the effects of his huge meal, and when he saw the man, he thanked him again and said, "Come with me now to Píta, which is my own country, and I will give you what you will of all my possessions."

Gopáni-Kúfa at first was afraid, thinking of what the antelope had said, but he finally consented and followed Insáto into the forest. For several days they traveled, and at last they came to a hole leading deep into the earth. It was not very wide, but large enough to admit a man.

"Hold onto my tail," said Insáto, "and I will go down first, drawing you after me."

The man did so, and Insáto entered.

Down, down, down they went for days, all the while getting deeper and deeper into the earth, until at last the darkness ended and they dropped into a beautiful country. Around them grew short green grass, on which browsed herds of cattle and sheep and goats. In the distance, Gopáni-Kúfa saw a great collection of houses, all square, built of stone and very tall, and their roots were shining with gold and burnished iron.

Gopáni-Kúfa turned to Insáto but found, in the place of the python, a man, strong and handsome, with the great snake's skin wrapped around him for covering. And on his arms and neck were rings of pure gold.

The man smiled. "I am Insáto," he said, "but in my own country I take man's shape—even as you see me—for this is Píta, the land over which I am king."

He then took Gopáni-Kúfa by the hand and led him toward the town.

On the way, they passed rivers in which men and women were bathing and fishing and boating, and farther on they came to gardens covered with heavy crops of rice and maize and many other grains that Gopáni-Kúfa did not even know the name of. And as they passed, the people who were singing at their work in the fields abandoned their labors and saluted Insáto with delight, also bringing palm wine and green coconuts for refreshment, as to one returned from a long journey.

"These are my children!" said Insáto, waving his hand toward the people.

Gopáni-Kúfa was much astonished at all that he saw, but he said nothing.

Presently, they came to the town. Everything here, too, was beautiful, and everything that a man might desire he could obtain. Even the grains of dust in the streets were of gold and silver.

Insáto conducted Gopáni-Kúfa to the palace and, showing him his rooms and the women who would wait upon him, told him that they would have a great feast that night. The next day, he might name his choice of the riches of Píta, and it would be given him. Then he went away.

Now Gopáni-Kúfa had a wasp called Zéngi-mízi. Zéngi-mízi was not an ordinary wasp, for the spirit of the father of Gopáni-Kúfa had entered it, so that it was exceedingly wise. In times of doubt, Gopáni-Kúfa always consulted the wasp as to what should be done, so on this occasion took it out of the little rush basket in which he carried it and said, "Zéngi-mízi, what gift shall I ask of Insáto tomorrow when he wants to know the reward he shall give me for saving his life?"

"Biz-z-z," hummed Zéngi-Mízi, "ask him for Sipáo the Mirror."

And it flew back into its basket.

Gopáni-Kúfa was astonished at this answer, but, knowing that the words of Zéngi-Mízi were true words, he determined to make the request.

So that night they feasted, and the next day Insáto came to Gopáni-Kúfa and, giving him joyful greeting, he said, "Now, my friend, name your choice among my possessions, and you shall have it!"

"King," answered Gopáni-Kúfa, "out of all your possessions, I will have the mirror, Sipáo."

The king started. "Oh friend, Gopáni-Kúfa," he said, "ask for anything but that! I did not think that you would request that which is most precious to me."

"Let me think it over again then, king," said Gopáni-Kúfa, "and tomorrow I will let you know if I change my mind."

But the king was very troubled, fearing the loss of Sipáo, for the mirror had magic powers, so that he who owned it had but to ask and his wish would be fulfilled. To it, Insáto owed all that he possessed.

As soon as the king left him, Gopáni-Kúfa again took Zéngi-Mízi out of his basket.

"Zéngi-Mízi," he said, "the king seems loath to grant my request for the mirror. Is there not some other thing of equal value for which I might ask?"

And the wasp answered, "There is nothing in the world, Gopáni-Kúfa, that is of such value as this mirror, for it is a wishing mirror, and it fulfills the desires of the one who owns it. If the king hesitates, go to him the next day, and the day after, and in the end he will bestow the mirror upon you, for you saved his life."

And that is what happened.

For three days, Gopáni-Kúfa returned the same answer to the king, and, at last, with tears in his eyes, Insáto gave him the mirror, which was of polished iron, saying, "Take Sipáo, then, Gopáni-Kúfa, and may your wishes come true. Go back now to your own country. Sipáo will show you the way."

Gopáni-Kúfa rejoiced and, saying farewell to the king, said to the mirror, "Sipáo, Sipáo, I wish to be back on the earth again."

Instantly, he found himself standing on the upper earth. But, not knowing the spot, he said again to the mirror, "Sipáo, Sipáo, I want the path to my own kraal."

And right before him lay the path. When he arrived home, he found his wife and daughter mourning for him, for they thought that he had been eaten by lions. But he comforted them, saying that while following a wounded antelope he had missed his way and had wandered for a long time before he had found the path again.

That night, he asked Zéngi-mízi, in whom sat the spirit of his father, what he had better ask Sipáo for next.

"Biz-z-z," said the wasp. "Would you not like to be as great a chief as Insáto?"

Gopáni-Kúfa smiled and took the mirror and said to it, "Sipáo, Sipáo, I want a town as great as that of Insáto, the king of Píta, and I wish to be chief over it."

Then all along the banks of the Zambezi River, which flowed nearby, sprang up streets of stone buildings, and their roofs shone with gold and burnished iron, like those in Píta. And in the streets men and women were walking, and boys were driving out the sheep and cattle to pasture. And from the river came shouts and laughter from the young men and women who had launched their canoes and were fishing.

And when the people of the new town saw Gopáni-Kúfa, they rejoiced greatly and hailed him as chief.

Gopáni-Kúfa was now as powerful as Insáto the king of the reptiles had been, and he and his family moved into the palace that stood high above the other buildings right in the middle of the town.

His wife was too astonished at all these wonders to ask any questions, but his daughter, Shasása, kept begging him to tell her how he had suddenly become so great, so at last he revealed the whole secret and even entrusted Sipáo the mirror to her care, saying, "It will be safer with you, my daughter, for you dwell apart, whereas men come to consult me on affairs of state, and the mirror might be stolen."

Then Shasása took the magic mirror and hid it beneath her pillow, and after that for many years Gopáni-Kúfa ruled his people both well and wisely, so that all loved him, and never once did he need to ask Sipáo to grant him a wish.

Now it happened that, after many years, when the hair of Gopáni-Kúfa was turning grey with age, there came white men to that country. Up the Zambezi they came, and they fought long and fiercely with Gopáni-Kúfa. But, because of the power of the magic mirror, he defeated them, and they fled to the sea coast.

Chief among them was Rei, a man of much cunning, who sought to discover whence sprang Gopáni-Kúfa's power. So one day he called to him a trusty servant named Butou and said, "Go to the town and find out for me what is the secret of its greatness."

And Butou, dressing himself in rags, set out, and when he came to Gopáni-Kúfa's town, he asked for the chief.

And the people took him into the presence of Gopáni-Kúfa.

When the white man saw him, he humbled himself and said, "Chief, take pity on me, for I have no home! When Rei marched against you, I alone stood apart, for I knew that all the strength of the Zambezi lay in your hands, and because I would not fight against you he turned me forth into the forest to starve."

Gopáni-Kúfa believed the white man's story, and he took him in and feasted him and gave him a house.

In this way the end came.

For the heart of Shasása, the daughter of Gopáni-Kúfa, went forth to Butou, the traitor, and from her he learned the secret of the magic mirror.

One night, when all the town slept, he felt beneath her pillow, and, finding the mirror, he stole it and fled with it to Rei, the chief of the white men.

So it happened that, one day, as Gopáni-Kúfa was gazing at the river from a window of the palace, he again saw the war canoes of the white men, and at the sight his spirit beset him.

"Shasása, my daughter!" he cried wildly. "Go get the mirror for me, for the white men are approaching!"

"My father," she sobbed, "the mirror is gone! For I loved Butou, the traitor, and he has stolen Sipáo from me!"

Then Gopáni-Kúfa calmed himself and drew out Zéngi-Mízi from its rush basket.

"Oh spirit of my father," he said, "what shall I do now?"

"Gopáni-Kúfa," hummed the wasp, "there is nothing now that can be done, for the words of the antelope that you killed are being fulfilled."

"Alas! I am an old man, I had forgotten!" cried the chief. "The words of the antelope were true words—my reward shall be of my own making— they are being fulfilled."

Then the white men fell upon the people of Gopáni-Kúfa and killed them, together with the chief and his daughter, Shasása. And since then, all the power of the earth has rested in the hands of the white men, for they have in their possession Sipáo, the magic mirror.

34

Nyajak[128]

Shilluk (Sudan)[129]

A woman was with child, and she bore a child; she was named Nyajak.

One day, the drum was beaten in a village far away. The people went to dance to the drum. This village where the drum was being beaten was the village of a lion.

And the child who had just been born also wanted to go to dance.

The people asked her, "Why are you saying that you also want to go? You are still so small!"

She said, "Never mind, I will go."

This child was a spirit. She went with the people.

When they arrived there, it began to rain, so they went into the house of the lion.

This lion was a man.

During the night, the other girls, who had come with Nyajak, slept, but the child who had just been born was awake. She knew that the man was actually a lion.

The lion wanted to open the house where the girls slept, but this child, Nyajak, asked from within the house, "Who is there?"

The lion replied, "Nyajak!"

The child answered, "Eh?"

The lion said, "Are you still awake?"

Nyajak said, "I am not yet asleep."

The lion asked, "Are you hungry?"

"Yes, I am."

The lion said, "Would you not like to have a ram killed?"

Nyajak answered, "Yes, I would."

So the lion killed a ram. He cooked it and gave it to Nyajak. Nyajak took it.

Then the lion said, "Nyajak!"

She replied, "Eh?"

"Do eat!" said the lion.

She said, "All right."

The lion said, "And then sleep."

Nyajak replied, "All right."

The lion went away and waited some time.

Then he returned and tried to get into the house.

But Nyajak again asked, "Who are you?"

The lion replied, "Nyajak, are you still awake?"

Nyajak said, "Yes, I am."

The lion asked, "Are you hungry?"

Nyajak replied, "Yes, I am."

"Would you not like to have an ox killed?" asked the lion.

Nyajak said, "Yes, I would."

So an ox was killed and was cooked by him and given to Nyajak.

The lion said, "Do eat!"

Nyajak replied, "All right."

The lion turned away.

After some time, he came back and tried to open the house.

Nyajak asked, "Who are you?"

The lion said, "Nyajak, are you still awake?"

Nyajak said, "Yes, I am."

The lion asked, "What do you want? Are you hungry?"

Nyajak replied, "Yes, I am."

The lion said, "Have a goat killed!"

Nyajak replied, "No, I won't have a goat killed. I am thirsty."

The lion asked, "In what shall I bring water?"

Nyajak said, "Why, bring it in a basket."

The lion ran to the riverbank with a basket. He dipped it into the water, but the water streamed down on the ground, and only leeches and small fish remained in the basket. He thrust them out and dipped the basket again, but the water flowed out on the ground, and the lion sat down a second time to pick out the leeches and the small fish.

In the meantime, Nyajak awakened the other girls, and they arose, asking, "What is the matter?"

Nyajak said, "Is not the lion going to eat us?" Then she said to them, "Eat this meat," referring to the sheep and ox that the lion had killed for her.

Nyajak knew the lion would not come back quickly.

When they had eaten, Nyajak said to the girls, "Run away!"

They ran away home to their country. Nyajak alone remained.

At last, the lion was tired of dipping water with the basket, and he came back, calling, "Nyajak, are you asleep?"

He came into the house, saying, "Nyajak!"

She remained silent.

The lion lighted a fire, and he found that the girls had gone.

He said, "This cursed Nyajak has led her comrades away."

Nyajak replied, "Why, am I not here?"

The lion sprang at Nyajak, but she disappeared.

The lion cried, "This cursed Nyajak, where has she gone?"

Nyajak replied, "Am I not here?"

The lion sprang again at her but did not catch her. Nyajak had disappeared.

At last, the lion was tired, and Nyajak went away. But the lion did not know it.

The girls arrived home.

And the lion came to them; he had turned himself into a beautiful big tree, an olam.[130] The girls liked him very much.

But Nyajak said, "Do not go under that tree! This tree is a lion!"

They replied, "Why, Nyajak begins to lie!"

Nyajak said, "All right, I shall say no more."

The girls climbed on the tree.

Suddenly, the lion seized them and fled with them.

Nyajak said, "What did I say just now?"

The people were much perplexed; they went away.

But Nyajak went to the lion. She turned into a very, very old man; she went limping on a crutch.

When the lion saw her, he said, "What kind of man is this old person?"

Nyajak replied, "A man begging for water."

And he gave her water.

Then she went back.

But presently she came back again; she had turned into a rat.

The lion had just gone to the riverside to fetch water in order to cook the girls whom he had caught. Nyajak drove the children away and brought them home.

When the lion came back, he asked, "Why, where have the children gone? Is it not this cursed Nyajak who has taken them away?"

And the lion came into the village of Nyajak; he had turned into a very fine girl. He came to converse with the brother of Nyajak.

The lion asked, "Where is the brother of Nyajak? Call him!"

The brother of Nyajak was called, and they conversed together.

But when Nyajak came, she exclaimed, "Oh dear, brother, how can you do such a wicked thing? Do you not know this is a lion?"

The boy said, "Go away, you are a great liar."

Nyajak replied, "It is your own affair, I shall say no more."

And Nyajak remained silent.

But while the boy slept, his eye was taken out by the lion.

That is all, and the lion went home to his village.

But the next morning, Nyajak found her brother weeping.

She asked, "Why?"

The boy answered, "My eye has been taken out."

Nyajak said, "Did I not tell you this man is a lion? What do you say now?"

He was silent.

Nyajak went away; she turned herself into an old woman; she went walking.

When she arrived at the home of the lion, she cried, "Here is a traveler at the gate!"

The lion said, "Welcome!"

She came in and exclaimed, "Oh, my brother, are you still here?"

The lion replied, "Who are you?"

Nyajak said, "Am I not your sister who had been carried away by the wind a long time ago?"

The lion said, "Ah! I had almost forgotten!" The lion wept; he was very glad.

And they talked together.

The lion did not know that it was Nyajak; he believed her to be his sister.

And Nyajak looked up and saw the eye of her brother.

She said, "My brother!"

The lion replied, "Eh?"

She asked, "What is it makes such a bad smell in the house?"

The lion answered, "It is the eye of the brother of Nyajak."

Nyajak asked, "Where did you find that?"

He answered, "I brought it; I had turned myself into a girl, and so I took out his eye."

Nyajak said, "As you have brought it, will you not take it down and show it to me?"

The lion took it down, saying, "But mind, lest it be taken by the crow!"

Nyajak said, "No, it will not be taken; we shall watch it." Then Nyajak asked, "But where is flour for cooking?"

The lion answered, "It is just being pounded."

Nyajak said, "Ah, that is good."

After some time, the lion said, "Sister, I am going to the riverside to fetch water."

Nyajak said, "Go."

The lion said, "Take heed, watch the eye of the brother of Nyajak, lest it be taken by the crow. We will cook it together with our meal."

So Nyajak was left in the house while the lion went to the river. But while he was gone, Nyajak took the eye of her brother and then turned herself into a crow. She flew up and returned to her native country.

She found her brother, put his eye back into its place, and so her brother was cured.

When the lion came back from the river, he found that the eye had gone, and he saw that the woman was also gone.

Then he said, "My heart is tired with this Nyajak, I shall never return to her."

That is all. And Nyajak was left alone by the lion; she lived with her brother. The lion remained in his place; he never returned anymore.

35

The Sultan's Wife[131]

Somali (Somalia)[132]

There was a sultan who had a son.

His son said, "I want to marry."

So the sultan gave him many presents and also a ship. The sultan's son set sail and came to a town. When he arrived at the town, he became friends with a sultan, and the sultan gave him a house.

The young man made a hole between the house he was in and the sultan's house, and he became friends with the sultan's wife.

One day, the young man said to the sultan's wife, "Make some food for me just as you are accustomed to make it for your husband." Then he went to the sultan and said, "Tonight, will you take food with me?"

The sultan said, "Well and good."

The young man said to the sultan's wife, "Tonight, when I and the sultan are having our food, I want you to serve us the food."

The woman said, "The sultan will know me."

He said, "He will not know you. I will say you are my wife."

She said, "If he does not know me, I will go with you and be your wife."

At night, the sultan came home and dressed himself, then went to the young man's house. And his wife passed through the hole in the house and came to the young man's house. Then she served the food to the sultan and the young man.

The sultan recognized his wife and got off his chair and went to his house. Before he reached his house, the woman passed through the hole and sat on her bed. And the sultan saw her.

When he saw her, he straightway came back to the house of the young man, while the woman came through the hole, and still he saw her.

The young man who was dining with him said to the sultan, "Did you think this woman who is serving our food was your wife? The woman is my wife," he said.

And the sultan sat down.

The next morning, the young man said, "I am sailing."

"Very good," the sultan answered.

And the young man arranged matters with the sultan's wife, saying, "In the morning, come through that hole; I am sailing."

So the woman came through and came to the young man, and he took her to the ship and sailed.

And the young man, having run away with the sultan's wife, married her.

36

Monyohe[133]

Sotho (Lesotho)[134]

There was a young woman called Senkepeng, the sister of Masilo.

Senkepeng refused to be married.

On a certain day, they went to a singing party at Morakapula's. They arrived, they sang, they sang the whole day.

In the afternoon, Morakapula called for rain, saying that Senkepeng refused to dance with him. It rained, it rained the whole night.

Morakapula gave the order to his people not to allow Senkepeng into their homes; they must drive her out.

Senkepeng went to an old woman and said, "Allow me to come into your house."

The old woman said, "My house is full."

Senkepeng said, "I shall kill you."

She said then, "Come into the house."

She went in and slept.

The night cleared up.

Then Masilo said, "Let us return home."

Morakapula said to Masilo, "All the rivers are full."

Masilo said, "We will cross them."

Masilo's people went away, returning home. They found that the river was full. They crossed.

Senkepeng was in their midst, but the river forced her back.

They came back, took her, held her fast, and went into the water with her. It forced her back again.

Then Masilo himself came. When he was near her, he said, "Senkepeng, why do you stay here?"

She said, "I cannot come. As soon as I go into the water, it forces me back."

Masilo said, "Come here, I shall hold you."

She came, he held her, going into the water with her.

It forced her back.

Masilo came back, fetched her, and went into the water with her.

It forced her back.

Masilo left her and went on.

Senkepeng said,

"Masilo of my mother, alas! alas! alas!
Masilo of my mother, alas! alas! alas!
Go and tell my mother at home, alas! alas! alas!
Tell her that all the rivers are full, alas! alas! alas!
Even the Motikoe River is full, alas! alas! alas!
I have refused the son of Morakapula, alas! alas! alas!"

Masilo said,

"Senkepeng, sister of Kali, son of Tsoloe, alas! alas! alas!
Senkepeng, sister of Kali, son of Tsoloe, alas! alas! alas!
Go down along the river of Motikoe, alas! alas! alas!
Go on, hiding yourself in the flotsam of the stream, alas! alas! alas!
All, all the rivers are full, alas! alas! alas!
Even the Motikoe River is full, alas! alas! alas!"

So they parted. Masilo went on. Senkepeng also went on, going down along the Motikoe River, still carrying her musical instrument. When she stopped, she found a heap of asparagus plants that the river had carried there. She opened the heap and entered. Her musical instrument remained outside, the staff of the musical instrument projecting above. This was near a fountain.

The next morning, 'Mamonyohe went to the fountain. She saw the musical instrument that was projecting.

She said, "What is it that projects so?"

She went, arrived, opened the heap of asparagus, and said, "Ah! I have found a beautiful wife for my son! Come out, my daughter-in-law, let us go home."

Senkepeng came out, still carrying her musical instrument.

They went home.

They arrived and entered 'Mamonyohe's house. 'Mamonyohe found that oxen and sheep had already been slaughtered, a quantity of strong beer had been brewed, much bread had been cooked. It was food that had been cooked for Monyohe.

Monyohe was living inside the roof of the house, seen by nobody.

'Mamonyohe said, "Take this food, carry it to your husband. There is the house of your husband."

Senkepeng took a full load of meat in the basket and carried it. She arrived, entered the house, put it down, and went out. She took a pot of beer, went and put it down. She went to take the bread; she arrived and put it down. She went to take thick milk; she arrived and put it down. She went out and returned to 'Mamonyohe.

Then she received this order: "Go and bring back the utensils on which you have taken the meat over there to your house."

She went there and found that nothing remained; only the bones were left.

She wondered, "What invisible thing is eating that food and finishing it off in an instant?"

She returned, and the mother said, "Take some corn, my dear, and grind it for your husband."

She took the corn, ground it, and cooked it. She took the bread out of the pots; she dished up the meat; she poured out the thick milk. She carried the food on her head and took it there.

Monyohe ate it, finishing it.

She was sent again to go and bring back the pots in which Monyohe's food had been sent. She found that nothing of it remained.

The sun set.

At sleeping time, she was told, "Go and sleep at your husband's."

She went, arrived, and slept on the ground; she did not see anything at all.

When the night was about to end, she felt Monyohe striking her with his tail, saying, "I am going to take snuff, I am going to creep."

She rose, went out, took a pitcher, went to the fountain, and drew water.

She found that 'Mamonyohe had already kindled a fire, that the meat was in the pot, that cattle had been slaughtered.

As soon as she arrived, 'Mamonyohe said, "Take some corn, grind it, and cook it for your husband."

She took corn, ground it, cooked it, and she dished up the meat, then carried the food on her head and brought it to Monyohe.

She was sent again and told that she must fetch the pots from Monyohe's house.

There was no rest all that day; cooking went on the whole day.

When the sun set, at sleeping time, she went to her house and slept.

When the night was about to end, she felt Monyohe striking her with his tail, saying, "I am going to take snuff, I am going to creep."

Senkepeng began to grow thin.

Some people of the village said to her, "Why do you stay here, you poor child? Why don't you go home? In all this big community, none of the girls has been able to stay at 'Mamonyohe's."

She said, "I don't know how to go home."

But on a certain day, she went out, took her pitcher, put it down near the fountain, and then went down. She was on her way home.

She went on, she went on, she went on. The sun rose when she was already far away.

Monyohe began to move over there in his house. A strong wind blew when he came out of his house.

The people shouted, "Come and see that big thing that comes out of 'Mamonyohe's house!"

Monyohe went in fiery haste, in pursuit of Senkepeng.

Senkepeng looked behind her and cried, "Oh! I am going to die today!"

The serpent drew near to her.

She said, "What can I do?" She said,

"Child of my sister, sing, and let us see.
Child of my sister, sing, and let us see."[135]

While the serpent was still singing, she went on and arrived at her home.

When she arrived at the courtyard of her parents, she fell down on her stomach.

The serpent arrived, it arrived tired, not having any more force, creeping on its belly.

The razors cut it, the knives divided it, and it then died.

'Mamonyohe arrived, and said, "Alas! my child, alas! my child has died quite alone. Where shall I take him?" She said, "Give me a black ox."

They gave her a black ox.

She said, "Kill it."

They killed it.

She drew together the body of her child, gathered it, wrapped it in the hide of the black ox, then burned it.

It was consumed; it became a black cinder.

She took the kaross she had brought from home; she gathered into it the ashes of her son; she gathered the ashes into the ox's kaross. She carried it on her head and went to the pool. She arrived, threw the kaross into the pool.

All the people were assembled there near the pool.

She began to go around the pool. She went around it, she went around it, she went around it.

Then, when her son came out of the water, he came out being now a man, no more a serpent, being a beautiful man.

Senkepeng said, "Oh! Oh, how beautiful my husband is!"

They went up, went to Senkepeng's parents.

They married her: he became her husband.

When they went away, they went to go and fetch cattle to pay Senkepeng's dowry.

She became the wife of Monyohe.

It is the end of the tale.

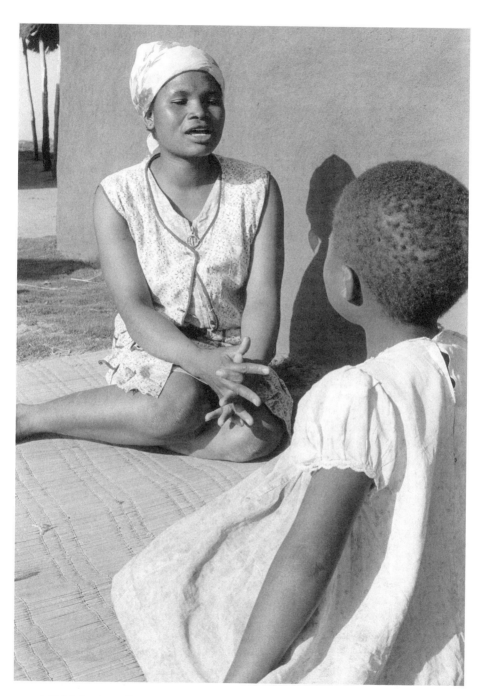

A Ndebele storyteller, 1976

37

The Physician's Son and the King of the Snakes[136]

Swahili (Tanzania)[137]

Once there was a very learned physician who died, leaving his wife with a little baby boy, who, when he was old enough, she named, according to his father's wish, Hasibu Karim Ed Din.

When the boy had been to school and had learned to read, his mother sent him to a tailor to learn his trade, but he could not learn it. Then he was sent to a silversmith, but he could not learn that trade, either. After that, he tried many trades but could learn none of them.

At last, his mother said, "Well, stay at home for a while."

And that seemed to suit him.

One day, he asked his mother what his father's business had been, and she told him he was a very great physician.

"Where are his books?" he asked.

"Well, it's a long time since I saw them," replied his mother, "but I think they are behind there. Look and see."

So he hunted around a little and at last found them. But they were almost ruined by insects, and he gained little from them.

At last, four of the neighbors came to his mother and said, "Let your boy go along with us and cut wood in the forest." It was their business to cut wood, load it on donkeys, and sell it in the town for making fires.

"All right," she said, "tomorrow, I'll buy him a donkey, and he can start fair with you."

So the next day Hasibu, with his donkey, went off with those four persons, and they worked very hard and made a lot of money that day.

This continued for six days, but on the seventh it rained heavily, and they had to get under rocks to keep dry.

Now, Hasibu sat in a place by himself, and, having nothing else to do, he picked up a stone and began knocking on the ground with it. To his surprise, the ground gave forth a hollow sound, and he called to his companions, saying, "There seems to be a hole under here."

Upon hearing him knock again, they decided to dig and see what was the cause of the hollow sound, and they had not gone very deep before they broke into a large pit that was filled to the top with honey.

They did not do any firewood chopping after that but devoted their entire attention to the collection and sale of the honey.

With a view to getting it all out as quickly as possible, they told Hasibu to go down into the pit and dip out the honey, while they put it in vessels and took it to town for sale. They worked for three days, making a great deal of money.

At last, there was only a little honey left at the very bottom of the pit, and they told the boy to scrape that together while they went to get a rope to haul him out.

But instead of getting the rope, they decided to let him remain in the pit and divide the money among themselves. So when he had gathered the remainder of the honey together and called for the rope, he received no answer. And after he had been alone in the pit for three days, he became convinced that his companions had deserted him.

Then those four persons went to his mother and told her that they had become separated in the forest, that they had heard a lion roaring, and that they could find no trace of either her son or his donkey.

His mother, of course, cried very much, and the four neighbors pocketed her son's share of the money.

To return to Hasibu:

He passed the time walking about the pit, wondering what the end would be, eating scraps of honey, sleeping a while, and sitting down to think.

While engaged in the last occupation, on the fourth day, he saw a scorpion fall to the ground—a large one, too—and he killed it.

Then he suddenly thought to himself, "Where did that scorpion come from? There must be a hole somewhere. I'll search."

So he looked around until he saw light through a tiny crack. He took his knife and scooped and scooped, until he had made a hole big enough to pass through. Then he went out and came upon a place he had never seen before.

Seeing a path, he followed it until he came to a very large house, the door of which was not fastened. So he went inside and saw golden doors, with golden locks and keys of pearl, and beautiful chairs inlaid with jewels and precious stones. And in a reception room he saw a couch covered with a splendid spread, and he lay down there.

Presently, he found himself being lifted off the couch and put in a chair, and he heard someone saying, "Do not hurt him. Wake him gently."

When he opened his eyes, he found himself surrounded by numbers of snakes, one of them wearing beautiful royal colors.

"Hello!" he cried. "Who are you?"

"I am Sultani wa Nyoka, king of the snakes, and this is my house. Who are you?"

"I am Hasibu Karim Ed Din."

"Where do you come from?"

"I don't know where I come from, or where I'm going."

"Well, don't bother yourself just now. Let's eat. I guess you are hungry, and I know I am."

Then the king gave orders, and some of the other snakes brought the finest fruits, and they ate and drank and conversed.

When the repast was ended, the king desired to hear Hasibu's story, so he told him all that had happened and then asked to hear the story of his host.

"Well," said the king of snakes, "mine is a rather long story, but you shall hear it. A long time ago, I left this place to go and live in the mountains of Al Kaf, for the change of air. One day, I saw a stranger coming along, and I said to him, 'Where are you from?' and he said, "I am wandering in the wilderness.'

"'Whose son are you?' I asked.

"'My name is Bulukia. My father was a sultan, and when he died I opened a small chest, inside of which I found a bag that contained a small brass box. When I opened this, I found some writing tied up in a woolen cloth, and it was all in praise of a prophet. He was described as such a good and wonderful man that I longed to see him. But when I made inquiries concerning him, I was told he was not yet born. Then I vowed that I would wander until I should see him. So I left our town and all my property, and I am wandering. But I have not yet seen that prophet.'

"Then I said to him, 'Where do you expect to find him, if he is not yet born? Perhaps if you had some serpent's water you might keep on living until you find him. But it's of no use talking about that, the serpent's water is too far away.'

"'Well,' he said, 'goodbye. I must wander on.'

"So I bade him farewell, and he went his way.

"Now, when that man had wandered until he reached Egypt, he met another man, who asked him, 'Who are you?'

"'I am Bulukia. Who are you?'

"'My name is Al Fan. Where are you going?'

"'I have left my home and my property, and I am seeking the prophet.'

"'Hm!' said Al Fan. 'I can tell you of a better occupation than looking for a man who is not born yet. Let us go and find the king of the snakes and get him to give us a charm medicine. Then we will go to King Solomon and get his rings, and we shall be able to make slaves of the genii and order them to do whatever we wish.'

"And Bulukia said, 'I have seen the king of the snakes in the mountain of al Kaf.'

"'All right,' said Al Fan, 'let's go.'

"Now, Al Fan wanted the ring of Solomon that he might be a great magician and control the genii and the birds, while all Bulukia wanted was to see the great prophet.

"As they went along, Al Fan said to Bulukia, 'Let us make a cage and entice the king of the snakes into it. Then we will shut the door and carry him off.'

"'All right,' said Bulukia.

"So they made a cage and put into it a cup of milk and a cup of wine and brought it to Al Kaf. And I, like a fool, went in, drank up all the wine and became drunk. Then they fastened the door and took me away with them.

"When I came to my senses, I found myself in a cage, with Bulukia carrying me, and I said, 'The sons of Adam are no good. What do you want from me?'

"And they answered, 'We want some medicine to put on our feet, so that we may walk upon the water whenever it is necessary in the course of our journey.'

"'Well,' I said, 'go along.'

"We went on until we came to a place where there were a great number and variety of trees, and when those trees saw me, they said, 'I am medicine for this,' 'I am medicine for that,' 'I am medicine for the head,' 'I am medicine for the feet,' and presently one tree said, 'If any one puts my medicine upon his feet he can walk on water.'

"When I told that to those men, they said, 'That is what we want,' and they took a great deal of it.

"Then they took me back to the mountain and set me free, and we said goodbye and parted.

"When they left me, they went on their way until they reached the sea, when they put the medicine on their feet and walked over. Thus they went many days, until they came to the place of King Solomon, where they waited while Al Fan prepared his medicines.

"When they arrived at King Solomon's place, he was sleeping and was being watched by genii, and his hand lay on his chest with the ring on his finger.

"As Bulukia drew near, one of the genii said to him, 'Where are you going?'

"He answered, 'I am here with Al Fan. He is going to take that ring.'

"'Go back,' said the genie. 'Keep out of the way. That man is going to die.'

"When Al Fan had finished his preparations, he said to Bulukia, 'Wait here for me.' Then he went forward to take the ring, when a great cry arose and he was thrown by some unseen force a considerable distance.

"Picking himself up, and still believing in the power of his medicines, he approached the ring again, when a strong breath blew upon him, and he was burned to ashes in a moment.

"While Bulukia was looking at all this, a voice said, 'Go your way. This wretched being is dead.'

"So he returned, and when he got to the sea again he put the medicine on his feet and passed over.

"And he continued to wander for many years.

"One morning, he saw a man sitting down, and said, 'Good morning,' and the man replied. Bulukia asked him, 'Who are you?'

"He answered, 'My name is Jan Shah. Who are you?'

"So Bulukia told him who he was and asked him to tell him his history.

"The man, who was weeping and smiling by turns, insisted upon hearing Bulukia's story first.

"After he had heard it, he said, 'Well, sit down, and I'll tell you my story from beginning to end. My name is Jan Shah, and my father is Twigamus, a great sultan. He used to go every day into the forest to shoot game. One day, I said to him, "Father, let me go with you into the forest today."

"'But he said, "Stay at home. You are better there."

"'Then I cried bitterly, and as I was his only child, whom he loved dearly, he couldn't stand my tears, so he said, "Very well, you shall go. Don't cry."

"'We went to the forest and took many attendants with us. And when we reached the place, we ate and drank, and then every one set out to hunt.

"'I and my seven slaves went on until we saw a beautiful gazelle, which we chased as far as the sea without capturing it. When the gazelle took to the water, I and four of my slaves took a boat, the other three slaves returning to my father. And we chased that gazelle until we lost sight of the shore. But we caught it and killed it. Just then, a great wind began to blow, and we lost our way.

"'When the other three slaves came to my father, he asked them, "Where is your master?" and they told him about the gazelle and the boat. Then he cried, "My son is lost! My son is lost!" and returned to the town and mourned for me as one dead.

"'After a time, we came to an island, where there were a great many birds. We found fruit and water, we ate and drank, and at night we climbed into a tree and slept until morning.

"'Then we rowed to a second island, and, seeing no one around, we gathered fruit, ate, and drank, then climbed a tree as before. During the night, we heard many savage beasts howling and roaring near us.

"'In the morning, we got away as soon as possible, and came to a third island. Looking around for food, we saw a tree full of fruit like red-streaked apples. But, as we were about to pick some, we heard a voice say, "Don't touch this tree. It belongs to the king." Toward night, a number of monkeys came; they seemed much pleased to see us, and they brought us all the fruit we could eat.

"'Presently, I heard one of them say, "Let us make this man our sultan."

"'Then another one said, "What's the use? They'll all run away in the morning."

"'But a third one said, "Not if we smash their boat."

"'Sure enough, when we started to leave in the morning, our boat was broken in pieces. So there was nothing for it but to stay there and be entertained by the monkeys, who seemed to like us very much.

"'One day, while strolling about, I came upon a great stone house, having an inscription on the door that said, "When any man comes to this island, he will find it difficult to leave, because the monkeys desire to have a man for their king. If he looks for a way to escape, he will think there is none. But there is one outlet, which lies to the north. If you go in that direction, you will come to a great plain that is infested with lions, leopards, and snakes. You must fight all of them, and if you overcome them you can go forward. You will then come to another great plain, inhabited by ants as big as dogs. Their teeth are like those of dogs, and they are very fierce. You must fight these, also, and if you overcome them, the rest of the way is clear."

"'I consulted with my attendances regarding this information, and we came to the conclusion that, as we could only die anyhow, we might as well risk death to gain our freedom.

"'As we all had weapons, we set forth, and when we came to the first plain we fought, and two of my slaves were killed. Then we went on to the second plain and fought again; my other two slaves were killed, and I alone escaped.

"'After that, I wandered on for many days, living on whatever I could find, until at last I came to a town where I stayed for a time, looking for employment but finding none.

"'One day, a man came up to me and said, "Are you looking for work?"

"'"I am," I said.

"'"Come with me, then," said he, and we went to his house.

"'When we got there, he produced a camel's skin, and said, "I shall put you in the skin, and a great bird will carry you to the top of that mountain over there. When he gets you there, he will tear this skin off you. You must then drive him away and push down the precious stones you will find there. When they are all down, I will get you down."

"'So he put me in the skin. The bird carried me to the top of the mountain and was about to eat me when I jumped up, scared it away, and then pushed down many precious stones. Then I called out to the man to take me down. But he never answered me, and went away.

"'I gave myself up for a dead man but went wandering about, until at last, after passing many days in a great forest, I came to a house, all by itself. The old man who lived in it gave me food and drink, and I was revived.

"'I remained there a long time, and that old man loved me as if I were his own son.

"'One day, he went away and, giving me the keys, told me that I could open the door of every room except one, which he pointed out to me.

"'Of course, when he was gone, this was the first door I opened. I saw a large garden, through which a stream flowed. Just then, three birds came and alighted by the side of the stream. Immediately, they changed into three most beautiful women. When they had finished bathing, they put on their clothes, and, as I stood watching them, they changed into birds again and flew away.

"'I locked the door and went away. But my appetite was gone, and I wandered about aimlessly.

"'When the old man came back, he saw that there was something wrong with me and asked me what was the matter. Then I told him I had seen those beautiful young women, that I loved one of them very much, and that if I could not marry her I would die.

"'The old man told me that I could not possibly have my wish. He said the three lovely beings were the daughters of the sultan of the genii and that their home was a journey of three years from where we were then.

"'I told him I could not help that. He must get her for my wife, or I would die.

"'At last he said, "Well, wait until they come again, then hide yourself and steal the clothes of the one you love so dearly."

"'So I waited, and when they came again I stole the clothes of the youngest, whose name was Sayadati Shems.

"'When they came out of the water, this one could not find her clothes. Then I stepped forward and said, "I have them."

""'Ah," she begged, "give them to me, their owner. I want to go away."

"'But I said to her, "I love you very much. I want to marry you."

""'I want to go to my father," she replied.

""'You cannot go," I said.

"'Then her sisters flew away, and I took her into the house, where the old man married us. He told me not to give her those clothes I had taken but to hide them, because if she ever got them she would fly away to her old home.[138] So I dug a hole in the ground and buried them.

"'But one day, when I was away from home, she dug them up and put them on. Then, saying to the slave I had given her for an attendant, "When your master returns, tell him I have gone home. If he really loves me, he will follow me," she flew away.

"'When I came home, they told me this, and I wandered many years, searching for her. At last I came to a town where one asked me, "Who are you?" and I answered, "I am Jan Shah."

""'What was your father's name?"

""'Twigamus."

""'Are you the man who married our mistress?"

""'Who is your mistress?"

""'Sayadati Shems."

"'I cried with delight, "I am he!"

"'They took me to their mistress, and she brought me to her father and told him that I was her husband, and everybody was happy."

"'Then we thought we should like to visit our old home, and her father's genii carried us there in three days. We stayed there a year and then returned. But in a short time, my wife died. Her father tried to comfort me and wanted me to marry another of his daughters, but I refused to be comforted and have mourned to this day.

"'That is my story.'

"Then Bulukia went on his way and wandered until he died."

Sultani wa Nyoka said to Hasibu, "Now, when you go home, you will do me injury."

Hasibu was very indignant at the idea and said, "I could not be induced to do you an injury. Please send me home."

"I will send you home," said the king, "but I am sure that you will come back and kill me."

"Why, I dare not be so ungrateful," exclaimed Hasibu. "I swear I could not hurt you."

"Well," said the king of the snakes, "bear this in mind: when you go home, do not go to bathe where there are many people."

And he said, "I will remember."

So the king sent him home, and he went to his mother's house. She was overjoyed to find that he was not dead.

Now, the sultan of the town was very sick, and it was decided that the only thing that could cure him would be to kill the king of snakes, boil him, and give the soup to the sultan.

For a reason known only to himself, the vizier had placed men at the public baths with this instruction: "If any one who comes to bathe here has a mark on his stomach, seize him and bring him to me."

When Hasibu had been home three days, he forgot the warning of Sultani wa Nyoka and went to bathe with the other people.

All of a sudden, he was seized by some soldiers and brought before the vizier, who said, "Take us to the home of the king of the snakes."

"I don't know where it is," said Hasibu.

"Tie him up," commanded the vizier.

So they tied him up and beat him until his back was all raw, and, being unable to stand the pain, he cried, "Let up! I will show you the place."

So he led them to the house of the king of the snakes, who, when he saw him, said, "Didn't I tell you you would come back to kill me?"

"How could I help it?" cried Hasibu. "Look at my back!"

"Who has beaten you so dreadfully?" asked the king.

"The vizier."

"Then there is no hope for me. But you must carry me yourself."

As they went along, the king said to Hasibu, "When we get to your town, I shall be killed and cooked. The first skimming the vizier will offer to you, but don't you drink it. Put it into a bottle and keep it. The second skimming you must drink, and you will become a great physician. The third skimming is the medicine that will cure your sultan. When the vizier asks you if you drank that first skimming, say, 'I did.' Then produce the bottle containing the first skimming, and say, 'This is the second, and it is for you.' The vizier will take it, and as soon as he drinks it he will die. And both of us will have our revenge."

Everything happened as the king had said. The vizier died, the sultan recovered, and Hasibu was loved by all as a great physician.

38

Untombinde, the Tall Girl[139]

Swati (Swaziland)[140]

BY ALBERTINE NXUMALO

It happened. . . .

There were some girls, they went to dip ochre. There were four of these girls.

The girls set out. Among them was one who was younger, smaller than the other girls. Her name was Ntombinde.

So they went, they walked and walked. At length, they arrived at the place where the ochre is dipped, and they dug it up, this ochre.

The youngest girl, Ntombinde,[141] was the favorite one at home, because she was youngest, she was the last born. And because she was the favored child, these other girls looked down upon her. So it was that, when they were at the ochre pit, they said, "If only she weren't here. We must do something to hurt Ntombinde. We'll finish her off here and leave her. When we get home, we'll say that we don't know where she disappeared to."

She did not hear them talking. She was absent for a while, having left the road for some reason. When she rejoined them—well, they went on and said nothing.

Then they dug up the ochre. They dug and dug at the pit. All the older ones dug first; Ntombinde was the last to do so. Then she went into the pit. While she was digging, before she finished, the other girls came back and filled in the pit over her. Then they departed with the dog. They buried her alive, despite the fact that she cried; they buried her and departed.

As they went on, the dog turned back to sniff out where Ntombinde remained. In spite of all its efforts to sniff out her, it could not locate her. The dog even tried to dig her up, but, because the soil was moist, it could not get anywhere. So it gave up and left. It went past these other three girls.

And Ntombinde remained there in the pit.

Time passed, and at length, another person came to dip ochre as well.

This person began to dig in this very spot where everyone had been digging, where the digging was usually done. As she was digging, she was surprised.

"Oh, as I dig, there seems to be movement! There is movement here!"

She dug and dug and again dug, thinking that she was digging for ochre. She was putting some of it into a dish, and she continued digging. Suddenly, she saw a head appear!

"Now what is this? It seems there is a human being here!"

The person ran away, leaving everything including the dish behind. She left, and Ntombinde remained inside there.

Ntombinde raised herself up then and came out. She went away.

The other person had gone, going to tell other people of this. She came and reported it, saying, "As I was digging over there, a human being suddenly appeared! First, I saw the hair appear! Maybe it is still there! Let's go and inspect!"

So they went. When they looked, they found that Ntombinde was not there anymore. She had gone away.

This person then said, "But it was here."

These others said, "You are lying! There never was a human being under the soil here!"

She protested, saying, "Truly, I swear! She was here! Look carefully, look and see, you'll find footprints!"

They looked closely, and they did indeed find where she had stepped as she came out.

They said, "A footprint means nothing! You're just telling tales!"

"Perhaps it's your own!"

She made a print of her foot and said, "Look at it! Does my footprint resemble this one in any way?"

They could see that it did not resemble it.

Ntombinde had departed—she had come to a forest and climbed a tree, and she remained there in the forest.

These people were persuaded now, and they said, "Where has this person disappeared to? What does all this mean?"

"How did it happen?"

Meanwhile, Ntombinde continued living in the forest there.

When the other three girls reached home, their mother asked, "Where is Ntombinde?"

They said, "She said she was going to visit uncle's homestead. She said she would return tomorrow."

"We don't know why she has not yet returned."

"Perhaps she decided to stay a little longer."

Their mother then said, "How could you let her go alone? Such a small child! How could she go to her uncle's place? Who showed her the way?"

They said, "She said she remembered from the time she traveled there with you."

Their mother said nothing, and they went to bed.

Ntombinde remained there in the forest.

And time passed.

By chance, a man came to that forest to chop wood. He came there and chopped. And he was hewing the very tree in which Ntombinde was sitting, she, in the upper reaches of the tree, said,

[sings] "Please help me!
Tell mother at home!
That they covered Ntombinde
With soil at the ochre pit!"

The man paid no attention. He did not take seriously what this might mean, and he went back to his chopping.

Again, Ntombinde said,

[sings] "Please help me!
Tell my mother at home!
That they buried, oh Lord, Ntombinde,
In the ochre pit!"

The man became nervous and looked around. But he could see no one.

"Who is it who's talking? There is someone who's talking here!" He leaned against the tree and stopped chopping. When he was not chopping, she not speak. But as soon as he began chopping, Ntombinde spoke, and said,

[sings] "Please help me!
Tell mother at home!
That they buried Ntombinde, oh Lord,
In the ochre pit!"

When the man looked up into the tree, he was surprised.

"There's a human being there!"

Hastily throwing away the axe, the man went away. He ran, he ran and ran, saying, "Ho! What kind of bad omens are these? Do people live here? Here I was, going to chop logs only to find that *people* live here! Hiii! What shall I do?" He tried to remember, "What did this person say?"

He was prepared to leave the forest, but then he thought, "Why do I run away? I should have stayed and listened to what this person said. That is what I shall do!"

He returned, thinking, "Let me go back so that I may hear well what she says. I'll sneak close, lay hold of my axe, seize it, and see if she won't speak."

The man crept closer and closer. He came into the area, found the axe that he had cast aside, and stood there for a time, all the while looking down, afraid to look up. He stood there, and there was no speaking.

Then he thought, "Let me chop again, or pretend to be chopping, to see if she will talk."

So he chopped.

She said,

[sings] "Do help me,
Tell mother at home!
That they buried Ntombinde, oh Lord,
In the ochre pit!"

And when he looked up, "Now that this person is talking about— It seems she is talking about this child who got lost. I heard it said that there is a child who got lost when they had gone to dig ochre. How did this happen? I wonder where this person belongs?"

So saying, he set out to go to that place, to the home of Ntombinde.

When he got there, he said, "There is a person whom I heard here in the forest. Did you ever find Ntombinde?"

They said, "No."

"Did she actually get lost?"

Her mother said, "Ntombinde did get lost when she went to the home of her mother."

This man then said, "Well, over there in the forest, I heard the voice of a person who mentioned the name of Ntombinde. She said that she had gone to dig ochre. It seems they buried her in the pit of ochre. But then, I may have heard badly."

Her mother said, "When they say my child is at the home of her mother, they mean that they buried her in the ochre pit. What will I do now? What can I do now?"

This person said, "We could go there and ask. Perhaps you too will be told. And perhaps I did not hear her words well, I don't know."

So her mother went along with the woodcutter, crying as she went.

This man said, "Don't cry. Just remain quiet. If you cry, this person won't talk."

At length, they arrived in the forest. And this man began to chop.

Again, Ntombinde said,

[sings] "You should help me
Tell mother at home!
That they buried Ntombinde, oh Lord,
In the ochre pit."

The mother said, "Oh, my child! Truly, they buried her in the ochre pit! Even though they said she is absent, even this child, my child, they buried her! But what will I do to them now? What will I do? That child is long dead; she is no more! But the one who is talking—who is it?"

They remained quiet and came close to this tree to inspect.

Then her mother said, "It is my child!"

She chopped down the tree with the help of this man; they chopped until the tree fell down. Ntombinde came down when the tree fell.

They asked her, "Ntombinde, what happened?"

She said, "They buried me in the ochre pit. As soon as I entered the pit to dig, they buried me and then departed. The dog that we had taken with us came back. I tried to dig myself out but was unable to do so. Finally, a person came along who tried to dig up the ochre, and then I suddenly appeared. This person ran away; she went and hid. I came out, I left the place and climbed this tree, because I feared to return home."

"Who is it who buried you?"

"It is they."

"Which one?"

"It was all of them. They suddenly decided to bury me. I don't know which one began it all."

They went home with her. When they got home, they shut her in a house so that those girls who had buried her should not see her.

When those girls came back, the mother asked, "Speak clearly! What did you do with Ntombinde?"

They said, "Did we not say, mother, that she's at uncle's home?"

It was said then, "Go and get her then, say that I want her here now!"

They went. They reached the home of their mother. They tried to think what they would say because, actually, their story was just talk.

"What plan shall we use so that mother will believe that she is there?"

When they reached that place, they sat down. They greeted them, and there was a response.

They said, "Where are you going?"

They said, "We're merely paying a visit."

Time passed; the sun set.

They slept there overnight. In the morning, they woke up and said, "Stay well. There is work to be done at home. They had said we should hurry and not stay many days."

They said, "Oh!"

The girls departed to return home. When they reached home, they were asked, "Where is Ntombinde?"

"We don't know where she disappeared."

They said, "And they too don't know. But when she left us, she said she was going to the home of uncle."

"You are mischievous!"

They dug a hole at home here, and they covered it with branches, they put branches over the hole. They said, "Now then, regarding this hole: As you jump over the hole, say, 'Ntombinde did go to the home of her uncle!' just as you jump over the hole. If you are telling the truth, you won't fall in. But if you did something to Ntombinde, as you are jumping over, you will fall in, and we will bury you and kill you!"

They refused to play, saying, "What shall we do?"

They were afraid to admit it.

So they said, "Make us jump! We don't care! After all, we knew nothing about it."

They were caused to stand in order. The first one tried, but she fell in. So did the second: she too fell in. And when the other one tried to run, they caught her and threw her in also and filled the hole with soil.

Then they brought Ntombinde out and gave her food. They gave thanks. The story has ended.

39

The Man Who Passed the Night in the Middle of the Sea[142]

Tigre (Ethiopia)[143]

Abunawas was very clever. And when the chief of his country heard of his cleverness, he sent messengers to him, saying, "Tell him: 'The chief says this to you: Come to me quickly and in a hurry. But do not come to me when the sun shines, nor come to me when there is shadow. And do not come to me walking on your feet, nor come to me riding on a beast. If you come to me in one of these ways, fear for your life!'" The messengers brought this word to Abunawas. Then Abunawas took a large net-bag, and he sat in it and tied it up. And he said, "The net-bag in which I am sitting, fasten it loosely with a rope to the neck of a camel." When they had fastened it, he went to the chief swinging on the camel's neck. And the chief was astonished at his cleverness.

Two men wagered in this way:

The one said to his companion, "If you pass one night in the middle of the sea, I'll give you these cattle of mine. But if you do not, then you will give me your cattle."

His companion said to him, "All right."

And they agreed to this.

But afterward, the one who had said he would pass the night in the middle of the water was afraid he would die. But not to pass the night in the water would mean he would have to pay what they had agreed upon.

So he asked an old woman, "I have made a bet. What, to you, seems the best thing that I should do?"

The old woman said to the man, "On the shore of the sea in which you are to pass the night, one of your relatives should kindle a fire, keeping it burning all night without letting it burn low. And you must always look into the flame of the fire. Then you will not die, but you'll be warm all night."

The man said, "Very well."

Then, during the night for which they had made the wager, he went down to the sea.

His mother made a fire on the shore opposite him, and she kept it burning all night long.

And her son, having his head above the water, passed the night looking at the fire.

To ensure that he did not come out of the water, there were watchmen standing near him on the land all night.

And when morning came, the man came out of the water, living.

And he said to the man with whom he had made the bet, "Now then, give me your cattle! I have been in the middle of the sea all night, until the morning."

But the other answered, "I shall not give you the cattle. You looked at the fire all night, and that is the reason you came out of it safely."

But the one who had passed the night in the water said, "When did I warm myself at the fire? Its heat was too far from me to reach me. I have fulfilled our wager."

The other replied, "I shall not give you anything, because you passed the night looking at the fire."

And all the people around them said, "That is true. Because you saw the fire, he need not give you anything."

They brought their case before the judge, and he said the same thing to them.

So the man who had passed the night in the water went home sad.

Afterwards, he went to Abunawas, saying, "This happened to me," and he told him all.

Abunawas said to him, "I have a remedy for you. You shall find it!"

Now Abunawas sent a message into all the land of his people, saying, "On such and such a day, I shall have a feast. I invite you to it."

On the day that he had named, he had cattle and goats killed, and rice was also boiled. To the servants at the table, he said, "Without my giving orders to you, do not pass even a gland! And all that you have boiled, hang up before the eyes of the people."

Then all the people gathered and seated themselves around the house of Abunawas.

But Abunawas sat in the house, keeping silent.

And the servants hung up in front of the people the meats that were cooked, and the people were glad and said, "Abunawas has prepared good meats for us."

But when it was dinner time, the servants did not bring the food near the people. So all the people became hungry. But they waited, saying, "Now, even now Abunawas will come out and have the meal given to us."

When the day waned and all the people complained of hunger, they said to a friend of Abunawas who was with them, "Go in for us to your friend, and tell him, 'They ask you: What have we done to you? Why have you done this to us?'"

The friend went in to him and said this to Abunawas.

And Abunawas answered, "Tell them, 'He says this to you: Are you not satisfied by all these meats that you have smelled while they were cooked and that are now hanging in front of you?'"

The friend of Abunawas returned to his company and reported to them what Abunawas had said.

They all said, "How do people become satisfied by sight? And what they have not eaten: in what way does it reach them?"

Then Abunawas came out to them and said, "If you know that men do not become satisfied by sight only, why have you kept back from the man who passed the night in the water the cattle of his wager, arguing, 'You have seen the fire'?"

All the people said, "That is right. No one becomes satisfied by sight, nor warm."

And they had the cattle given to the man who had passed the night in the middle of the sea.

Then Abunawas had the meal given to the people.

And after they had eaten, they went each to his family.

In this way, Abunawas, by his cleverness, made justice be done to the man.

This is what they say.

40

The Hare and the Lion[144]

Tswana (Botswana)[145]

The hare once said to the lion, "Come, let us make a fold for the beasts."

The lion agreed.

The hare cried, "Fold, make yourself!"

And the fold made itself.

Then the hare said to the lion, "You lie down and pretend to be dead, and I will call all the beasts together. Then rise up and kill them."

The lion lay down as if he were dead, and the hare climbed the poles at the opening into the fold and cried, "Beeee! Come and see Malacwi dead!"

Malacwi is the name by which the lion was known to the hare and the other beasts of the field.

All the beasts of the field came and entered the fold.

But the tortoise took a stalk of grass and poked it into the lion from behind, and the lion thereupon drew itself away from the stalk.

Then the tortoise said to its young one, "Little tortoise, my child, let us get away from here, for there is no dead thing that can draw itself in on being touched."

And they went away.

Then Malacwi arose and killed the beasts.

The hare said, "Let us say, 'House, build yourself.'"

The lion replied, "Just speak. You're the one who knows everything."

Then the rain came, and the lion said, "Let the house be roofed."

To this, the hare answered, "I know how to call the grass."

And the lion asked that the grass be called.

The hare then said, "Grass, mow yourself."

And the grass was not only mown, it brought itself to the place where they were.

Then the lion said, "Let the roof be thatched."

But the hare answered, "Ah, that is far beyond me."

The lion was astonished, and said, "What do you mean? Is it possible that one who knows how to make things make themselves does not know how to make a thatch put itself on?"

Then the lion climbed on the roof while the hare remained below twisting sinews together.

While he was doing this, he said to the lion, "Let sparks come through the rafters lest you perish with cold."

To this, the lion agreed.

So the hare made a fire, and on the coals he grilled some fat meat. When the meat was cooked, he tied the sinew to the lion. Then he placed a piece of the fat meat on the end of a stick and said to the lion, "May I swallow this, my elder brother?"

But the lion, in a fierce voice, cried out, "Put it down!"

The hare pulled the sinew with which he had tied the lion, and the lion, feeling the pain, cried out, "Oshe! Oshe!" whereupon the hare broke off the branch from a piece of wood and said to it, "May this piece of wood kill my elder brother."

He went on doing this until the lion was dead.

When he had killed the lion, the hare ate all the food, and after the lion's skin had become dried up and all the flesh and bones had fallen out of it, he entered the skin in the evening and went to the house of the hyena.

Speaking in a gruff voice, he said, "Push out your food, push out your food!"

The hyena pushed it out, and the little hyenas spent the night hungry. This went on for some time, until the little ones became quite thin.

Now one day, when the sun was well up and the mother hyena was away, the little ones saw the hare come out of the shriveled-up skin and dance and sing, "I am a great hare. I have conquered the hyena and the lion. I conquer the hyena."

When evening came, the little hyenas told their mother what they had seen and heard, and she said, "Well, we shall see."

Later, the hare in the lion's skin came speaking as formerly, but the hyena took no notice, just remained at ease. But she took the stone on which her pot stood on the fire, and threw it at the skin, whereupon came a hollow sound from the skin. And the hare burst out and fled, leaving the skin behind.

The hare fled in earnest and went to visit another hyena. He found the hyena's wife weeding in the garden patch and said to her, "Mother, seeing you are alone, please let me nurse your children for you. Afterward, I'll cook for you."

The hyena agreed.

The next day, the hyena went to her garden as usual and left the hare with the children. The hare looked well after them that day.

On the next day, she again left the children in the charge of the hare. The young hyenas were all of one color, all being very dark skinned.

And on this day, the hare killed one of them.

When, toward evening, the mother returned home, the hare set flesh before her. She asked where the meat had come from, to which the hare replied that while the children were playing he had gone out and hunted young duiker.

"Well! well!" said the hyena.

When the hyena had eaten, she called for her children that she might suckle them. The hare went to bring the children.

Now, as there were ten children, he brought one twice.

The next day, he remained with them again and killed a second one. This he also cooked and gave to the mother, and once more she ate.

When she called for her young ones to be brought, he brought the eighth one three times, thus making up the number ten.

Day after day, he killed one of the cubs and acted as formerly.

At last, when none was left, the hare was told to bring his younger brothers, that they might suck his mother.

The hare appeared as if he did not understand and asked who were his younger brothers.

The hyena replied, "Your younger brothers, whom you know."

"I don't know them, mother," was the hare's reply.

"Oh, hare," said the hyena, "they are those little black younger brothers of yours."

To which the hare answered, "Don't you know that you have eaten them all, and the last of them is the one now in your mouth?"

The hyena snatched up something, saying she would kill him, but the hare ran away with the hyena on his heels.

The hare found a hollow tree and hid himself in it.

Then the hyena came to the tree. She asked whether anyone was inside, saying to the hollow of the tree, "Mmamorotoroto of the hollow, have you seen a hare pass this way?"

She asked this because she saw protruding eyes, though not the body of the hare.

Then an answer came from the hollow of the tree: "Where see we the hare, we of the protruding eyes?"

The hyena drew near and said, "May this not be it?"

Whereupon the hare leaped out and ran for his life. The hyena followed hard behind him and drove him in the direction of the river.

When he got to the river, the hare changed himself into a large round stone on the bank of the river. Along came the hyena, and she saw the stone.

She cried out, "Oh, one might possibly see the hare on the other side of the river."

So she took the stone and threw it across the river, saying as she did so, "Freeeeee! Tee!"

The hare stood up on the other side, stood upright, and said, "I knew that it would be you, my mother, who would help me to cross the river. Has not my elder sister helped me across the swollen stream"?

And the hyena's heart almost broke.

A Xhosa storyteller, October 20, 1975

41

Spider[146]

Vai (Liberia)[147]

There was a spider. And a great famine came into the country so that there was no rice, no cassadas, no plantains, no palm-cabbage, no meat, no victuals: a great famine had come into the country. The spider and his wife had been begetting children for a long time: a hundred children. There was no food in the country for them to give to the children.

The spider became sick—it was a feigned sickness.[148]

He said to his wife, "I shall die."

And his wife said, "Do not die. We will work."

The spider said, "No, I shall die." And he said to his wife, "When I have died, do not place me in a reclining position. Instead, set me upright in the hole and lay boards on me, then put earth on the boards."

His wife consented. The spider died. The woman said to her children, "Dig a hole."

And they dug a hole, and they set the spider in the hole: they did not place him in a reclining position, they *set* him in the hole. With boards, they covered the hole.

Then, when evening came, the spider came out of the hole and went to a marsh far away.

He was still alive: he had not died.

He went and met a great woman, a chief. The woman possessed very much rice, very much rice was in her farm, and very much was in the store, and there were very many cassadas in the farm. But the woman was barren; she had no children.

The spider asked, "My mother, where are your children?"

She said, "I have no children."

He said, "I have a medicine. I will give it to you. Drink it, and you will become with child and give birth."

The woman said, "Give me the medicine. When I give birth, if I give birth to a child, I will give you a whole shed full of rice, two farms of cassada, and a great many plantains."

The spider, because of the famine, agreed. He went away to take out the medicine by the way, and then he returned to the woman. She killed a goat and cooked rice for the spider and said, "Spider, here is rice for you."

The spider ate the rice; he was satisfied.

Then he put the medicine into a bowl, put water into the bowl, mashed the medicine into a bowl, put water into that bowl, then mashed the medicine.

He said to the woman, "Bring a strip of cloth."

He tied it around the woman's eyes and said, "Drink the medicine. And when you have drunk the medicine, you will see me no more. I am going far away. In six months, you will give birth to a male child. Then I shall return so that you can give me my rice and all my victuals."

The woman agreed. She took the bowl and drank the medicine.

The spider jumped into the bowl, and the woman swallowed the spider.

The spider was inside the woman.

And the woman brought forth a child: it was the spider himself.

The woman gave him water to drink; she cooked excellent rice and gave it to the spider to eat. The spider had been within her: her baby was the spider.

The woman did not know that her baby was the spider.

There is an animal in the forest, his name is deer. He is cunning.

The deer said, "I shall go and see the woman's child; he has been eating the woman's rice for six months." The deer arrived and said, "My mother, I have come to see your child."

The woman handed her child to the deer.

The deer looked at the child, and he saw that it was a spider. He handed the child to the woman. The woman took the child and laid it within cloths.

The deer went far away to a town, took a switch, returned, then took the cloth from on the baby and flogged him well. The baby ran and went far away. The deer said to the woman, "It was a spider, it was no child. The spider was an impostor."

The spider went to his wife, hear!

All his wife's rice had become ripe, she had very many fowls, she beat rice, and her children killed animals for meat. The woman cooked the rice, she cooked the meat, she put the rice into a bowl and put the meat into the rice.

The spider came in one evening and met his wife while she was eating rice. He pushed his wife's hand, passed on, and stood there. The wife put her hand into the rice. The spider struck his wife's hand again and said to his wife, "I died long ago and have now returned."

The wife did not reply.
The wife's child said, "My mother, it is my father."
The wife said, "No, your father died long ago."
The spider came, and said to his wife, "I am the spider."
The wife said, "The spider died long ago."
The spider is an impostor, hear!
Finished.

42

In Quest of a Wife[149]

Xhosa (South Africa)[150]

BY NONGENILE MASITHATHU ZENANI

Now for a story. . . .

In a certain homestead was a young man who wanted a wife. But his father did not want to take a wife for him. His father wanted the youth to work for himself, to get his own dowry.

The young man spoke to some other men: "Let's go and find work! My father doesn't want to get a wife for me; he wants me to work for myself."

The other young men agreed to take this journey. That group traveled then, and after a while, as they walked along, they heard something speaking: "Beneath the rock! Beneath the rock!"

The youth who had gathered the others together said, "Something's talking. It says, 'Beneath the rock!' Do you hear it? It keeps saying, 'Beneath the rock!'"

One of the others said, "What do we care about something that says, 'Beneath the rock'? We're looking for work!"

"Don't bother us about things that are beneath a rock," said another. "We care nothing about them!"

Again, this thing said, "Look! Look, beneath the rock! Please look beneath the rock!"

These men started smoking. They lit their pipes, then continued their journey.

But the other young man looked about, and he finally saw the thing that had been speaking. He saw just a portion of it; he saw its eyes.

It said, "Remove this rock! It's crushing me!"

He took pity and removed the rock. But it was a snake! This thing that was being crushed by the rock was a snake.

The young man went on his way—and the snake followed him. It wanted to eat this man!

It said, "Stop!"

He said, "What do you want?"

"I was caught beneath that rock for a long time! Now I'm starved! I'm going to eat *you!*"

The young man ran then; he fled from the snake.

"What's the matter with this snake? I helped it, and now it wants to eat me!"

The youth hurried on then, and he happened to meet a cow—an old cow, eating alone. There were no other beasts around, and this cow was very thin.

He said, "Cow! Cow, please help me! Please trample on this snake for me! It's coming to eat me! It's chasing me—even though I helped it! The snake was being crushed by a rock, and I pulled the rock off, I removed the rock! The snake was being crushed by the rock! And now it wants to eat me!"

The cow said, "That's what happens to do-gooders! Their good deeds boomerang on them! Look at me, see how I've ended up! All alone here! I used to be a milk cow, I gave a lot of milk! And I was loved by the children; milk was squirted from my teat into their mouths! Now, I've become thin, my milk has dried up, and they've discarded me, they've left me alone here! They don't even think of me now; they don't come out here to bring me home. They drive the others home and leave me here by myself. They say I'm nothing, I'm worthless. Go on your way, young man! I'm where I am today because of my kindness. Go on your way!"

That fellow passed on then, and he could no longer see his comrades. They had left him when he had remained behind listening to that snake. Now he traveled alone.

Further along, he saw a horse. It was standing, head up, and was as feeble as the old cow. It was an old horse.

The young man went up to the horse: "Horse."

It said, "Hnn?"

"Help me, I'm being pursued by a snake!"

"Why is the snake chasing you?"

"It was under a rock—under a rock, over there! It asked me to lift the rock, because the rock was crushing it. I raised the rock, and now the snake says that it wants to eat me!"

The horse said, "Well, fellow of my father, look at me! I used to be a race horse! I used to be yoked to a cart by myself! that's how strong I was! Whenever there was a race, I used to gallop ahead, and they would come back with much money because of me! But when my strength began to ebb, and when I became the decrepit thing that you see here, they discarded me, threw me away! They used to feed me maize; they don't do that anymore. They just stare at me. They don't bring me home from the veld now; they just stare at me. If I should die, they wouldn't care. That's the reward for kindness! It just turns on the doer! Look after yourself, my friend, there's no way I can help you!"

The young man passed on then; he journeyed on. Then he saw a dirty young fellow walking along, walking and playing his harp.

He said, "You, playing on your harp! Wait for me!"

But this thing was an *imbulu*.[151] The *imbulu* said, "Who are you?"

"Well, I'm a stranger. As I was journeying along with some friends of mine, I heard something that said, 'Beneath the rock! Beneath the rock! Look beneath the—' and when I looked, I saw only the eyes. This thing said, 'Lift the rock!' So I lifted the rock, and it came out. But it was a snake! The rock had been crushing a snake! Now that snake wants to eat me— even though I saved it from that rock!"

The *imbulu* said, "What a fool you are! What's the matter with you? You know that snakes bite humans! Why, then, go ahead and lift the rock that's crushing a snake? You should have poked at the snake while it was under the rock, you should have killed it there! Well, this is what happens when you're generous. You're a fool, young man! But I do have a suggestion. Let's just allow this snake to catch up with us here. I want to see it for myself. Just stop running now."

The young man stopped there, and the snake arrived.

The *imbulu* said, "Snake, what is this? What do you want?"

"Well, I'm hungry! I want to eat this person!"

"What has he done?"

"We're supposed to be traveling together, but he keeps walking ahead of me!"

"What happened in the beginning?"

"I was trapped under a stone. I was caught there; a rock was crushing me."

"Where's that rock? Let's just investigate this; let's see if you're telling the truth! He'll not run away from you anymore while I'm here."

They departed then; they went back to that rock to clarify precisely what had occurred. They had come a great distance from that rock, and finally they came to it again.

The young man said, "Here's that rock."

The *imbulu* said, "Now tell us, snake, in what position were you when this fellow relieved you? Just simulate the way it was."

The snake went under the rock and simulated the way it had been.

"It was just like this. It was this way!"

The *imbulu* said, "And the rock—how was it placed?"

The snake said, "My body's aching! It's just too painful! Let's not include the rock!"

The *imbulu* said, "No, don't worry, we'll put the rock on your body very gently. I just want to see how the rock was placed on you."

This fellow took the rock and put it on the snake. "It was just like this. This is the way the rock was."

The *imbulu* immediately jumped on the stone!

He said, "Crush the snake! Let it die here! That's what you should have done to begin with! That's what you should have done in the first place! What was the matter with you—that you released the snake? Have you no brains? Well, go on your way!" So they departed.

Then the *imbulu* said, "What will you give me? You were about to be killed by the snake that you saved from the rock, and I rescued you."

"Well, I'll give you something when I return."

"Do you know my homestead?"

"Why don't you tell me where it is?"

They journeyed on, and passed by the *imbulu*'s homestead. When they got there, the young man saw that the *imbulu* had two children there.

The *imbulu* said, "This is my homestead. Look, here are my children. When you've fulfilled your work contract, come back here and show me what you're thanking me with."

The young man went on his way; he went and found his job without seeing the other men he had been traveling with. He arrived at the homestead of an important person.

He arrived and said that he was looking for work, that he had started off as a member of a group and had been left behind. He had not seen the others again; he did not know the direction they had traveled. He had not seen them again because they were two days ahead of him. And they had not waited for him.

That man said, "I'm glad that you want work, young man. I do have work here. I'll hire you. This is what you must do: go and get for me two feathers from Nine-Feathers."

"Nine-Feathers?"

"That's right."

"Where is he?"

"You must find him! He lives in big forests. Return here with two feathers. If you do that, you'll have done the equivalent of ten years of work! And you'll receive payment!"

The young man traveled then, carrying provisions, seeking that thing. His provisions consisted of roasted mealies and ground boiled corn. He journeyed, seeking that head, the head that had nine feathers. He walked and walked, traveling, asking about Nine-Feathers again and again.

Finally, he came to some stumps that were fighting—by themselves! No one was manipulating them!

He said. "This is the first time I've seen stumps fighting! What can I do about this?"

He went on, and came to an old woman.

She said, "Please wipe these eyes of mine, child who is in difficulty! I'm in difficulty, too, because of my eyes!"

It happened that this young man was a respectful fellow, not haughty. He had reverence for old people; he was deferential to her. He went to her and wiped her eyes; he wiped her eyes with his coat.

The old woman said, "The thing that you're wiping me with, your coat, it's rather rough on my skin. It's making my eyes ache!"

So he wiped her eyes with his hand; he wiped her gently.

She said, "You see, my child, I know where you're going even without your telling me. You're going to Nine-Feathers! You are to get two of his feathers. But nobody ever returns from Nine-Feathers' place! No one has ever gone there and returned! Now this is what you must do: there is a tree, a big tree at Nine-Feathers' place. If you're lucky, you'll find him asleep. Don't go directly to the house. If you don't see him, go to this tree and cut bits from the tree and put them into your pocket. Then go to the house. You'll be asked where you have come from, and you should answer that you're looking for work. If he is there, don't say that you're looking for feathers! If he isn't there, tell the woman that you've come for those feathers, and tell her the number of feathers that you want. Then chew on the piece of the tree a little—don't chew a lot! Then wipe yourself with it. You must keep this piece of the tree! When Nine-Feathers appears, he'll want to fight you outside. Go out then, and he'll follow you with his sticks. If you don't have your own sticks, he'll give you some—and he'll insist that you fight. Now I must warn you that all he has to do is to beat a human being once, and that's it—you're dead! Now then, before you go outside with him, take a bite of this piece of the tree, and swallow it. When he's ready to fight with you, he'll first go to that tree and take a bite from it. If he's the one who bites the tree first, you'll die. If *you* bite first, then you'll not die."

The young man said, "Thank you, grandmother! Thank you for telling me something I didn't know. I didn't even know where his homestead is,

I've never been there before. I don't know this person; I don't know what kind of person he is. I just want work because I'm in difficulty. My father won't get a wife for me; he wants me to work for myself. He had to work for himself; that's how he came to have my mother. And that's what I'm working at now."

The young man went on then; he journeyed. And when he was close to Nine-Feathers' house, he saw that tree, the one that the old woman had mentioned. She had told him, "There is a tall tree at that homestead, but there's no name for it." He went carefully, watching to see whether Nine-Feathers was about.

"How can I get that bark from this tree?"

He walked on slowly, slowly, looking this way and that, and then he went directly to the tree and cut off two pieces of bark. He put them into his pocket. Then he went to the house. When he got there, he greeted the woman who was there. This woman responded softly; she raised her hand and gestured to him; she pointed to her sleeping husband behind her. She gestured to the young man, indicating that he should not speak loudly.

She said, "Where are you from?"

He said, "I've come here to find work."

"Why?"

"I want some feathers."

The woman said, "Yu! How many?"

This child said, "I want four." He asked for more than he had been sent for; he had been told to get two feathers. But he said, "I want four."

She said, "Mhm!" Then, "Come around here," and she covered him up. She covered him and said, "I'm afraid this man's about to wake up!"

This youth sat there.

The thing with many feathers on his head woke up suddenly. "What's that smell? I smell a human being!"

The woman said, "It's a person who's come here seeking work."

He said, "Where is this person?"

She said, "Here he is!" and she produced him.

He said, "So, we've met today! You've come to seek work? Well then, you've got it!" So he said, and he went outside. He went outside; he went out with his sticks. He had four of them, two for one, two for the other. He said, "Let's fight!"

The young man had already taken a bite of this tree and swallowed it. This other one went over to the tree and chopped off a piece. He chewed it and swallowed it.

Then he said, "Let's fight!"

This young man hit Nine-Feathers; he showered him with blows. And so that person died; he passed out.

When Nine-Feathers had died, this woman said, "This is a great day! Finally, someone has come here and helped me. I've really become tired of living with this thing that eats people. I've grown tired of it. I've been rescued now; I've been saved by this child—where has he come from? This is the one, friends, who attacked this thing that has been destroying the people who come to this home. It has been said that the feathers are valuable; people have come here again and again for those feathers."

The young man then plucked ten feathers, and he went home.

When he came to that old woman who had spoken with him, the one whose eyes he had wiped, she spoke to him: "My child, go well. Do you see now that you got the work you sought? You got even more than you wanted. You'll never have to work again, ever! From this day, you'll never have to work again. And your children, too, they won't have to work. How many feathers do you have?"

The young man said, "There are ten."

She said, "As I said, with all those feathers, you'll never have to work!"

"Don't you have any humor in your eyes now, grandmother? Is there anything in your eyes that I can wipe for you?" So said this young man.

She said, "Yes, you may do that. You may wipe my eyes, my child."

And he wiped her eyes again; he wiped her eyes with his hand. He wiped her eyes; he wiped the eyes of this old woman.

Then he journeyed on, and again he passed by those two stumps that were fighting.

He went straight home. He arrived at that homestead, and as he arrived he hid eight of the feathers. He produced only two of them.

He said, "I've come back, my lord."

"Oh, you've returned, my child!"

"Yes."

"Did you get them?"

"Yes."

"Let me see."

And he produced the feathers.

When this fellow saw them, he said, "I can't speak with you while I'm alone. The family of this homestead must also be present when I speak with you, young man. Sleep! The others aren't here right now. They've gone about their separate businesses. They'll return tomorrow, so please sleep now. I want them all to be here; I want all the people of this home to be here when I speak with you about the work that you've done for me."

So that young man slept.

The next morning, the children of this home were all gathered together there.

This man addressed his oldest son, and said, "My servant has returned, my son."

Then, when they had all arrived: "My oldest son, the young man whom I hired has come back. And now that he has returned, I want you to see with your own eyes the great thing that he has done. All of you are familiar with this business."

So saying, he took those two feathers of Nine-Feathers. He put them down and said, "Here's the achievement of this young man. Now tell me what I should give him. Speak, tell me, boys."

These young men answered him, "Well, father, this is too much for us. Even one feather—"

"Not to mention two!"

"Well, we're unable to talk about it."

"Sometimes we're able to offer opinions, but regarding this matter— it's just too much for us."

"We'll just listen to what you say, and we'll agree with whatever you decide to do."

Their father said, "Well, my children, I'm going to move from this homestead. I'll leave this young man here; this'll be his homestead from now on. He has purchased it completely with his deed. As for me, I'll build my own homestead, and I'll build homesteads for you, too. The two feathers will take care of all that. We'll ask him to allow us to have one room in this homestead while we prepare the places where we'll build our homesteads."

That was the father's speech; that is what he said to his sons.

One of the young men said, "I hear you, father."

Then the father said to the young man who had obtained the feathers, "Young man, this homestead is yours now—all of it. Everything that is here is yours, no matter what it is—the fields are yours, the garden, everything at home here, the stock. You take it all! Everything that is in this homestead is yours. The only thing that is mine is my eating dish and my sleeping blankets. That is all. The things that I have already planted, those that have ripened I've already taken; those that I've planted over there, the ones that aren't ripe yet, those belong to you! You may give me some of those things when I ask for them, but that is up to you. The things are yours! For now, I would like to borrow one house to stay in temporarily."

The young man said, "No, father, I would not ask you to stay in a cramped place, as if you had been driven out of this homestead. You haven't been driven out; you're just recognizing the value of my labor. Stay as you have been staying, and build your new homesteads. Leave only when you have finished the construction, when you are ready to move into the new houses, when everything has been completed. I shall just ask one more thing of you, father. I shall request that you suggest a young woman for me to marry. You know the homesteads around here. It is not good just to marry a young woman for her looks, if her background and history are not proper. One must know the lions from which she has come. Now I am asking you, father, get such a woman for me."

That old man agreed to do so. He said, "All right, my fellow."

And he got a young woman for him, a young woman he thought proper. He knew her home, he knew the people of her homestead, and the character of those people.

The young man married that woman then, and she came with her bridal party. She became the wife of the young man. She was very deferential to the old man; it was as if she were his daughter-in-law. And the old man treated the young man as if he were his own son.

Time passed, and they were very happy in this homestead. That daughter-in-law was very respectful to the older people; she treated them as if they were her husband's own parents.

The old man built his own homestead; he built it well. He even planted the fields in his new homestead before he moved. By the time he went there, nothing was lacking. He remained here with this young man during the period before he moved and became his friend. They remained friends even after the old man had departed and gone to his own home. The young man had never gone back to his own home; he remained here.

After a long time, he journeyed with his wife to visit his father.

When he got to his home, he said, "Well, father, I have come to visit you. When I left here to go to work, I actually worked for only one month. I took a wife that very month, because I had got very heavy work—it was piece work. On the day that I escaped with my life, I obtained everything that I had lacked. If you weren't my father, I'd even say that I'm above you. I'm very much ahead of you; you'll never come anywhere near me. No one will come near me. Even your son can never come close to me in wealth. You must come and visit my homestead, see what it is like, take a look at it. I lack nothing. And I want to give you some things that you do not have. You shall never lack anything as long as I am living."

His father thanked him and said, "Child, I thank you. I did not get you a wife back then because I wanted you to grow up a little, to mature. I did not get a wife myself until I was mature. I wanted you to grow up a little; it wasn't that I didn't want you to have a wife."

His father journeyed then; he went to see his son's homestead. When he got there, he looked it over; he walked about throughout that homestead, admiring this, leaving that alone, going over to the cattle folds. There were some cattle that were away at the outposts, cattle that do not come back home, that stay out there by themselves. The only time he would fetch cattle from their number was when he was going to slaughter. The father of this young man went to the outposts as well; he saw everything.

Then his father departed. He was given six milk cows by his son, cows that would nourish him.

He said, "Go home with them, father, and don't eat food without milk. You're getting old."

His father thanked him again and felt very good. He went home.

The young man remained happy and expressed respect for the people of the homestead at which he had worked. They were all very fond of each other, as if they were people who had always been together.

The story has ended; it has ended.

43

Children of the Anthill[152]

Xhosa (South Africa)

BY NONGENILE MASITHATHU ZENANI

Now for a story . . .

A woman of a certain homestead was pregnant. Because she had become pregnant before getting married, she realized that her condition was shameful. She hid her growing stomach, she attempted to disguise her pregnancy.

The months went by and her stomach became bigger; her breasts also revealed that she was pregnant. She tended now to remain by herself, to hide her condition from other people. Time passed for her, time passed and she continued her efforts to conceal her situation.

Then, after a time, she began to feel birth pains. When she experienced those severe pains, she knew that something was going to happen. She therefore left her home, and journeyed a great distance. She went a long way from her home.

She came to a certain place, and the pains were becoming stronger. She began to dig into an anthill; she dug, she dug and dug, making a kind of house in that anthill. When she had finished digging, the birth pains quickened, and she struggled to give birth. Finally, she gave birth to two children, a boy and a girl. And when she had delivered these children, she wrapped some of her rags about them, and left them there in that anthill.

Now that she was no longer pregnant, she presented an appearance of someone who was blameless, one who had done nothing wrong. She remained at her home.

As for the children, they grew up there at the anthill; they became older, and in time were able to crawl. They had to eat soil, because there was no one in that place to feed them. The children grew up, eating the soil. They crawled, after a time they walked, and finally they developed into children who were mentally awake. They observed the things that passed by, as they remained in the anthill.

After a long time, the boy began to travel about, hunting. He hunted birds: he would strike them down, then bring them to his sister. They would roast the birds.

Time passed, time passed, and the boy realized that something might happen to them at this stage of their lives. They were still alone, and their minds were developing, even though they continued to live in this anthill. He contemplated what he should do, because they were getting more and more mature.

This child said, "Sister, this land that we live in contains a great many things. You know that I've been wandering about every day, then returning here at dusk. I have found that just about everything is present in this country. There are ogres here, too, creatures that eat people! There are dangers in this land. You must continue to close the door of this place until I return from my trips. Don't open that door until you hear *my* voice! Whenever I've gone off, for the sake of your security, you should not open the door until I say a certain thing. You know my voice. I'll stand by the door, and say,

'Open! Open!
Open! Open!
At the rock with two openings,
Open!
Where no swallows dwell,
Open!'

Now, just in case someone overhears me saying this, and attempts to imitate my voice, note the tone of my voice carefully."

His sister understood his warning.

So it was that he continued to travel about, seeking various things to eat. He would go hunting, then return. When he returned, he would stand there at the door which his sister had closed, and would say,

"Open! Open!
Open! Open!
At the rock with two openings,
Open!
Where no swallows dwell,
Open!"

And his sister would open the door.

"Child of my mother!" he would say, and they would eat then and be happy.

And so time passed for them.

But these children had already been smelled by the fabulous beasts that dwelled in this land, these ogres. The smells of the children were very pleasant to these creatures. They sensed the presence of people by their odors, and they would hunt these people. One of these creatures had heard the song that was sung at the anthill, that the song would be sung, then the anthill would be opened. He told his fellow beasts, and they determined to go to that anthill when the sister was alone, when the other one had departed.

One of the beasts went there, it stood by the door and said,

"Open! Open!
Open! Open!
At the rock with two openings,
Open!
Where no swallows dwell,
Open!"

But the girl refused to open the door

The beast tried again, it tried and tried and tried, but the girl utterly refused to open the door, hearing quite clearly that the singer was not her brother.

The beast departed then, and after he had gone, the girl's brother returned.

"Open! Open!
Open! Open!
At the rock with two openings,
Open!
Where no swallows dwell,
Open!"

She opened the door, his sister opened the door, and the boy entered.

His sister told him, "Oh, child of my mother, something came by here! It spoke with a gruff voice here at the doorway, saying that I should open the door and let it in. I determined not to open the door, because I knew that it wasn't you! Then that thing left, it shuffled off!"

Her brother said, "Do not open the door, even a little!"

That creature went back to its fellows, and asked some of its companions for advice. Did they, perhaps, have a plan that would enable him to get this "bird" that refused to open the door? How could he obtain a voice that resembled that of the bird? He heard the song, he saw the way the door was opened. He realized that the girl recognized that the beast's voice was that of a beast, that that was the reason the door was not opened.

One of those creatures gave him some advice then: "Your voice is too gruff, too loud! You must heat an axe, heat it until it's red-hot. Then, while it's still red-hot, swallow it. It'll come out below, through your anus."

That creature swallowed the axe then because it wanted that "bird"; it swallowed the axe. But the axe was not very hot; he swallowed it just as it was turning red. Consequently, the axe did not go right through his body and come out of the anus.

The beast traveled, he went over there to that place. Again he sang the song, but this time, too, its voice was gruff:

"Open! Open!
At the rock with two openings,
Open!
Where no swallows dwell,
Open!"

The girl did not open the door. She realized again that the voice was not that of her brother.

That beast departed once more, frustrated again. Then the girl's brother arrived:

"Open! Open!
At the rock with two openings,
Open!
Where no swallows dwell,
Open!"

She opened the door.

The girl again narrated to him what had occurred: "Once again, during your absence, a creature arrived." She thought it was a different creature, she did not realize that it was the same one as before. "This thing also had a rough voice, as it told me that I should open the door. I didn't open it. Then the creature departed."

"You were right not to open the door. You must never open it, except for me!" her brother said emphatically, again instructing her that she must not open the door.

When the beast arrived at his home, he told the others that the door was again not opened by the girl. It was clear that his voice was not yet what it should be.

The other one said, "You didn't do it right. I said that you should heat an axe until it's red-hot, then to swallow it so that it comes out below."

He heated the axe, then, and it was truly red-hot this time. He swallowed it, and the axe came out of his anus. Then he went again to this "bird"; he arrived there and stood at the door:

"Open! Open!
At the rock with two openings,
Open!
Where no swallows dwell,
Open!"

The girl opened the door, thinking that it was the voice of her brother.

But something else entered! It was a thing that had furry ears that reached down to its legs! The child was alarmed.

It came right inside, then took her and put her into a sack. It carried her off on its shoulder, taking her to its home.

She was crying, and, as she was being taken away, she took a handful of ashes from the hearth. She dropped those ashes as they were going, making a line with them that trailed after them, sprinkling the ashes until she came to the house of the ogre. When they had arrived at the ogre's house, he uncovered her, and found that the girl was exceptionally beautiful. Obviously, she should not be eaten. She ought to become his wife, "because this woman is lovely! and she might produce a fine breed of children for me!"

She was kept by the ogre then, and became his wife. She blossomed, she became even more beautiful when they decided not to eat her, when they kept her alive and appreciated her. She preferred to become the wife of this creature than be cooked. So it was, then, that she became a wife and acquired a married name: she became Nojikolo, the wife of this homestead.

Time passed, time passed for her, and she remained a wife there.

Her brother, in the meantime, had come home, and had discovered immediately the ashes in the doorway.

He said, "Oh!" It was bad news, he knew that she had been kidnapped. Still, no matter what he thought might have happened, even though he was certain that she was gone, he decided to try the song again anyway. He said,

"Open! Open!
At the rock with two openings,
Open!
Where no swallows dwell,
Open!"

Nothing happened.

He opened the door himself, and said, "My mother's child is gone! They got her today!"

Her brother sat there and cried, he cried and cried. Then he took his sticks and prepared to travel. He closed the door behind him, knowing that he could not live comfortably until he knew precisely what had happened to his sister, until he knew whether she was dead, or alive.

He followed the trail of ashes that she had dropped, and finally arrived in that country where she had been taken. When he came to the other side of a valley, his sister had a glimpse of him as she sat outside her home with her husband. She looked at her brother, and recognized his gait; she knew that it was her mother's child.

She thought, "I wonder what will be done to him?" Then she said to her husband, "My lord, do you see that person?"

The creature said that he indeed saw him.

She said, "It's a child from my country, from the neighborhood of my home. It's my minion. You see, he knows that I parted from him a long time ago, and he has come now to rejoin me. His coming should be welcomed warmly. He will do nice things for me, so that my prestige will be heightened. I must have that minion next to me."

"Oh," said her husband. "Do you say so, wife? Is that your minion?"

"Yes," the wife said. Then she said, "Ki ki ki ki ki! The wife's minion has arrived! the minion of Nojikolo!"

"Oh!" So said the great man, her husband. "Come, minion of Nojikolo! Minion of my wife, my wife of the great house!"

The "servant" approached them then, the brother played the role of the minion very well. He arrived, and was immediately welcomed and provided with privileges. A mat was spread out for him. He sat by the door, he was treated with dignity because he was valued by the wife, Nojikolo.

The next day, the creatures went hunting, and the "minion" had an opportunity to talk with his sister, discussing the possibility of escape. "I want us to go home."

His sister agreed. She had two children already, one of whom was a boy. Nojikolo said, "All right, don't worry. The people will leave this place and go off to hunt. During such hunting expeditions, my husband must go along as well. Because I don't eat human flesh, my husband must see to it that animals that I can eat will be caught. That's why he can't remain behind, he can't even think of remaining behind. So don't worry about him, he'll be gone. And I shall tell him that this minion of mine doesn't eat human flesh either."

They whispered these things to each other when the husband had gone out.

When he returned, his wife said to him, "Lord, this minion doesn't put human flesh into his mouth at all. He eats the kind of meat that I eat."

"All right, wife. We'll try to accommodate him."

So it was that the husband also went off on the hunt. And when they had all departed, only a little old woman was left behind, a woman who no longer knew how to walk, who limped and crawled along the ground. That little old woman was left behind when the others departed, going off on their hunting expedition.

When Nojikolo and her minion estimated that the creatures were far away on their hunt, the brother stopped playing the role of minion; he stood on both feet, and gathered together everything that was movable in this homestead. The wagons were inspanned, and they loaded everything that they needed on the wagons; they left behind only what they did not need. And they also rounded up all the livestock of this homestead.

The little old woman realized that something was going on when she heard the rattling of the wagons: "Really! Something is clattering!" She crawled along the ground, then peeked through the door at all the movement and commotion, the shiki-shiki and the ngxashi-ngxashi here in this homestead. Yet she knew that there was no one here except Nojikolo, a person who was unable to go anywhere. Then she saw that all of the livestock of this home was being rounded up, that it was being lined up. Nothing was being left behind!

She shuffled along, trying to reach a more or less elevated place, a hill. Then she called out, "The homestead is being robbed by the minion of Nojikolo!"

One of the creatures, far below, said, "Something seems to be calling to us from that mountain."

The little old woman repeated, "The homestead is being robbed by the minion of Nojikoooooolo!"

A creature said, "What is she saying?"

"She says that the game is below, going directly towards the forest!"

The creatures hurried off then, in groups of varying sizes and speeds.

Then the old woman called out again, "The homestead is being robbed by the minion of Nojikoooolo!"

One of them said, "What is she saying?"

"The old woman over there says that we should exchange legs! She says that a tall person should take a leg of a short person!"

They did that, then. The leg from a tall creature was snapped off and was affixed to a short creature, and the short leg was taken and attached to a tall creature. Then they walked off, each creature with one tall leg and one short leg; they limped now, they limped, and they had no speed at all because they were not moving on their own legs. Each creature moved with one long leg and one short leg.

The little old woman called out, and in the meantime the boy and his sister were far off, having completely disappeared by now.

The woman called out, "The homestead is being robbed by the minion of Nojikoooooolo!"

"What is she saying?"

"She says, 'The homestead is being robbed by the minion of Nojikolo!'"

Then, in a rush, they began to take off those legs, they fell over each other, limping, hurrying. Finally, they arrived at their home. And the little old woman told then what had happened.

They pursued the brother and sister. After a long time, the sister looked back and saw them coming: "We're in big trouble now," she said. "There are the ogres! What will happen to us?"

The ogres were all pursuing them. Their box of ogre was emptied out, they were trying everything to capture these humans.

Then the brother said, "All right, let come what may!" He was carrying a spear, so he took no action until they caught up with him. But the creatures were in disarray, some were ahead of others. He stabbed the first one that came to him. And when he had stabbed it, all the creatures died. They were all destroyed, even though he had done nothing to the others.

The brother and sister went on, then, traveling now in happiness. They arrived at their home, and, because of what they had brought back with them, they now had a homestead that was more elegant than others.

The story has ended, it has ended.

44

The King and the
Kini-kini Bird[153]

Yoruba (Nigeria)[154]

The Yoruba folk-lore tales are very numerous. The word now commonly used to mean one of these popular fables is *alo*, which more properly means a riddle, or something invented, literally something twisted, or inverted. A reciter of tales, called an *akpalo* (*kpa-alo*) 'maker of alo,' is a personage highly esteemed, and in great demand for social gatherings. Some men, indeed, make a profession of story-telling, and wander from place to place reciting tales. Such a man is termed an *akpalo kpatita*, 'one who makes a trade of telling fables.' . . .[T]he professional story-teller very often uses a drum, with the rhythm of which the pauses in the narrative are filled up. When he has gathered an audience around him, he cries out, 'My *alo* is about so-and-so,' mentioning the name of the hero or heroine of the tale; or 'My *alo* is about a man (or woman) who did so-and-so,' and, after this preface, proceeds with the recital.[155]

My *alo* is about a certain king.

One day, the king called all the birds to come and clear a piece of ground. But he forgot to call the *kini-kini* bird.[156]

All the birds came. They set to work, and they cleared a large piece of ground.

In the middle of the piece of ground was an *odan* tree. At midday, when the sun was hot and all the birds had left their work for the way, the *kini-kini* bird came and perched on the *odan* tree and began to sing:

"The king sent to invite my companions, *kini-kini.*
He assembled all the children of the folk with wings, *kini-kini.*
  Grow grass, sprout bush, *kini-kini,*
  Come, let us go to the house, *kini-kini,*
  And there we can dance the *bata*, *kini-kini.*
If the *bata* will not sound, we will dance the *dundun*, *kini-kini.*
If the *dundun* will not sound, we will dance the *gangan*, *kini-kini.*"[157]

238

Next morning, when the birds came to work, they found the grass they had cleared all grown over with grass and bush.

They went and told the king.

The king said, "That is nothing. Clear it again."

The birds went to work and cleared it again and at midday went away.

The *kini-kini* bird came back and sang his song again:

"The king sent to invite my companions, *kini-kini*.
He assembled all the children of the folk with wings, *kini-kini*.
  Grow grass, sprout bush, *kini-kini*,
  Come, let us go to the house, *kini-kini*,
  And there we can dance the *bata*, *kini-kini*.
If the *bata* will not sound, we will dance the *dundun*, *kini-kini*.
If the *dundun* will not sound, we will dance the *gangan*, *kini-kini*."

And again, the grass and bush sprang up.

Next day, the birds, when they saw what had happened, went and informed the king.

"No matter," said the king." "Clear the ground again."

A third time, the birds cleared the ground and went away, and a third time the *kini-kini* bird came and sang:

"The king sent to invite my companions, *kini-kini*.
He assembled all the children of the folk with wings, *kini-kini*.
  Grow grass, sprout bush, *kini-kini*,
  Come, let us go to the house, *kini-kini*,
  And there we can dance the *bata*, *kini-kini*.
If the *bata* will not sound, we will dance the *dundun*, *kini-kini*.
If the *dundun* will not sound, we will dance the *gangan*, *kini-kini*."

And the grass and bush sprang up.

The next day, when the birds found the ground covered with bushes, they went to the king. They asked him to give them authority to seize the person who was playing this trick.

The king said, "Very well."

Then all the birds went back to the piece of ground, and they put a great quantity of bird-lime on the *odan* tree. Then they went home.

Next morning, they came and cleared the ground again and at midday went and hid in the bushes close by.

The *kini-kini* bird came and perched on the *odan* tree. He sang his song:

"The king sent to invite my companions, *kini-kini.*
He assembled all the children of the folk with wings, *kini-kini.*
   Grow grass, sprout bush, *kini-kini,*
   Come, let us go to the house, *kini-kini,*
   And there we can dance the *bata*, *kini-kini.*
If the *bata* will not sound, we will dance the *dundun*, *kini-kini.*
If the *dundun* will not sound, we will dance the *gangan*, *kini-kini."*

And the grass and bush grew up.
   Then he wanted to fly away, but he found himself held by the bird-lime.
   All the birds flocked to the tree and saw the *kini-kini* bird. They seized him and brought him to the king. They said, "Here is the one who has caused us so much trouble."
   The king made the *kini-kini* bird come near.
   "What have I done to you," he asked, "that you should act like this?"
   The *kini-kini* bird said, "When you called all my companions to clear the ground, you left me out. Therefore, I have avenged myself."
   When the king heard this, he raised his hand to give the *kini-kini* bird a slap.
   "Pardon, pardon," said the *kini-kini* bird. "If I find any cowries, I shall give them to you. When I get any kola-nuts, I shall bring them to you."
   The king gave the bird a slap, and the *kini-kini* bird defecated cowries until the room was filled.
   "What is this?" said the king, much astonished.
   And he raised his hand again to give the *kini-kini* bird a slap.
   "I beg pardon," said the bird. "If I find any cowries, I shall give them to you. When I get any kola-nuts, I shall bring them to you."
   The king gave him a slap, and the *kini-kini* bird defecated from his body still more cowries than the first time.
   The king sent messengers through all the country and summoned all his people to assemble on the fifth day to see a marvel.
   All the people promised to come.
   Then the king put the *kini-kini* bird into a basket. He covered the top of the basket and went out. His little son, who wanted to give the *kini-kini* bird a slap himself, uncovered the basket.
   And the bird flew away.
   When the king came home, he went to the basket. He found no bird in it, and he called his son. "Where is the *kini-kini* bird?" he asked.
   The little boy answered that he had gone to play with it and that the

bird had flown away. The king took the little boy and beat him. He beat him, he beat him, and, in his anger, he cut off one of his ears.

"Go quickly!" he said. "Go quickly, and find the bird!"

He pushed him out of the house.

The boy made a little drum and went on the road to the forest. He sat down in a place in the forest where the birds were accustomed to come. And he began to beat on his drum.

The drum said,

"Tinliki, tinliki, tinli—puru.
Tinli—puru."

All the birds flocked around, and each danced in turn.

When it came to the turn of the *kini-kini* bird to dance, the *kini-kini* bird did not want to dance. All the birds begged him to dance, but he refused.

Then the boy played more quickly on the drum; he beat and beat and beat. And all the birds begged the *kini-kini* bird.

At last, the *kini-kini* bird began to yield. He twisted here and he twisted there. He flew three times around the head of the little boy. The boy continued beating as if had not noticed anything, and the *kini-kini* bird began to dance.

He turned here and twisted there. He turned, and twisted, and turned, until he came up quite close to the drum.

Then the little boy thrust out his hand and seized the *kini-kini* bird by the leg.

All the other birds flew away.

The boy brought the *kini-kini* bird to his father.

"I have caught him," he said. "Here he is. Won't you do something now to restore my ear?"

The king got up.

He took a dead leaf and put it in the place of the ear. And the dead leaf softened and changed into an ear.

45

Untombi-yaphansi[158]

Zulu (South Africa)[159]

BY LYDIA UMKASETHEMBA

There was a certain king who had dug a large field. At the proper season, many men went to dig the garden.

That king had only three children. The eldest was called Usilwane,[160] the second Usilwanekazana,[161] and the other Untombi-yaphansi.[162]

But Usilwane and Usilwanekazana loved each other.

It happened at a certain time that Usilwane went to hunt. He returned, carrying in his hand a leopard. He said, "This is my dog. Give it milk, mix the milk with boiled corn and make porridge, and give it its food cold, so that it may eat. But it will die if you give it hot food."

They did as he directed them.

At length, the leopard grew. It was a great dog, and the people were very much afraid because it was a leopard. They said, "It will devour the people. Usilwane will become a wizard. Why does he domesticate a leopard and call it his dog?"

But Usilwanekazana, troubled because she heard the people say that a child of her family would become a wizard, said, "With what can I kill this leopard?"

Then, one day, all the people went to harvest in the garden of the king. Usilwane had gone to visit the young women, and Usilwanekazana remained alone. That morning, she heated milk until it boiled and added to it some pounded corn. She gave this to the dog of Usilwane. It ate and ate, and, because the food was hot, when it had finished eating it died.

Usilwane returned at noon and found his dog dead.

He said, "Usilwanekazana, what has killed my dog?"

She replied, "It ate food while it was still hot and died."

Usilwane said, "Why did you kill my dog? Long ago, I told you not to give it hot food, for it would die. You have killed my dog on purpose."

Usilwane took an assegai and said to Usilwanekazana, "Raise your arm, that I may stab you."

Usilwanekazana replied, "For what evil have I done?"

He said, "You have killed my dog."

Usilwanekazana said, "I killed it because the people said you would practice witchcraft by it."

Usilwane said, "No, you killed it because you did not love it. Make haste; raise your arm so that I may stab you."

But Usilwanekazana laughed, thinking that Usilwane was merely jesting. But he angrily laid hold of her, raised her arm, and stabbed her below the armpit. Then Usilwane took a pot and put into it the blood of Usilwanekazana. He then wiped her carefully and washed her and laid her on her mat. He took a pillow and placed it under her head. He set her head in order, putting scents on it and placing a fillet on her brow. He put armlets on her arms and anklets on her legs; he anointed her with fat and covered her with a blanket. It was just as though she were asleep.

He then went out and took one of his sheep and brought it home and killed it. He poured its blood into the vessel that contained that of Usilwanekazana and mixed it together. He skinned the sheep and cut out the lungs, the heart, and the liver and chopped them up with the entrails and the caul. He cooked it together. When it was done, he placed it at the lower side of the fireplace and washed himself and sat down.

When the sun was declining, Untombi-yaphansi came. She entered her mother's house and found Usilwane sitting and Usilwanekazana lying down.

Usilwane said, "Take, there is food, Untombi-yaphansi. Eat."

Untombi-yaphansi said, "Why is Usilwanekazana sleeping?"

He said, "I do not know. She is merely sleeping."

Untombi-yaphansi said, "Oh, where did this food come from?"

Usilwane replied, "Do you not see that sheep?"

Untombi-yaphansi said, "Why was it killed?"

He said, "It was merely killed."

Then Usilwane went to his own house to wait there.

Untombi-yaphansi took some food. When she was about to eat, a large fly came to her and made a great noise and said, "Boo! boo! give me, and I will tell you!"

She drove it away with her hand.

When she was again about to eat, the fly came immediately and said, "Boo! boo! give me, and I will tell you!"

When it did this a third time, Untombi-yaphansi shouted, "Here, Usilwane! Here, Usilwane! There is a fly that says, 'Boo! boo!' and asks me to give it, and it will tell me."

Usilwane replied, "Kill it. It is deceiving you. Do not give it."

Again, Untombi-yaphansi took some of the food, and again the fly made a great noise, saying, "Boo! boo! give me, and I will tell you."

She drove it away with her hand.

Again, it said, "Boo! boo! give me, and I will tell you."

When it did so the third time, she gave it food.

It licked the food and said, "Take care, do not eat this food, for Usilwane has killed Usilwanekazana. He said that she killed his leopard without cause. See, Usilwanekazana is dead; this is her blood. And the leopard is dead."

Untombi-yaphansi at once arose. She took off the blanket with which Usilwanekazana was covered and saw the blood flowing from beneath her armpit.

Untombi-yaphansi rushed out; she ran to her fathers and mothers. When she was at the upper part of the village, Usilwane left his house and saw her.

He called her, saying, "Here, attend to me, Untombi-yaphansi! Where are you going?"

Untombi-yaphansi fled with haste. Usilwane pursued her, taking an assegai in his hand, thinking that when he caught her he would stab her with it.

When Usilwane was very near her, Untombi-yaphansi said, "Open, earth, that I may enter, for I am about to die this day."

The earth opened, and Untombi-yaphansi entered.

When Usilwane came there, he sought her but could not see where Untombi-yaphansi had descended.

He said, "Oh! oh! Where did she descend? for I thought when I was over there that she was here."

He was no longer able to see her. He went back again.

Untombi-yaphansi went on. When it was evening, she slept, not having come out from the earth.

In the morning, she awoke and again went on. When it was midday, she came out of the earth and went and stood on a small elevation and shouted, "There will be nothing but weeping this summer! Usilwaneka-zana has been murdered by Usilwane! He says she killed the prince's leopard without cause."

An old woman who was in the royal garden said, "It sounds as though someone was shouting afar off, saying, 'Usilwanekazana has been killed by Usilwane. She has killed the prince's leopard without cause.'"

The king said, "Seize her, and cast her outside the garden."

They seized the old woman, killed her, and cast her outside the garden, saying that she was prophesying evil against the king's child.

Untombi-yaphansi passed onward from that place and went to another small elevation and cried, "There will be nothing but weeping this summer! Usilwanekazana has been murdered by Usilwane! He says she killed the prince's leopard without cause."

An old man said, "There is some one shouting afar off. It sounds as if someone is saying, 'There will be nothing but weeping this summer. Usilwanekazana has been killed by Usilwane. He says she has killed the prince's leopard without cause.'"

The king said, "Seize him, and cast him outside the garden."

They seized him and cast him out.

Untombi-yaphansi again departed and went near them and shouted, "There will be nothing but weeping this summer. Usilwanekazana has been killed by Usilwane. He says she has killed the prince's leopard without cause."

When all the people heard that, they cried and ran toward her, saying, "What do you say?"

She replied, "Usilwanekazana has been killed by Usilwane. She has killed the prince's leopard without cause."

All the men went home. When they arrived, Usilwane fled.

They called him, saying, "Come back! Do you think there is any reason why all the people should be killed? You are not about to be killed!"

Usilwane came back and went into the house. They laid hold of him and bound him and said, "What is to be done with him?"

The king said, "Close the door, and set fire to the house that we three may be burned. But you, Untombi-yaphansi, go to your sister, and live with her, for I and your mother will be burned with this house. We do not wish to live, because Usilwanekazana is dead, and we too will die with her."

Usilwane said, "Listen to me. Do not burn me with the house; stab me with an assegai."

The king said, "No, my child, I will cause you to feel very great pain, for it is you who have murdered my child."

Untombi-yaphansi said, "With whom shall I go?"

Her father replied, "Take an ox; mount it, and go. When you are on the top of the hill, you will hear the great roaring of the burning village. Do not look back, but go on."

She departed, riding on the ox. When she was on hill, she heard the roaring of the fire. She wept, saying, "So then I hear this great roaring. My mother and father are burning."

She went on and came to a great river.

When she came to it, there appeared an *imbulu*,[163] which said, "Princess, Untombi-yaphansi, just come down here from your ox, so that I may get up and see whether it becomes me or not?"

She replied, "No, I do not wish to dismount."

The *imbulu* said, "What is the matter?"

But Untombi-yaphansi knew beforehand that an *imbulu* would appear at that place, for her mother had told her, "If the ox treads on a stone, an *imbulu* will come out at that place."

She was therefore afraid to dismount from the ox. So she said, "Get out of the way, and let me pass on."

The *imbulu* said, "Oh! Lend me the ox, so that I may see whether it is suitable for me."

She dismounted.

The *imbulu* said, "Hand me your things, so that I may put them on and see whether they are suitable for me."

She gave the *imbulu* all her things. The *imbulu* put them on and mounted the ox and said, "Oh, how they become me!"

Untombi-yaphansi said, "Dismount now and give me my things, so that I may get up."

The *imbulu* said, "I do not wish to get down. Why did you lend the ox to me?"

She replied, "You asked me to lend it to you."

The *imbulu* said, "I do not wish to get down. Let us leap here on the stones and see which will have wet feet."

The *imbulu* leapt, but Untombi-yaphansi walked in the water, because she was not mounted on any thing.

When they had crossed, the *imbulu* said, "It is your feet that are wet. Now your name is Umsila-wezinja, Dogs'-tail. And I am now Untombi-yaphansi."

But Untombi-yaphansi made no answer; she was silent.

The *imbulu* went on, riding on the ox, and Untombi-yaphansi came after on foot.

They went on and came to the place where the sister of Untombi-yaphansi was married. They entered the village and went to the upper part of it.

The *imbulu* went into a house, and Untombi-yaphansi also went in.

The *imbulu* said, "Don't come in. Hold my ox."

Untombi-yaphansi held the ox, and the *imbulu* went in and sat down.

The sister of Untombi-yaphansi asked, "Who are you?"

The *imbulu* replied, "It is I, child of our house. Oh! Do you not recognize me?"

She said, "No, I do not recognize you, for the child of our house I left when she was still young. I know nothing but her name. But her body glistened; she was like brass."

The *imbulu* said, "I was very ill. I no longer have that body of mine that was like brass."

Her sister wept, saying, "Oh! Is this truly the child of our house?" She said, "And she who is at the doorway, where does she come from?"

The *imbulu* said, "It is a mere thing. I fell in with it at the river, it was merely going on foot."

She said, "May I give you food?"

The *imbulu* replied, "Yes, I am hungry."

She gave the *imbulu* porridge, and it ate.

She said, "Call your servant over there so that I may give her some food as well. Here is some whey."[164]

The *imbulu* said, "Give it to her there in the doorway."

Her husband said, "No, do not give food to the person outside. Bring her into the house so that she may eat here."

She called her, saying, "What is her name?"

The *imbulu* replied, "Umsila-wezinja."

Her sister said, "Come and eat, Umsila-wezinja."

She went in. Her sister took a child's vessel and gave her some whey in it.

The *imbulu* said, "No! no! Child of our house, do not give it to her in the vessel of your children. Pour it for her on the ground so that she may eat it there."

Her brother-in-law said, "No, do not pour food for a person on the ground. Give it to her in her hands."

Her sister dipped it out with a spoon and poured it into her hands.

But Untombi-yaphansi put her hands around the pillar of the house, and her sister put it into her hands. When she had finished, she separated her hands, and the milk[165] was spilled.

Her sister scolded her, saying, "How is it that I pour my milk into your hands and you throw it away?"

She replied, "It is because, when I stretched out my hands, I placed them on each side of the pillar."

The sister gave her boiled mealies,[166] and Untombi-yaphansi ate, and then they retired to rest.

In the morning, the sister of Untombi-yaphansi said, "I am in trouble because there is no one to watch for me: the birds are troubling me in my garden."

The *imbulu* said, "There is Umsila-wezinja; let her go with those who watch, keeping the birds from the garden, that she may watch for you."

She said, "Well, go."

Untombi-yaphansi went with Udalana.[167]

When they came outside the village, Untombi-yaphansi stopped and said, "You go ahead, Udalana."

Udalana went ahead, and they reached the gardens. Udalana went to the garden belonging to her house, which was high up. The garden that was watched by Untombi-yaphansi was low down, and the watch-houses were opposite each other.

The birds were very numerous. As they were entering the garden, the birds came. Udalana threw stones at them and said, "There they are, Umsila-wezinja."

Untombi-yaphansi said,

"Tayi, tayi, those birds that devour my sister's garden,
Although she is not my sister truly,
For I am now Umsila-wezinja.
I was not really Umsila-wezinja,
I was Untombi-yaphansi."

The birds went away immediately in accordance with her word. The girls remained there the whole day, and no birds came. Udalana wondered much when she saw that there were no birds, since they troubled her so much every day.

When it was midday, Untombi-yaphansi said, "You throw stones at the birds for me, Udalana. I am going now to bathe."

She went to the river. When she came to the river, she went into a pool and washed, and she came out with her whole body shining like brass, and she was holding in her hand her brass rod.

She hit the ground and said, "Come out, all you people of my father, along with the cattle of my father and my food."

At once, there came out of the earth many people,[168] many cattle, and her food. She ate.

Her own ox also came out. She mounted it and said,

"In my father's cattle-pen we used to sing e-a-ye,
Among the white-tailed cattle we used to sing e-a-ye."

All the people, together with the trees, took up the song, singing in unison with her.

When she had done all this, she descended from her ox. She hit the ground with her rod and said, "Open, earth, that my father's things and his people may enter."

And truly the earth opened, and all the things and men entered.

Again, she took some black earth and smeared her body with it and was as she was before. She went up from the river to the garden and went into the watch-house.

She said, "Have the birds been here?"

Udalana said, "Oh! By the council! Did she leave me with a lot of birds?"

As they were speaking, a large flock of birds came.

Udalana said, "There they are, Umsila-wezinja."

Untombi-yaphansi said,

"Tayi, tayi, those birds that devour my sister's garden,
Although she is not my sister truly;
Although I am now Umsila-wezinja.
I was not really Umsila-wezinja,
I was Untombi-yaphansi."

The birds at once went away in accordance with her word.

But Udalana wondered much at those words of his and said, "I say, Umsila-wezinja, what are you saying?"

Untombi-yaphansi replied, "I say nothing."

Udalana descended from her watch-house and went to that of Untombi-yaphansi and said to her, "Oh! Where have you eaten, Umsila-wezinja?"

Untombi-yaphansi said, "Why do you ask?"

She replied, "I ask because I do not see the refuse of the sugar-cane where you have eaten."

Untombi-yaphansi said, "I have eaten."

The sun set, and they returned home.

When they arrived, the king asked, "Were there any birds there, Umsila-wezinja?"

Untombi-yaphansi said, "Yes, there were very many indeed."

The *imbulu* said, "This is her way. Umsila-wezinja will just sit on the ground until the garden is utterly destroyed by the birds. And when it is all gone, she says she has been worsted by the birds."

They sat; they retired to rest.

In the morning, the girls went to watch for birds in the gardens. When they were at the gateway, Untombi-yaphansi stood still and said, "You go ahead."

Udalana replied, "Oh! What happens to you if you go first? Every day I go in front."

But Untombi-yaphansi was afraid to go first because the dew would wipe off that with which she smeared her body, and then her brass color would glisten and people would recognize her.

Udalana went in front.

They came to the garden and sat down.

Udalana said, "There they are, Umsila-wezinja."

Untombi-yaphansi said,

"Tayi, tayi, those birds that devour my sister's garden,
Although she is not my sister truly,
But she was my sister."

She said, "Stay and watch, Udalana. I am going now to bathe."

She went.

When Untombi-yaphansi had gone, Udalana went after her; she too went to the river.

When Untombi-yaphansi came to the river, she entered the pool and came out with her body glistening, carrying in her hand her brass rod.

Udalana wondered when she saw this.

But Untombi-yaphansi did not see Udalana, for she had concealed herself.

Untombi-yaphansi took her rod and struck the ground with it and said, "Open, earth, that I may see the things of my father, that all may come out, my father's people and my things and the cattle."

All these things came out in accordance with her command. Food also came out, and she ate. She took her garment, which was ornamented with brass balls, and put it on. Then, having adorned herself, she mounted her ox.

She said,

"In my father's cattle-pen we used to sing e-a-ye,
Among the red-tailed cattle we used to sing e-a-ye."

All the people and the trees took up the song.

Udalana was afraid. She trembled; it was as if the very earth was moving.

When Untombi-yaphansi was getting down from her ox, Udalana hurried back ahead of her and arrived first at the garden.

And Untombi-yaphansi said, "Let it all sink into the ground."

Everything sank into the ground.

She smeared her body, then returned to the garden.

When she arrived, she said, "Have the birds been here long, Udalana?"

Udalana said, "Why did you stay so long at the river?"

Untombi-yaphansi replied, "Do you not see that I cannot wash quickly, that my body is dirty and very black?"

Udalana arose and went to the watch-house where Untombi-yaphansi was. She sat beside her, looking earnestly at the whole of her body, but she did not see anywhere a glistening spot. She wondered what she had smeared herself with.

The king came to the garden and said, "Good day, Umsila-wezinja. Are there any birds here?"

She said, "Yes, sir, there are."

Untombi-yaphansi descended from the watch-house, afraid because the king was on it.

The king said, "Why do you get down, Umsila-wezinja?"

She replied, "No, I merely get down, sir."

The king came down from the watch-house and returned home.

Untombi-yaphansi and Udalana also went home. When they arrived, they ate and lay down.

In the evening, Udalana went to the king and said, "King, awaken very early in the morning, and go and stay at my watch-house. Then, at noon, when Umsila-wezinja has gone to bathe, we shall follow her. You will see her with her body glistening. She comes out of the pool with her brass rod, and she hits the ground with it and says, 'Open earth, that all the things of my father may come out.' And there come out cattle and men and food and all her ornaments. You will see her mount an ox and sing. And the men and the cattle and the trees take up the song, and everything sings in unison with her."

The king said, "If I go in the morning, shall I see that?"

Udalana said, "Yes, king, you will see it."

They retired to rest.

When the king rose in the morning, he went to the watch-house of Udalana.

When the sun was up, Udalana and Untombi-yaphansi set out. When they were at the gateway, Untombi-yaphansi said, "You go on ahead, Udalana."

Udalana said, "Why do you not go first? Why are you afraid to go in front?" Udalana went on.

Untombi-yaphansi said, "Oh! How is it that today there is no dew?"

Udalana said, "Perhaps a deer has passed."

Untombi-yaphansi said, "But why has the dew dried up so much?"

They went on and came to the garden. They sat down. The birds came.

Udalana said, "There they are, Umsila-wezinja."

She frightened them in the same way as all other people. But they did not go away; they troubled them very much.

The king said, "How is it that the birds have troubled you so much today?"

Udalana replied, "On other days, Umsila-wezinja frightens them in a different way. But today, I do not know why she has departed from her usual method."

Udalana went to Untombi-yaphansi and said, "Why do you not go to bathe today?"

She said, "No, I am lazy today."

But Untombi-yaphansi perceived that there was someone in the garden, because she saw that there was no dew.

At length, the sun set. The king came down from the watch-house and returned home, and Untombi-yaphansi and Udalana returned after him.

When they reached home, Untombi-yaphansi said, "The birds trouble us."

Her sister said, "Watch the birds with great care, Umsila-wezinja, that they not destroy my corn."

They retired to rest.

In the morning, the king left home and went by another way to the garden. He hid himself in the midst of the corn.

When it was light, Udalana and Untombi-yaphansi went to watch. When they came to the gateway, Untombi-yaphansi said, "Go on ahead."

Udalana replied, "No, I don't like to go first, either. You go in front."

Untombi-yaphansi went first. As they went, she looked at her legs and saw that the dew was beginning to wash off that with which she had smeared herself.

She refused to walk first, saying, "You go on ahead, Udalana."

Udalana went in front.

They came to the garden.

Udalana said, "And today, too, are you not going to bathe?"

She replied, "I am going."

Untombi-yaphansi came down from her watch-house and went to the watch-house of Udalana; she sat down there.

The birds came.

Udalana said, "Scare them, Umsila-wezinja."

Untombi-yaphansi said,

"Tayi, tayi, those birds over there that eat my sister's garden,
Although she is not my sister truly;
Since I became Umsila-wezinja.
I used not to be Umsila-wezinja indeed,
I was Untombi-yaphansi."

The birds immediately went away.

And the king wondered when he saw it.

At noon, Untombi-yaphansi said, "I am going now to bathe, Udalana. You watch the birds for me in the garden."

Untombi-yaphansi departed and went to the river.

And the king, too, along with Udalana, went to the river. They hid in the underwood.

Untombi-yaphansi went into the pool and came out with her body glistening like brass, and she carried her brass rod.

She struck the ground with it and said, "Open, earth, that my father's things may come out, and my father's people, and his cattle, and my things."

Everything came out, and her food came out as well. She ate and put on her garments and her ornaments; then she mounted the ox and sang,

"In my father's cattle-pen we used to sing e-a-ye,
Among the white-tailed cattle we used to sing e-a-ye,
Among the red-tailed cattle we used to sing e-a-ye."

All the people and the trees took up the song.

The king wondered when he saw this. He said to Udalana, "I will go out and lay hold of her, so that she will no longer be able to hide herself."

Udalana assented.

When all those things had again sunk into the ground, the king went out.

When Untombi-yaphansi saw the king, she was very frightened.

The king said, "Do not fear, my sister-in-law. For a long time, you have been troubled without ceasing, because since you arrived here you have been concealing yourself."

The king took her and went with her and Udalana to the garden.

The king said, "When it is quite dark, come back with her, Udalana, and put her in your house. I will come with her sister when you are there."

The king went home.

When it was dark, Udalana and Untombi-yaphansi returned and went to Udalana's house.

The king came, and he called the sister of Untombi-yaphansi. They then went into the house, and he brought Untombi-yaphansi to her.

Her sister cried, saying, "Long ago, I said, 'How is it that her body does not glisten?'"

They inquired of Untombi-yaphansi what that thing was. She told them it was an *imbulu* and gave a full account of what the *imbulu* had done.

The king said, "Go, Udalana, and tell the boys to awaken in the morning and make a deep pit in the cattle-pen, and tell the women to boil water early in the morning."

Udalana took the message to them.

They retired to rest.

Early in the morning, the boys arose and dug a deep pit. They put some milk in a pot, which they let down by a cord into the hole.

The king said, "Go and call all the women and the bride[169] to come here."

All were called, and all arrived.

The king said, "All of you jump across this hole."

The *imbulu* said it was afraid to leap.

The king said, "No, you leap!"

The *imbulu* refused.

The king boiled over with anger and said, "Leap! Leap immediately!"

The other women leapt.

When the *imbulu* was leaping, its tail saw the milk, and it went into the hole, throwing itself in with violence.

The king said to the women, "Run and fetch the boiling water and pour it into the hole."

They fetched the water and poured it into the hole.

The *imbulu* was scalded. With earth, they covered it up in the hole.

Then the king told the people, "Go and tell the whole nation to come here, because I am the chosen husband; my sister-in-law has come."

The whole nation was told, and the people came.

The marriage company entered the village. Untombi-yaphansi danced together with her people. She lived in happiness with her sister. Many cattle were killed, and they ate meat.

They all lived together happily.

Nongenile Masithathu Zenani

46

Combecantsini[170]

Zulu (South Africa)

BY LYDIA UMKASETHEMBA

There was a certain king of a certain country. He used to have children who were crows, he had not one child that was a human being. In all his houses, his children were crows.

But his queen had no child; it was said that she was barren. She remained a long time without having any child. All used to jeer her, and even the very women who gave birth to crows said, "We indeed do give birth only to crows, but you give birth to nothing. Of what use then do you say you are?"

She cried, "But did I make myself? For even you are mothers, because it was said, 'Be you mothers.'"[171]

At length, she went to dig. When she was now nearly finished, two pigeons came to her as she was sitting on the ground and weeping.

One said to the other, "Vukuthu."

The other said, "Why do you say, 'Vukuthu,' and not ask why she is crying?"

She said, "I am crying because I have no child. The other wives of the king give birth to crows, but I give birth to nothing."

One said, "Vukuthu."

The other said, "Why do you say, 'Vukuthu,' and not ask her what she will give us if we give her power to have a child?"

She replied, "I would give all I possess."

One said, "Vukuthu."

The other said, "Why do you say, 'Vukuthu,' and not ask what food she will give us?"

She said, "I would give you my corn."

One said, "Vukuthu."

The other said, "Why do you say, 'Vukuthu,' since we do not eat corn?"

She said, "I will give you arum."

One said, "Vukuthu."

The other said, "Why do you say 'Vukuthu,' and not tell her we do not like arum?"

She mentioned all the kinds of food she had.

They refused it all.

At length, she said, "That is all the food I have."

The pigeon said, "Vukuthu. You have corn, but for our part we like castor-oil seeds."

She said, "Oh, I have castor-oil seeds, sir."

One said, "Vukuthu."

The other said, "Why do you say, 'Vukuthu,' and not tell her to hurry home at once and fetch the castor-oil seeds?"

The woman ran home at once. On her arrival, she took the castor-oil seeds which were in a pot, and she poured them into a basket, placed the basket on her head, and went with the seeds to the garden.

On her arrival, one of the pigeons said, "Vukuthu."

The other said, "Why do you say, 'Vukuthu,' and not tell her to pour the seeds on the ground?"

She poured the castor-oil seeds on the ground. The pigeons picked them all up.

When they had eaten them all, one said, "Vukuthu."

The other said, "Why do you say, Vukuthu,' and not ask her if she has brought a horn and a lancet?"

She said, "No."

One said, "Vukuthu."

The other said, "Why do you say, 'Vukuthu,' and not tell her to go and fetch a horn and a lancet?"

She ran home, and fetched a horn and a lancet, and came back immediately.

On her arrival, one of the pigeons said, "Vukuthu."

The other said, "Why do you say, 'Vukuthu,' and not tell her to turn her back to us?"

She turned her back to them.

One said, "Vukuthu."

The other said, "Why do you say, 'Vukuthu,' and not scarify her on the loins?"

The pigeon cupped her, and when he had finished cupping her, he took the horn and poured the clotted blood into it.

One said, "Vukuthu."

The other said, "Why do you say, 'Vukuthu,' and not tell her on reaching home to find a large vessel, pour the clotted blood into it, then let two moons die, and then uncover the vessel?"

She went home and did so.

She remained two months. When the third new moon appeared, she found two children. She took them out of the vessel, and placed them into a large pot.

She remained three moons without looking into it. When she looked on the fourth moon, she found them now large, and laughing.

She greatly rejoiced.

She went to dig. When she reached the garden, she sat down until the sun went down. She said, "Can it be that my children can live? For I am jeered by the other women, and even they do not give birth to human beings, they give birth to crows."

In the afternoon, she would return home. When it was evening, and she was about to lie down, she shut up the doorway with the wicker door and with a mat, saying, "Then, if anyone passes by the door, he will see nothing."

She waited, and when she saw that the people no longer went up and down in the village, she took her children, and placed them on a mat. She took milk and gave it to them. The boy drank it, but the little girl refused it.

When she had remained with them a long time, she put them back again into their place, and slept.

As regards their growth: both grew very fast. At length, they crawled on the ground, not having been seen by anyone. After a time, they walked, their mother concealing them from the people. They remained in the house, not going out, their mother not allowing them to go out, saying that if they went out they would be seen by the crows, and the crows would kill them, for they used to vex her in her very house. She would rise in the morning and fetch water, then go out to dig. When she would return in the afternoon she would find water spilled over the whole house, and the ashes taken out of the fireplace and the whole house white with the ashes. She said, "This is done to me because I do not give birth, even to these crows. If I too had given birth, I should not be treated in this way. I have been afflicted for a long time in this way, and even with my husband who married me it is the same. He no longer regards me as a human being, because I have no child."

Both grew until they were great children. The little girl was at length a grown-up young woman and the boy a young man.

The mother said to them, "You are now so big, my children, but you have no name." She said to the girl, "As for you, your name is Combecantsini."[172]

The boy said, "For my part, do not give me a name, for I will receive my name of manhood, when I have grown up, from my father. I do not wish to have a name now."

The other agreed.

It happened at noon, when the mother was not there: the girl said, "Let us go and fetch water, since the crows have spilled the water of our mother."

The boy said, "Did our mother not forbid us to go outside?"

The girl said, "By whom shall we be seen, since all the people have gone to dig?"

The boy agreed.

The girl took a water-vessel. She went to the river, both going together.

The boy's peculiarity was that he was white, but the girl was very shining.

So they went, and reached the river and dipped water. When she had filled the vessel, she said to the boy, "Put it on my head."

When he was just about to put it on her head, they saw a line of people coming to them.

When they came to the river, they said, "Give us water to drink."

The boy dipped water with a cup, and gave it to the first.

The second asked also, saying, "Give me water to drink."

He gave him water to drink.

All asked in like manner, until the boy had given them all water to drink.

They said, "To what village do you belong?"

They replied, "To that one on the hill."

They said, "Is there anyone at home?"

They said, "No, there is no one."

They said, "To which house do you belong?"

They said, "To that which is last, near the main entrance."

They said, "Who is the queen?"

They replied, "The queen was our own mother, but it happened that, because she had no child, her house was removed and placed near the entrance."

The children inquired of them, "And you, to what nation do you belong?"

They replied, "We came from over there. We are looking for a very beautiful woman, for the king of our nation is going to be married."

They said, "Is he about to take his first wife?"

They assented.

They asked, "Of what nation are you?"

They said, "We are Hwebu."

The girl said, "And the king of your nation, is he a Hwebu?"

They replied, "No, he is not of the same race as ourselves. We only are Hwebu. And we are not many, we are but one troop."

So the Hwebu departed.

The boy put the water-vessel on her head. They went up the hill to their home, and sat down.

In the afternoon, when the mother returned from digging, she asked, "By whom was this water fetched?"

They said, "By us."

She said, "Did I not forbid you to go outside? By whom, then, were you told to go and fetch water?"

The boy said, "I refused, for my part, but Combecantsini said, 'Let us go and fetch water.'"

The mother said, "Did no man see you?"

They replied, "We were seen by some Hwebu, who formed a very long line. They asked us whose children we were. We said we belong to this village." They were silent then.

They remained for many days. But they were unknown to anyone of their own village; they were known by the Hwebu only.

It happened that, on another occasion, there came very many cattle in the afternoon with very many people.

All the people of the village said, "It is an army. Into what place has it made a foray, and taken so many cattle as these?"

They saw many men coming to their village. These men left many of the cattle outside, then they entered the village with some of the cattle.

On their arrival, they drove the cattle into the cattle-pen, and went to the upper part. They stood there, and respectfully asked for his daughter from the father.

All the people of the village were silent, being silent from wonder, saying, "Is there a man who would come and select from among crows one to be his bride? For there is not a girl who is a human being in this village."

But the men asked, as though they knew the young woman.

At length, the women said, "If you have come to select a bride, which is the young woman among all these of ours? That mother will be glad whose daughter shall be selected with so many cattle as these."

All the women went out of the houses and stood outside. Some ran to the entrance, saying, "Ye, ye! Is the woman who has no child satisfied as to whose are these bridegroom's men?" They said this for the purpose of jeering the childless one, for they had given birth to crows only.

The men went out in anger, together with the father of the crows. He was enraged with the women, and said to them, "Away with you, away with you! For which girls of yours do you make this huzzahing? since you have given birth only to crows? Who would cast away so many cattle as these for a crow's dowry?"

The men said, "Make haste into your houses, and cease this noise."

The owner of the village went to the bridegroom's men, and said, "As for me, I have no girl. I am the father of mere crows, and of nothing else. Take your cattle, and go home to your people with them."

They replied, "We ask you not to refuse us, for we know that at this place there is a young woman who is a human being."

The head of the village swore that there was no young woman at his home.

At length, the bridegroom's people looked at each other, being desirous of inquiring of the Hwebu who had come there at first. They asked them, "Did you in truth see a young woman at this place?"

The Hwebu replied, "We did see one at this place. We can point out the house that she went into."

They asked which one it was.

They said, "It is that which is the last but one."

They said, "Chief of this village, we are indeed acquainted with your daughter. We can even point out the house in which she is."

The chief of the village replied, speaking in anger, "Are these men then truly so very wise? For I, the father of the children, tell you, in this place there is not a girl who is a human being. But you dispute the matter with me, because you have come to laugh at me because I am not a father of human beings. That house to which you point, the occupied of it has not given birth to so much as a crow."

The woman of that house, when she heard her husband saying this, left her house, and said, "Behold the bridegroom's people of our princess! Come into the house, and have cattle killed for you, my sons-in-law. For though I have had no child, yet you have seen that I have a child."

Her husband went to the house and said, "I thought you had no child, but, since you have come out and shouted, have you a child?"

She replied, "Since I do not have children, where could I get a child?"

He said, "I ask then, my child, tell me why you shouted?"

She replied, "I have shouted for my children, who are not the children of a man, but mine only."

Her husband said, "Where are they?"

She said, "Come out, so that he may see you."

The boy and girl came out.

When the father saw them, he fell on the boy and embraced him, crying and saying, "*Hawu! hawu!* Have women such great courage? How is it that you have hidden the children until they are as big as this, they being unknown to anyone?" He said, "Where did you get these children?"

She replied, "The pigeons gave them to me. They scarified me on the loins, there came out a clot, it was placed in a vessel, and at length it became human beings. I nourished them. I did not want to tell you, for the crows might have killed them."

The father agreed, and said, "Which bullock shall be slaughtered for them? As for the goats, they must not have a mere goat killed. It is proper that they kill a young ox."

She went out of the house and came to the bridegroom, now laughing and happy, saying, "Come out, that I may point out to you your bullock."

Kakaka, the bridegroom, went out alone. She pointed out to him the young ox. It was killed and eaten.

On the next day, the father said, "It is proper that the girl, too, have a bullock killed for her, together with that which she is about to dance[173] before her bridegroom's people."

So the mother agreed.

The father arose, and said, "It is proper that all the customs of this child be fully carried out, for it is my wish that her bridegroom's party take her with them on the day of their departure, for the crows may kill her."

So all her customs were completed. Goats were killed for her, for when she came to puberty she had nothing killed for her, because no one knew of her. She danced for the bridegroom's party. The cattle were killed and the flesh eaten.

The father said, "Set aside a leg, my children, so that you and your wife will have food on your journey."

They replied, "Yes, father, and we are desirous of going in the morning."

They were entirely of one heart.

The mother said to the bridegroom's party, "When you have set out on your journey, you will see a green animal in the path. It will make its appearance on the high land. Do not pursue it, just leave it alone. Then the marriage of my child will be fortunate."

On the following morning, they set out. Two large oxen were selected for the bridegroom and his bride, and they were placed upon them, their soldiers going before them, they following alone with many young women who had been summoned from her father's people.

At length, they reached the highland, and then they saw that animal about which the mother had warned them, telling them not to kill it.

All the soldiers ran and pursued the animal.

The bride said, "Forbid them to pursue the animal. Did my mother not tell you not to pursue it?"

Kakaka, the bridegroom, answered, "Of what consequence do you say it will be? Just let them pursue it, it is no matter."

The bride and bridegroom and the bridesmaids remained them a long time, waiting.

After a time, the bridegroom said, "We're tired standing here in the sun. Let me go at once and bring back the men, so that we may go on our way. It is now noon."

So he departed.

After that, the others remained a long time without seeing the bridegroom. Finally, the bride said to the bridesmaids, "I am tired of waiting. And I am longing for water."

As she was speaking these words, an *imbulu*[174] came to them, and said, "Good day, beautiful princesses."

They acknowledged the salutation.

The *imbulu* said to the bride, "Just come down, so that I may see if your dress is suitable for me."

She replied, "I do not wish to come down."

The *imbulu* said, "*Hawu!* Just come down, you will get up again at once."

After a time, the bride descended.

The *imbulu* took her dress and put it on, and said, "How well it fits me!" Then it said, "Bring me your veil, so that I may see if it becomes me."

The bride refused, saying, "I am afraid of the sun, princess."

The *imbulu* said, "Lend it to me. I'll return it to you at once."

She gave it the veil.

The *imbulu* put on the veil, and said, "Just let me get on your ox, so that I may see if that too would become me."

She said, "Get up, but come down again immediately."

So the *imbulu* mounted, and said, "*Ncinci!* How admirably it suits me!"

She said, "Come down now."

The *imbulu* said, "I do not wish to come down, I shall never come down."

The bride said, "Get down, so that I may mount."

The *imbulu* replied, "You gave me permission to get up. I shall never come down again."

Then the bridesmaids and the bride departed. They turned into finches, and the bride turned into a fly-catcher bird. They went to the forest and remained there, now being birds.

The bridegroom's men arrived with the skin of an animal that they had skinned. They went in front. When they were still at a distance from the young women, Kakaka said, "*Hawu*! My men! Do you see the bride, how small she has become, and that she no longer shines? What has happened to her? And where are the bridesmaids?"

They replied, "Oh sir, perhaps the bridesmaids were tired of sitting in the sun and went back to their own homes. We see what the sun has done to the bride, for she was not accustomed to sit in the sun."

He replied, "And if that were so, that which is done by the sun would be evident. My body is weak, it seems to me that this is not my bride."

They came in front of her, and said, "Where are the bridesmaids?"

The bride answered as though her tongue were tied, speaking rapidly and thickly, saying, "They have gone home."

So they went forward, the soldiers going in front, and the bridegroom himself went in front with his soldiers. The bride[175] remained behind, going alone with the ox.

When they were at some distance from that place, they saw many birds pitched on the grass in front of them, saying, "Kakaka, the king's child, gone off with an animal!" They said "Out upon him, the groom is running off with an *imbulu*!"

He said, "*Hawu*! my men! Do you hear what these birds say? What are they saying? Did you ever hear birds speak?"

They said, "Sir, the manner of birds of the thorn country: they speak."

So he was silent. They went forward.

The birds went before them, and said, "Kakaka, Kakaka, the king's child gone off with an animal! Out upon him, he runs off with an *imbulu*."

That troubled the heart of Kakaka very much.

When they were near home, the birds turned back and remained in the forest.

They entered their home, all the men going in front, leaving the bride alone behind them.

In the cattle-pen there were many men sitting with the king, Kakaka's father.

The bride entered, going alone. She went to the upper part of the enclosure.

All the men who were in the enclosure said, "What is that which has come with the prince?"

The king spoke in anger. He called his son, saying, "Come here, you boy."

Kakaka went in fear, because he saw that his father was very angry.

The king said, when Kakaka came to him, "What is that with which you have come? Is that thing the young woman who the Hwebu said was beautiful?" He said, "Hurry, call all of them to come here to me. All the Hwebu shall be killed, because they lied when they said that they had seen a beautiful woman."

Kakaka said, "No, king, my father, I too saw the woman, when she was very beautiful."

The father replied, "What, then, is the matter with her now?"

He said, "I do not know. We were told at her home on no account to kill a certain animal. But we killed it, and when we returned from killing it, on our arrival the young woman was as she is. And the other young women of her people were no longer there. As we went along, I too saw that it is not the young woman with whom I left her home."

So the father was silent.

They tarried a few days. But Kakaka would not allow her to be called his wife, saying that he did not have a wife yet. The time would come when he should marry a beautiful woman.

And all the people wondered at this woman, and said she was not like a human being.

There was an old woman who lived at that village. She had no legs, only arms. She remained at home, doing nothing. Her name was Thlese. She was so called because when walking she rolled along with her body only.

The people had gone to dig. When they were gone, the bridesmaids again turned into human beings, and came to that place.

They went to Thlese and said, "Will you say that you have seen any young women here at home?"

Thlese said, "No, my children. I will say, how could I see people here since I am but Thlese?"

They went out and took all the vessels from one side of the village, and they went to fetch water. They came with the water. Then they crushed maize for making beer for the whole village. They fetched water again and again, and boiled it for the beer. They fetched water, and daubed the floors of the houses of the whole village. They went and fetched firewood, and placed it in the whole kraal.

Then they went to Thlese and said, "Thlese, who will you say has done all this?"

She said, "I will say that I did it."

They went to the open country, and on their arrival again became birds.

In the afternoon, when the people returned, all the women of the village said, "*Hawu*! Who has been daubing the floors here at home? And who has fetched water? and firewood? and crushed maize for beer? and heated the water?"

All went to Thlese, and asked her by whom it was done.

She said, "It was done by me. I shuffled and shuffled along, and went and fetched water. I shuffled and shuffled along, and went and fetched firewood. I shuffled and shuffled along, and crushed the mealies, and I shuffled and shuffled along, and heated the water."

They said, "*Hawu*! Was all this done by you, Thlese?"

She said, "Yes."

They laughed and were glad, saying, "Thlese has helped us by making beer for the whole village."

They retired to rest.

On the following morning, they went to dig.

All the bridesmaids came to the village, carrying firewood.

Thlese said, "Ye, ye, ye! See the daughters-in-law of my father. It is well that the wedding party should come home."

They placed the firewood for the whole kraal. They ground the maize that they had crushed the day before for the beer, and they made beer in every house in the kraal. The fetched water. They ground malt, being about to make beer, they mixed the malt with the maize-mash.

They went to Thlese and said, "Goodbye, our grandmother."

She replied, "Yes, bridal party of my mother's mother."

So they departed.

In the afternoon, all the women came home, and they again went to Thlese, and said, "Who has ground the mash? who has cooked?"

Thlese said, "I shuffled and shuffled, and went and fetched wood. I shuffled and shuffled, and ground the mash. I shuffled, and fetched water. I shuffled, and boiled water. I shuffled and shuffled, and ground malt. I shuffled, and mixed it with the maize-mash. I shuffled, and came back here to the house, and sat down."

They laughed, saying, "Now we have got an old woman who will work for us."

They sat down, they retired to rest.

On the following day, when no one was there, the bridesmaids arrived. Thlese was sitting outside. They went to her, and said, "You are a good creature, Thlese, because you do not tell anyone."

They went into the houses, they ground malt, they mixed the mash, they strained the beer they had set to ferment rapidly on the day before, they poured the grains into the mash they had mixed, that it might quickly ferment. They collected into large earthen vessels that which they had strained. They took another vessel, and went with the beer that was in the vessel to Thlese. When they came to her, they drank, and gave also to Thlese.

She laughed and was joyful, and said, "I will never tell, for my part. You shall do just as you like."

Again, they departed and went into the open country, again turning into birds.

In the afternoon, all the women came and saw that all the mash was mixed. They said, "Thlese is wearied with us for asking by whom it was done. Let us just say nothing. There is something wonderful which is about to happen here at home."

But in the evening, Kakaka went to Thlese and earnestly asked her, "*Hawu*! Grandmother, tell me by what means this is done."

Thlese replied, "By me, child of my child."

He said, "*Hawu*, grandmother! You could not do it. Tell me by whom it has been done!"

She said, "At noon, when every one of you are gone, there come many women. But among them there is one most beautiful, her body is glistening. It is they who make beer here at home."

Kakaka said, "Grandmother, did they not say they would come tomorrow?"

Thlese replied, "Oh, they will come."

Kakaka said, "I too will come at noon, and see the women." He said, "But do not tell them, grandmother."

She replied, "No, I will not tell them."

So they retired to rest.

On the following day, all the people departed, going to dig.

Then the women came. They went into the houses, they strained the beer in the whole kraal. When they had strained it all, they poured it into vessels in the whole kraal. They took a very large earthen vessel, and poured into it, collecting the beer of the whole kraal with a vessel. They filled the earthen vessel.

They went out with it, and went to Thlese. On their arrival, they set it down on the ground. They took cow-dung, and daubed the floors of the whole kraal. They swept the whole kraal, they fetched firewood and put it in the courts of the whole kraal. They went into the house in which was Thlese, they took vessels and drank beer.

When they had drunk a great deal of beer, Kakaka entered the kraal. When they saw him, they went to the doorway, thinking to go out and then escape without his seeing them.

But he blocked the doorway, saying, "*Hawu*, child of my father, Combecantsini, what great evil have I done you, that you have troubled me to this degree?"

Combecantsini laughed, and said, "Eh, eh, out upon Kakaka! Was it not you who took me from my father's kraal, and left me on the high lands, and went away with an *imbulu*?"

He replied, "I saw it was not you. And because I no longer saw you, I did not know what you had done."

So they remained, Kakaka rejoicing greatly and saying, "I said, 'I shall soon die,' when I no longer saw you."

When it was afternoon, the people came.

Kakaka went out to his father, smiling with joy, and saying, "Today then, my father, the woman who was lost to me on the high lands has come."

His father asked, laughing for joy, "Where is she?"

He said, "Over there, in the house."

His father said, "Tell all the people here at home, that all the men are to dig a pit immediately here in the cattle enclosure, and tell the women to boil water in all the pots."

So he told them.

When all that was done, all the women were ordered to come out and leap over the pit which had been dug in the cattle enclosure. Some milk had been put in the pit.

And the bride, too, was called. It was said, "You go too to the cattle enclosure. All the women are going to jump over the pit."

This was done because, it was said, when the *imbulu* sees the milk, it will throw itself in and go to drink the milk.

They went to the kraal.

The bride said, "I am afraid to go into the cattle-pen of strangers."

They said, "Go, it is no matter."

So she went, and came to the cattle-pen.

The other women leapt.

She was about to leap, too. When she was about to leap, she saw the milk, her tail unfolded, and she threw herself into the pit on seeing the milk.

Then all the people ran and took the boiling water, and came with it and poured it into the hole.

The *imbulu* died.

All the people were told that the true bride had come. They rejoiced, and men were sent and told to go to the whole nation and tell the people to assemble for a dance, for the prince had been accepted by a young woman.

On the following day, men and youths, and girls and women assembled. They danced, and the bride and her bridesmaids also danced. Many cattle were killed, and they ate meat for several days.

The king ordered Kakaka's kraal to be built. The wattles were cut, and the kraal built at once. It was a very large kraal.

And the bride was appointed, it being said it is she who is queen.

The bridesmaids picked grass and thatched the whole village of the bride. They then departed and went back to their people.

And she then reigned, together with her husband.

Notes

Bibliography

Notes

1. Richard Burton, tr. *The Book of the Thousand Nights and a Night* (London: Burton Club, 1886).

2. Melville J. Herskovits and Frances S. Herskovits, *Dahomean Narrative* (Evanston: Northwestern University Press, 1958), 6.

3. Henry Callaway, *Nursery Tales, Traditions, and Histories of the Zulus* (Springvale, Natal: John A. Blair, and London: Trübner, 1868), i.

4. Quoted in Leo Frobenius and Douglas C. Fox, *African Genesis* (New York: Stackpole Sons, 1937), 16.

5. Edward Steere, *Swahili Tales* (London: Society for Promoting Christian Knowledge, 1869), v.

6. E. Jacottet, *The Treasury of Ba-Suto Lore* (Morija: Sesuto Book Depot, 1908), xxii.

7. See number 51 for a story collected by Bleek from another San.

8. Callaway, *Nursery Tales, Traditions, and Histories of the Zulus*, in the "Preface to the First Volume," pages unnumbered.

9. R. Sutherland Rattray, *Akan-Ashanti Folk-Tales* (Oxford: Clarendon Press, 1930), 132–37.

10. The Asante live in south central Ghana in West Africa. They are linguistically related to the Akan; together with the Asante, the Fante, and the Akuapem, the Akan make up about half of the twenty million people of Ghana. There are approximately 1.2 million Asante living in Ghana.

11. That is, they ate out of the same dish.

12. Paul B. DuChaillu, *Adventures in the Great Forest of Equatorial Africa and the Country of the Dwarfs* (New York: Harper, 1899), 392–94.

13. The Apinji, or Pinji, live in Ngounie Province in Gabon (population: 1.2 million) in Central Africa. There are about five thousand Apinji, and they largely adhere to traditional Apinji religion.

14. "Never goes twice to the same place."

15. A kind of antelope.

16. A. H. Sayce, "Cairene Folklore," *Folk-Lore* 11 (1900): 361–64.

17. Arabic is the language of the majority of the population (sixty-eight million) of Egypt in North Africa.

18. Feridah Kirby Green, "Folklore from Tangier," *Folklore* 19 (1908): 443–53. Feridah Kirby Green wrote that the stories were told "in Arabic, and written down by me a few hours after hearing. I have striven more to get the idea than the exact words, and in *no case* have I drawn on my imagination. The Moor who related them to me is an ordinary well-to-do villager, who has never been further from Morocco than Gibraltar, and then only for one day, and can speak no word of any language but his own. He attended the village school when a boy, but since his father's death, when he was about fifteen, was obliged to leave it, and attend to, first the cares of his farm, then his trade of a mason, and finally to enter the services of my family [Kirby Green's father was the British minister in Morocco] as groom" (440–41).

19. Arabic is the language of about 70 percent of the population (28.5 million) of Morocco, in North Africa.

20. Shumshen N'har, Light of Day, Aurora.

21. Tajur: a merchant.

22. *Haik*: a long, white, woolen outer garment that covers the body and the head.

23. *Amareeyah*: "a large cage-like box in which a bride is carried to her husband's house" (Kirby Green, "Folklore from Tangier," 447).

24. Dehhor: "the first call to prayer after midday, about 2 p.m." (Kirby Green, "Folklore from Tangier," 447).

25. *Tajjins*: "a dish of meat and vegetables; a stew" (Kirby Green, "Folklore from Tangier," 452).

26. Compare this with a Hausa story, "Yarima, Atafa, and the King," in Harold Scheub, *The African Storyteller* (Dubuque, Iowa: Kendall/Hunt, 1999), 339–41. (Originally from Frank Edgar, *Litafina Tatsniyoyi Na Hausa* [Belfast: W. Erskine Mayne, 1911–1913]. Tr. from Hausa by Neil Skinner, *Hausa Tales and Traditions* [Madison: University of Wisconsin Press, 1977], 269–79.)

27. R. H. Nassau, "Batanga Tales," *Journal of American Folklore* 28 (1915): 24–27.

28. There are about seven thousand Batanga in Cameroon (which has a population of 15.2 million); Cameroon is located in western Africa.

29. P. P. H. Hasluck, "Algerian Folktales, II," *Folk-Lore* 36 (1925): 173–77.

30. Fourteen percent of the approximately thirty million Algerians speak Berber languages.

31. "Mozabites are Berbers living almost due south of Algiers. They are most industrious, but hated by the Arabs" (Hasluck, "Algerian Folktales, II," 174).

32. Andrew Lang, ed., *The Grey Fairy Book* (New York: Longmans, Green, 1900), 38–60. Originally in Hans Stumme, *Märchen und Gedichte aus der Stadt Tripolis in Nordafrika* (Leipzig: J. C. Hinrichs, 1898).

33. Ninety percent of the 5.5 million population of Libya is composed of people of Arab and Berber ancestry.

34. René Basset, *Moorish Literature* (New York: Colonial Press, 1901), 234–37.

35. Approximately 99 percent of the 28.5 million population of Morocco is Arab-Berber.

36. Adolph N. Krug, "Bulu Tales from Kamerun, West Africa," *Journal of American Folk-Lore* 25 (1912): 109–11.

37. About 175,000 Bulu live in Cameroon (which has a population of 15.2 million and 280 languages).

38. Albert D. Helser, *African Stories* (New York: Fleming H. Revell, 1930), 124–30.

39. Two hundred fifty thousand Bura live in Nigeria (which has a population of 130 million and 470 languages).

40. Richard Edward Dennett, *Notes on the Folklore of the Fjort (French Congo)* (London: David Nutt, for the Folk-lore Society, 1898), 60–64.

41. There are five to six thousand Fiote, or Vili, living in the Republic of Congo (which has a population of 3.1 million).

42. "Nzambi Mpungu made the earth and sent Nzambi there. Then he came down and married his creation, thereby becoming the father of us all. Nzambi became the great princess who governed all on earth" (Harold Scheub, *A Dictionary of African Mythology, The Mythmaker as Storyteller* [New York: Oxford University Press, 2000], 191).

43. Blaise Cendrars, "La Geste de Samba Guêladio Diêgui, in *Anthologie nègre* (Paris: Sans Pareil, 1927), 133–47. From Cendrars, "The Great Deeds of Samba Gueladio Diegui," in *The African Saga*, tr. Margery Blanco (New York: Payson and Clarke, 1927), 171–88.

44. The Peuhl make up 40 percent of the 7.7 million population of the West African country of Guinea.

45. Griot: poet.

46. Compare this part of the story with the story collected in Gambia in 1977 by Sonja Fagerberg (Scheub, *The African Storyteller*, 388–93). The storyteller was Malick Secka. The story was performed on June 19, 1977, in Basse, Gambia.

47. Blaise Cendrars, "Les Méfaits de Fountinndouha," in *Anthologie nègre* 248–52. From Cendrars, "Fountinndouha," in *The African Saga*, 301–6.

48. About forty-three thousand Gourmanchéma live in the West African country of Niger, which has a population of 10.6 million.

49. Oral poets.

50. Harry Johnston, *Liberia* (London: Hutchinson, 1906), 2: 1085–87.

51. There are about 150,000 Grebo who live in Liberia, a West African country with a population of 3.3 million.

52. J. F. Schön, *African Proverbs, Tales and Historical Fragments* (London: Society for Promoting Christian Knowledge, 1886), 76–82.

53. About 21 percent of the population of Nigeria in West Africa is Hausa. Nigeria, the most populous nation in Africa, has a population of 130 million.

54. Dodo is not human, but he speaks human languages and often marries human wives. He is an ogre with creative potential. He has married the younger sister and kept her prisoner under the water.

55. H. Beiderbecke, "The Fleeing Girls and the Rock, a Herero Legend," *Folk-Lore Journal* 2 (1880): 76–85.

56. The Herero live in the southwest African country of Namibia, constituting about 7 percent of the population of 1.82 million.

57. The Herero, "a pastoral nation, are nomads. When, on one place, the water and grass for the cattle fail, they remove to another. Hence they have only temporary dwelling-places" (Beiderbecke, "The Fleeing Girls and the Rock, a Herero Legend," 82–83).

58. "The eldest unmarried daughter of a Chief is called 'The big girl,' and 'Favorite,' occupying also a 'privileged' position. She is the guardian and carrier of the sacred fire" (ibid., 83).

59. "I.e., the undertaker of the hunting expedition, to whom his followers have to deliver all the proceeds of the hunt" (ibid., 83).

60. "When the Herero set out on dangerous expeditions, they are first painted on the forehead, with the ashes of the sacred fire, by the 'big woman' or by the 'big girl'" (ibid., 84).

61. "This stone lies near the sacred fire, the place of sacrifice. Only the chief or priest sits down upon it" (ibid., 84).

62. "This magic sentence cannot be translated. Perhaps it is very old Otyihereró" (ibid., 85).

63. "The Ovahereró girls have sometimes a small iron bell fastened to their clothes" (ibid., 85).

64. "It is the custom of the Ovahereró, when walking in a line, to keep the order of their respective ages and rank" (ibid., 85).

65. "Literally: 'She has spoken the language of the youngest,' which has no weight" (ibid., 85).

66. Friedrich Wilhelm Traugott Posselt, *Fables of the Veld* (London: Oxford University Press, 1929), 30–34.

67. There are about 350,000 Jindwi in the south-central African country of Zimbabwe, the population of which is 11.5 million.

68. Basset, *Moorish Literature*, 267–69.

69. About three million Kabyle live in northern Africa.

70. Sigismund Wilhelm Koelle, *African Native Literature* (London: Church Missionary House, 1854), 151–53.

71. There are about four million Kanuri in western Africa.

72. W. H. I. Bleek, *Reynard the Fox in South Africa, or Hottentot Fables and Tales* (London: Trübner, 1864), 85–89.

73. There are about fifty-five thousand Khoikhoi in Namibia and in western South Africa.

74. Satirically meaning he has seen wrongly.

75. Again, satirically.

76. W. E. H. Barrett, "A'Kikuyu Fairy Tales (Rogano)," *Man* 12 (1912): 183–85.

77. The Kikuyu make up 22 percent of the population of the East African country of Kenya, which has a total population of 31.2 million.

78. Sundiata Modupe Broderick, "The Tori: Structure, Aesthetics and Time in Krio Oral Narrative-performance," Ph.D. diss., University of Wisconsin, 1977, 310–16.

79. Krio is the first language of 10 percent of the 5.7 million people of Sierra Leone; it is understood by almost all people in that West African country.

80. Clement M. Doke, *Lamba Folk-lore* (New York: G. E. Stechert, 1927), 45–51.

81. The Lamba compose about 2.5 percent of the central African nation of Zambia, which has a total population of some ten million.

82. The young woman is waiting on the other side of the tree.

83. Emil Torday, *On the Trail of the Bushongo* (London: Seeley, Service, 1925), 92–97.

84. About 6.5 million of the Democratic Republic of Congo's 55.2 million population are Luba.

85. Torday, *On the Trail of the Bushongo*, 40.

86. James Sibree, "The Oratory, Songs, Legends, and Folktales of the Malagasy," *Folk-Lore Journal* 1 (1883): 202–8.

87. About ten million of the 16.5 million population of Madagascar, located off the southeastern coast of Africa, are Malagasy. Malagasy and French are the country's official languages.

88. "These are not strictly proper names, but are rather words denoting the eldest and youngest daughters in a family. The latter, however, is frequently retained as a proper name" (Sibree, "The Oratory, Songs, Legends, and Folktales of the Malagasy," 202).

89. *Ànamàmy*: a vegetable.

90. *Tòaka*: rum.

91. "The old Hova villages, generally built on top of hills, were all thus enclosed within a series of deep fosses, for the sake of security, in the former warlike times" (Sibree, "The Oratory, Songs, Legends, and Folktales of the Malagasy," 204).

92. *Làloména*: a fabulous creature. "This animal is like the ox, but lives in the water. It has two horns, and they are very red, and it is said to be amongst the strongest of the animals which live in the water. It is difficult to say exactly what its appearance and qualities are, for there is much of the fabulous mixed up with the accounts of it" (ibid., 173).

93. Horn: the ordinary drinking vessel.

94. Lit., lies.

95. Alfred Claud Hollis, *The Masai: Their Language and Folklore* (Oxford: Oxford University Press, 1905), 202–15.

96. About 450,000 Masai (Maasai) live in Kenya, which has a population of 31.2 million.

97. Heli Chatelain, *Folk-Tales of Angola* (Boston: American Folklore Society, 1894), 64–81.

98. About 25 percent of the population of the southwestern African country, Angola, are Mbundu. Angola has a total population of 10.6 million.

99. The Lukala "is the largest affluent of the Kuanza River, which it joins at Massangano" (Chatelain, *Folk-Tales of Angola*, 273).

100. I.e., the space and the ground around a tree.

101. Loanda, also spelled Luanda, and formerly known as São Paulo de Luanda, is a city in northern Angola, situated on the coast of the Atlantic Ocean. It is the capital of Angola.

102. About midnight.

103. Alfred Claud Hollis, *The Nandi: Their Language and Folk-lore* (Oxford: Clarendon Press, 1909), 104–5.

104. Nandi is a part of the Kalenjin language family spoken by 12 percent of Kenya's 31.2 million population.

105. The ground-hornbill (*Bucorax caper*) is a large black bird with red gills and white markings on its wings (Hollis, *The Nandi: Their Language and Folk-lore*, 104).

106. R. Sutherland Rattray, *Some Folk-lore Stories and Songs in Chinyanja* (London: Society for Promoting Christian Knowledge, 1907), 133–36.

107. Malawi is in east-central Africa. It has a population of 10.7 million, of whom 3.2 million are Nyanja.

108. "Lit. the case is finished at the mouth" (Rattray, *Some Folk-lore Stories and Songs in Chinyanja*, 136).

109. Eugène Hurel, *La Poésie chez les primitifs; ou, contes, fables, récits, et proverbes du Rwanda (Lac Kivu)* (Bruxelles: Goemaere, 1922), 27.

110. More than 98 percent of the people who live in Rwanda are Nyarwanda (Kinyarwanda); this includes the Hutu, Kiga, and Twa. Rwanda's population is 7.4 million.

111. Imana is the supreme being, the creator. (See Scheub, *A Dictionary of African Mythology, The Mythmaker as Storyteller*, 77–78).

112. In a Venda story, a father's three sons set out serially to marry the beautiful daughter of a man who lives in a community nearby. When each of the two eldest sons is returning home with her, she sings that she has no teeth, and indeed they discover that what she says is true. Each of the two sons then returns her to her father. But when the youngest son goes to claim her as his bride, when she sings her song he asks her to open her mouth. He sees the black ridge in her mouth, but when they come to the middle of a stream, he scrubs the girl's mouth with sand, and a beautiful set of teeth is revealed. Now the two elder brothers, who had made fun of their youngest brother when he set out on his quest, are shamed: "All spoke of her beauty and her excellent teeth, but the two brothers never saw for themselves, their shame being too great" (Hugh Arthur Stayt, *The Bavenda* [London: H. Milford, 1931], 339–41).

113. Herbert L. Bishop, "A Selection of Šironga Folklore," *South African Journal of Science* 19 (1922): 394–400.

114. About half a million Ronga live in the southeastern African country of Mozambique, which has a population of 19.6 million.

115. "It is, unfortunately, impossible to reproduce the vivacity, the interpretative gesture, the free use of 'descriptive complements,' and the very evident enjoyment of the stories shown by the narrator" (Bishop, "A Selection of Šironga Folklore," 383).

116. W. H. I. Bleek and L. C. Lloyd, *Specimens of Bushman Folklore* (London: George Allen, 1911), 174–91.

117. About sixteen thousand San live in Namibia in southwestern Africa. Namibia has a population of 1.82 million.

118. In another version of this story, the unusual sleepiness is caused by the lion. (Notes for this story are from Bleek and Lloyd, *Specimens of Bushman Folklore.*)

119. A large tree with yellow flowers and no thorns.

120. The tree hurt the back of the man's head; therefore, he moved it a little.

121. The man cried quietly, because he saw himself in the lion's power, and in great danger.

122. The narrator explains that the stick was one of those pieces that had broken off, fallen down, and lodged in the bottom of the tree.

123. The lion came back a little way (after having gone out of sight) to look again.

124. The lion, this time when it came back to look at the man, had only its head and shoulders in sight.

125. He did not run straight but ran first in one direction, then sprang to another place, then ran again, and so on.

126. Andrew Lang, *The Orange Fairy Book* (New York: Longmans, Green, 1906), 16–23.

127. There are about 1.1 million Sena who live in Mozambique in southeastern Africa; Mozambique has a population of 19.6 million.

128. Diedrich Westermann, *The Shilluk People, Their Language and Folklore* (Philadelphia: Board of Foreign Missions of the United Presbyterian Church of N.A., 1912), 213–17.

129. About 175,000 Shilluk live in the southern part of Sudan, which has a total population of thirty-seven million.

130. Olam: a sycamore fig.

131. J. W. C. Kirk, "Specimens of Somali Tales," *Folk-Lore* 15 (1904): 321–22.

132. Somali is spoken by 85 percent of the population (7.75 million) of Somalia.

133. Jacottet, *The Treasury of Ba-Suto Lore*, 126–34.

134. The Sotho make up 85 percent of the 2.2 million population of the land-locked southern African country Lesotho.

135. Jacottet note: "Her song is a kind of spell which keeps Monyohe behind" (133).

136. George W. Bateman, *Zanzibar Tales* (Chicago: A. C. McClurg, 1901), 197–224.

137. Swahili is spoken by 94 percent of the people in the East African country of Tanzania, which has a population of 37.2 million. It is the official language of the country.

138. Compare the Ndau (Mozambique) story, "The Sky Princess and the Poor Youth" (Franz Boas and C. Kamba Simango, "Tales and Proverbs of the Vandau of Portuguese South Africa" [*Journal of American Folk-Lore* 35 (1922)]: 200–201).

139. The storyteller was Albertine Nxumalo, a twenty-one-year-old Swati woman. The performance (2S-2004) took place in a home in Zombodze, Swaziland, on October 24, 1972. In the audience were two women, two men, and twenty children and teenagers.

140. Swaziland, in southern Africa, has a population of 1.1 million people, of whom about 90 percent are Swati.

141. Ntombinde: lit., the tall young woman.

142. Enno Littmann, *Publications of the Princeton Expedition to Abyssinia* (Leyden: E. J. Brill, 1910), 1: 34–38.

143. Of the 67.6 million people who live in Ethiopia, 32 percent speak Tigre and Amhara.

144. J. Tom Brown, *Among the Bantu Nomads* (Philadelphia: J. B. Lippencott, 1926), 181–85.

145. The Tswana make up 70 percent of the population of the southern African nation of Botswana, which has a total population of 1.6 million.

146. Sigismund Wilhelm Koelle, *Outlines of a Grammar of the Vei Language* (London: Church Missionary House, 1854), 69–72.

147. About ninety thousand Vai live in the West African nation of Liberia, which has a population of 3.3 million.

148. Lit., a lie-sickness.

149. This story (1S-657) was performed on September 15, 1967, at about 3:30 P.M., along a path in Mboxo (Nkanga) Location, Gatyana District, the Transkei. In Mrs. Zenani's audience were five women and fifteen children.

150. Of South Africa's population of 43.7 million, 17.5 percent speak Xhosa, one of the eleven official languages of the country.

151. The *imbulu* is frequently a mischievous character in the oral narratives of southern Africa. It is a fantastic creature, half-animal and half-human.

152. The story was performed on September 19, 1967, at about 12:30 P.M., in a home in Mboxo (Nkanga) Location, Gatyana District, the Transkei. In the audience were several women.

153. Alfred Burdon Ellis, *The Yoruba-Speaking Peoples of the Slave Coast of West Africa* (London: Chapman and Hall, 1894), 253–58.

154. Twenty-one percent of Nigeria's 130 million population are Yoruba.

155. Ellis, *The Yoruba-Speaking Peoples of the Slave Coast of West Africa*, 243.

156. The *kini-kini* bird: "A small black and white bird, sometimes called the

doctor-bird. It is named from its cry, which resembles the words *the kini-kini bird*" (ibid., 253).

157. "*Bata, dundun,* and *gangan,* are the names of different kinds of drums. The *bata* is a tall drum, the *dundun* is hung with little bells, and the *gangan* is properly a war-drum. These names are onomatopoeic. Each drum has its own measure and rhythm. . ." (ibid., 254).

158. Callaway, *Nursery Tales, Traditions, and Histories of the Zulus,* 296–316. Callaway refers to "another version of this tale in which the names are different. Usilwane is called Unkoiya; Usilwanekazana, Ulukozazana,—Little-hen-eagle; and Untombi-yapansi, Umabelemane,—Four-breasts" (296).

159. The Zulu constitute 22.4 percent of the population of South Africa (43.7 million). Zulu is one of the eleven official languages of South Africa.

160. Usilwane: the beast-man.

161. Usilwanekazana: the little beast-woman.

162. Callaway notes, "*Untombi-yapansi,* The damsel-of-beneath, or of-the-earth. It may have reference to three things:—1. To poverty or distress; 2. To origin,—from the earth; 3. To her having traveled underground" (*Nursery Tales, Traditions, and Histories of the Zulus,* 296).

163. The *imbulu* is a fantasy character that frequently appears in girls' puberty rite of passage stories. It is usually a male, has four legs but attempts to walk upright like humans, has a lisp, and has a tail that often betrays it when, in the presence of milk or meat fat, it points directly at the food.

164. Callaway notes, "The story makes it clear however that we are not to understand simple whey, but whey mixed with ground mealies [corn]. Poor people and dependents only eat ground mealies mixed with whey; superiors use amasi [curdled milk]" (*Nursery Tales, Traditions, and Histories of the Zulus,* 305).

165. It was not proper for Untombi-yaphansi to drink the milk belonging to her brother-in-law.

166. Mealies: corn.

167. Udalana, Little-old-one.

168. In another version of the story, the dead include her mother, father, and sister.

169. I.e., the *imbulu.*

170. Callaway, *Nursery Tales, Traditions, and Histories of the Zulus,* 105–30.

171. Callaway note: "It is a reference to the word which Nkulunkulu [God], when he broke off all things from *utlanga* in the beginning, uttered, determining by an ordinance all future events" (106).

172. The mat-marker.

173. Callaway note: "This ceremony is for the purpose of openly acknowledging the bridegroom to the bride. A mat is placed on the ground in the middle of the cattle-pen; the bridegroom and his party sit at the upper end of the enclosure. The bride and her maids pass, dancing, from the entrance to where they are sitting. One then takes the bridegroom by the hand, and leads him down to the mat,

and leaves him standing on it. The mat is not afterwards touched by the bride's party, because the bridegroom's feet have stood on it. It is . . . respected by them, but it is taken away by someone belonging to him" (117).

174. An *imbulu* is a semi-human creature: it has difficulty walking on two legs and it has a tail. It has a speech impediment. It frequently occurs in stories having to do with girls' puberty rites of passage, when it takes the identity of the girl.

175. That is, the *imbulu*, the false bride.

Bibliography

Baissac, Charles. *Le Folklore de l'Ile-Maurice*. Paris: Maisonneuve et Ch. Leclerc, 1888.

Barrett, W. E. H. "A'Kikuyu Fairy Tales (Rogano)." *Man* 12 (1912): 183–85.

Basset, René. *Moorish Literature*. New York: Colonial Press, 1901.

Bateman, George W. *Zanzibar Tales*. Chicago: A. C. McClurg, 1901.

Beiderbecke, H. "The Fleeing Girls and the Rock, a Herero Legend." *Folk-Lore Journal* 2 (1880): 76–85.

Benjamin, Walter. *Illuminations*. Trans. Harry Zohn. Glasgow: William Collins, 1973.

Bérenger-Féraud, Laurent-Jean-Baptiste. *Les Peuplades de la Sénégambie*. Paris: Ernest Leroux, 1879.

Bishop, Herbert L. "A Selection of Šironga Folklore." *South African Journal of Science* 19 (1922): 394–400.

Bleek, W. H. I. *Reynard the Fox in South Africa, or Hottentot Fables and Tales*. London: Trübner, 1864.

Bleek, W. H. I., and L. C. Lloyd. *Specimens of Bushman Folklore*. London: George Allen, 1911.

Boas, Franz, and C. Kamba Simango. "Tales and Proverbs of the Vandau of Portuguese South Africa." *Journal of American Folk-Lore* 35 (1922): 200–201.

Broderick, Sundiata Modupe. "The Tori: Structure, Aesthetics and Time in Krio Oral Narrative-Performance." Ph.D. diss., University of Wisconsin, 1977.

Brown, J. Tom. *Among the Bantu Nomads*. Philadelphia: J. B. Lippencott, 1926.

Burton, Richard, tr. *The Book of the Thousand Nights and a Night*. London: Burton Club, 1886.

Callaway, Henry. *Nursery Tales, Traditions, and Histories of the Zulus*. Springvale, Natal: John A. Blair, and London: Trübner, 1868.

Cendrars, Blaise. *Anthologie nègre*. Paris: Sans Pareil, 1927.

———. *The African Saga*. Tr. Margery Bianco. New York: Payson and Clarke, 1927.

Chatelain, Heli. *Folk-Tales of Angola*. Boston: American Folklore Society, 1894.

Dennett, Richard Edward. *Notes on the Folklore of the Fjort (French Congo).* London: David Nutt, for the Folk-lore Society, 1898.

Djebar, Assia. *Fantasia: An Algerian Cavalcade.* 2 vols. Portsmouth, NH: Heinemann, 1993.

Doke, Clement M. *Lamba Folk-lore.* New York: G. E. Stechert, 1927.

DuChaillu, Paul B. *Adventures in the Great Forest of Equatorial Africa and the Country of the Dwarfs.* New York: Harper, 1899.

Dupuis-Yakouba, A. *Les Gow ou Chasseurs du Niger.* Paris: Ernest Leroux, 1911.

Edgar, Frank. *Litafina Tatsuniyoyi Na Hausa.* Belfast: W. Erskine Mayne, 1911–1913. Tr. from Hausa by Neil Skinner, *Hausa Tales and Traditions.* Madison: University of Wisconsin Press, 1977.

Ellis, Alfred Burdon. *The Yoruba-Speaking Peoples of the Slave Coast of West Africa.* London: Chapman and Hall, 1894.

Ennis, Merlin. *Umbundu, Folk Tales from Angola.* Boston: Beacon Press, 1962.

Equilbecq, Victor Français. *Contes populaire d'Afrique occidentale.* Paris: G.-P. Maisonneuve et Larose, 1972.

———. *Essai sur la littérature merveilleuse des noirs.* Vol. 3. Paris: E. Leroux, 1916.

———. *La Légende de Samba Guélâdio Diêgui prince du Foûta.* Dakar: Nouvelles éditions africaines, 1974.

Frobenius, Leo, ed. *African Nights.* New York: Herder and Herder, 1971.

Frobenius, Leo, and Douglas C. Fox. *African Genesis.* New York: Stackpole Sons, 1937.

Hasluck, P. P. H. "Algerian Folktales, II." *Folk-Lore* 36 (1925): 173–78.

Helser, Albert D. *African Stories.* New York: Fleming H. Revell, 1930.

Herskovits, Melville J., and Frances S. Herskovits. *Dahomean Narrative.* Evanston: Northwestern University Press, 1958.

Hollis, Alfred Claud. *The Masai: Their Language and Folklore.* Oxford: Oxford University Press, 1905.

———. *The Nandi: Their Language and Folk-lore.* Oxford: Clarendon Press, 1909.

Hurel, Eugène. *La Poésie chez les primitifs; ou, contes, fables, récits, et proverbes du Rwanda (Lac Kivu).* Bruxelles: Goemaere, 1922.

Jacottet, E. *The Treasury of Ba-Suto Lore.* Morija: Sesuto Book Depot, 1908.

Johnston, Harry. *Liberia.* Vol. 2. London: Hutchinson, 1906.

———. *The Uganda Protectorate.* Vol. 2. London: Hutchinson, 1904.

Jordan, Archibald Campbell. *Towards an African Literature: The Emergence of Literary Form in Xhosa.* Berkeley: University of California Press, 1973.

Kirby Green, Feridah. "Folklore from Tangier." *Folklore* 19 (1908): 440–58.

Kirk, J. W. C. "Specimens of Somali Tales." *Folk-Lore* 15 (1904): 316–26.

Koelle, Sigismund Wilhelm. *African Native Literature.* London: Church Missionary House, 1854.

———. *Outlines of a Grammar of the Vei Language.* London: Church Missionary House, 1854.

Krug, Adolph N. "Bulu Tales." *Journal of American Folklore* 62 (1949): 348–74.

———. "Bulu Tales from Kamerun, West Africa." *Journal of American Folk-Lore* 25 (1912): 106–24.

Lang, Andrew, ed. *The Grey Fairy Book.* New York: Longmans, Green, 1900.

———. *The Orange Fairy Book.* New York: Longmans, Green, 1906.

Littmann, Enno. *Publications of the Princeton Expedition to Abyssinia.* Vol. 1. Leyden: E. J. Brill, 1910.

Monteil, Charles. *The Bambara of Ségou and Kaarta.* Tr. Kathryn A. Looney. New Haven: Human Relations Area Files 1960.

———. *Less Khassonké: monographie d'une peuplade du Soudan français.* Paris: E. Laroux, 1915.

Nassau, R. H. "Batanga Tales." *Journal of American Folklore* 28 (1915): 24–27.

Parsons, Elsie Worthington Clews. *Folk-Lore from the Cape Verde Islands.* New York: American Folk-lore Society, 1923.

Patterson, J. R. *Stories of Abu Zeid and the Hilali.* London: Kegan Paul, Trench, Trübner, 1930.

Payet, J. V. *Récits et traditions de la Réunion.* Paris: L'Harmattan, 1988.

Petrie, W. M. Flinders, ed. *Egyptian Tales.* London: Methuen, 1895.

Posselt, Friedrich Wilhelm Traugott. *Fables of the Veld.* London: Oxford University Press, 1929.

Rattray, R. Sutherland. *Akan-Ashanti Folk-Tales.* Oxford: Clarendon Press, 1930.

———. *Some Folk-lore Stories and Songs in Chinyanja.* London: Society for Promoting Christian Knowledge, 1907.

Roscoe, John. *The Baganda, An Account of Their Native Customs and Beliefs.* London: Macmillan, 1911.

Sayce, A. H. "Cairene Folklore." *Folk-Lore* 11 (1900): 354–95.

Scheub, Harold. *The African Storyteller.* Dubuque, Iowa: Kendall/Hunt, 1999.

———. *A Dictionary of African Mythology, The Mythmaker as Storyteller.* New York: Oxford University Press, 2000.

———. "A Review of African Oral Traditions and Literature." *African Studies Review* 28, 2/3 (1985): 1–72.

———. *The Tongue Is Fire.* Madison: University of Wisconsin Press, 1996.

———. *The Xhosa Ntsomi.* Oxford: Clarendon Press, 1975.

Schlenker, Christian Friedrich. *A Collection of Temne Traditions, Fables and Proverbs.* London: Church Missionary Society, 1861.

Schön, J. F. *African Proverbs, Tales and Historical Fragments.* London: Society for Promoting Christian Knowledge, 1886.

Schreider, Jules. *Manuel de la langue tigraï parlée au centre et dans le nord de l'Abyssinie.* Vienne: Alfred Hoelder, 1887.

Sibree, James. "The Oratory, Songs, Legends, and Folktales of the Malagasy." *Folk-Lore Journal* 1 (1883): 200–211.

Smith, Edwin W., and Andrew Murray Dale. *The Ila-Speaking Peoples of Northern Rhodesia.* Vol. 2. London: Macmillan, 1920.

Stayt, Hugh Arthur. *The Bavenda.* London: H. Milford, 1931.

Steere, Edward. *Swahili Tales*. London: Society for Promoting Christian Knowledge, 1869.

Stumme, Hans. *Märchen und Gedichte aus der Stadt Tripolis in Nordafrika*. Leipzig: J. C. Hinrichs, 1898.

Talbot, P. Amaury. *In the Shadow of the Bush*. London: William Heinemann, 1912.

Torday, Emil. *On the Trail of the Bushongo*. London: Seeley, Service, 1925.

Torrend, J. *Specimens of Bantu Folk-lore from Northern Rhodesia*. London: Kegan Paul, French, Trübner, 1921.

Tounsy, Mohammad ibn ʿUmar el. *Voyage au Ouadây*. Paris: Chez M. Duprat, 1851.

Tremearne, A. J. N. "Hausa Folklore." *Man* 10–11 (1911): 20–23.

Westermann, Diedrich. *The Shilluk People, Their Language and Folklore*. Philadelphia: Board of Foreign Missions of the United Presbyterian Church of N.A., 1912.

Zeltner, Fr. de. *Contes du Sénégal et du Niger*. Paris: E. Leroux, 1913.

Zemp, Hugo. "La Littérature des Dan (Côte d'Ivoire)." Ph.D. diss., University of Paris, 1964.

Zenani, Nongenile Masithathu. *The World and the Word: Tales and Observations from the Xhosa Oral Tradition*. Madison: University of Wisconsin Press, 1992.